Socialism

Socialism

A Logical Introduction

SCOTT R. SEHON

OXFORD
UNIVERSITY PRESS

Oxford University Press is a department of the University of Oxford. It furthers
the University's objective of excellence in research, scholarship, and education
by publishing worldwide. Oxford is a registered trade mark of Oxford University
Press in the UK and certain other countries.

Published in the United States of America by Oxford University Press
198 Madison Avenue, New York, NY 10016, United States of America.

© Oxford University Press 2024

All rights reserved. No part of this publication may be reproduced, stored in
a retrieval system, or transmitted, in any form or by any means, without the
prior permission in writing of Oxford University Press, or as expressly permitted
by law, by license, or under terms agreed with the appropriate reproduction
rights organization. Inquiries concerning reproduction outside the scope of the
above should be sent to the Rights Department, Oxford University Press, at the
address above.

You must not circulate this work in any other form
and you must impose this same condition on any acquirer.

CIP data is on file at the Library of Congress
ISBN 978–0–19–775334–7 (pbk.)
ISBN 978–0–19–775333–0 (hbk.)

DOI: 10.1093/oso/9780197753330.001.0001

Paperback printed by Sheridan Books, Inc., United States of America
Hardback printed by Bridgeport National Bindery, Inc., United States of America

For my mother, Vera Dellwig, and in memory of my grandfather, Will H. Hayden.

Contents

Acknowledgments	xi

PART I. INTRODUCTION

1. Logic and Arguments	3
Argument *Ad Hominem*	4
What Is an Argument?	6
A Sample: Socialism and Starvation	10
A Look Ahead	15
Key Takeaways	16
2. Defining "Socialism"	18
Don't Argue about Words	18
It All Comes in Degrees	19
The Classical View	25
Some Rough Distinctions	29
Scandinavia and Democratic Socialism	32
Key Takeaways	38
3. Moral Philosophy Background and the Master Arguments	39
The Fundamental Question	39
A Moral Framework	41
Promoting Well-Being	43
Rights	50
Key Takeaways	61

PART II. RIGHTS-BASED ARGUMENTS

4. Does Socialism Violate Rights?	65
Socialism and Political Rights	65
Socialism and Economic Rights	70
Self-Ownership and the Nonaggression Principle	73
Self-Authorship and Economic Rights	79
Key Takeaways	85
5. Does Capitalism Violate Rights?	87
Extraction of Surplus Value: The Basic Idea	87

viii CONTENTS

Initial Attempts at an Argument	89
Filling the Gap in the Argument: The Exploitation Principle	92
Final Version of the Argument	96
Evaluating Premise (2) of *Capitalism Exploits*: Is the Distribution Undeserved?	98
Evaluating Premise (1) of *Capitalism Exploits*: Is It Unfair?	104
Key Takeaways	108

PART III. SOCIALISM AND HUMAN WELL-BEING

6. The Progress Argument	113
Empirical Evidence and the Master Arguments	113
Humanity's Spectacular Progress	115
Capitalism as the Explanation?	117
Correlation versus Causation and the Capitalist Argument	120
Testing the Capitalist Hypothesis: Data from 20th-Century Communism	123
Science and Technology as the Real Explanation	129
Key Takeaways	130
7. Redistribution: Inequality and Envy	131
The Pettiness of Envy	131
Diminishing Marginal Utility versus Incentives	133
The Empirical Evidence: Optimal Rates of Taxation	137
Inequality Is Toxic	141
Key Takeaways	149
8. Collective Control: The Democracy Argument	151
Empirical Correlations: Scandinavia Again	151
Community versus Competitiveness	153
Why Is Democracy Good? The *All Affected Principle*	160
Democracy and Traditional Governmental Functions	163
Democracy and Economic Decisions	167
Market Socialism	169
Markets and the Capitalist Reply to the *Democracy Argument for Socialism*	171
Key Takeaways	173

PART IV. CAPITALISM AND HUMAN WELL-BEING

9. The Case for Markets	177
Hayek: The Better Information Argument	178
Friedman: The Better Incentives Argument	182
Key Takeaways	188

CONTENTS ix

10. Market Failures I: Public Goods — 190
    The Argumentative Situation — 190
    Hayek and the Diffuse Benefit of Some Services — 192
    Applications — 196
    Key Takeaways — 201

11. Market Failures II: Monopolies and Monopsonies — 203
    Monopolies — 203
    Where Shopping Is Impractical — 208
    Monopsony and Labor — 212
    "Government Is Not the Solution"? — 216
    Key Takeaways — 219

12. Market Failures III: Neighborhood Effects and Climate
    Change — 220
    Negative Externalities and Neighborhood Effects — 220
    Other Examples — 223
    The No-Brainer? Future Generations and Climate Change — 226
    Key Takeaways — 239

13. Conclusion — 240

A Brief Annotated Selection of Suggested Readings — 249
Index — 253

Acknowledgments

As will be discussed in the introduction, this book has a pedagogical as well as a philosophical aim: I hope to help readers to see how to think critically about socialism and capitalism. Even if I convince no one of my beliefs, the book will have served a purpose if it helps any reader to better use the tools of argument and analytical thought.

Accordingly, I will begin by acknowledging some of the most influential people in my own education in this realm. My very first philosophy class in college was a course on formal logic taught by Warren Goldfarb. Although I was always very argumentative (as my mother, brothers, and high school friends can attest), learning symbolic logic from Warren was like having the scales fall from my eyes: by better understanding the nature of logical inference, I began to really grasp what made an argument good or bad. My next philosophy teacher, Paul Hoffman, first showed me the amazing utility of breaking a philosopher's argument down into numbered steps. OK, I will not go on, teacher by teacher, enumerating and elaborating on what each did for me, but I will name a few of them: Paul Benacerraf, Mark Johnston, John Rawls, Michael Smith, Jennifer Whiting, and George Wilson.

Returning closer to the present day, I would like to thank friends, family, and colleagues who read parts of the manuscript and gave me valuable comments: Vera Dellwig, Kristiana Filipov, Michael Morrison, Hayden Sartoris, Josephine Sehon, Donald Stanley, and anonymous referees for Oxford University Press. I also benefited from detailed written discussion (often on Facebook, of all places) with many interlocutors, most notably Steve Davis. Three readers of the entire manuscript stand out for their insightful and detailed comments, comments that saved me from many a misstep: Sam Arnold, Kristen Ghodsee, and Kristi Olson.

My institution, Bowdoin College, has been helpful in a number of ways. First and foremost, they have provided me with a steady supply of intelligent and motivated students from whom I have learned a great deal while I was trying to teach them. I am particularly grateful to the students I taught in a class called Socialism, Capitalism, and Democracy, in which I tried out many of the ideas and arguments in this book. Bowdoin also granted me a

xii ACKNOWLEDGMENTS

sabbatical leave during which I wrote most much of the first draft. I have also been blessed with wonderful colleagues, both present and past, in the Department of Philosophy at Bowdoin.

This book never would have come close to happening were it not for my partner, Kristen. Not only did she provide much needed emotional support throughout the writing and editing process, though that would be reason enough for substantial gratitude. Beyond that, the whole idea of writing this book was hers, and she gave me expert advice and substantive comments throughout the whole process. She remains my inspiration, my mentor, and my beloved.

PART I
INTRODUCTION

1

Logic and Arguments

This book is a *logical* introduction to socialism. As opposed to what? you might ask. An *illogical* introduction? By promising a logical introduction, I mean that I plan to introduce you to the *arguments* for and against socialism, where an argument is characterized by clearly identified premises that purport to logically imply a conclusion. (More on the nature of arguments below.)

One way of introducing the arguments about socialism would be to stay studiously neutral: present the reasons and inferences offered by the opposing sides but take no stand on who is right. That will not be my approach. I will indicate which arguments I think work and which do not, and I will ultimately come down on the side of socialism: that we should move our political and economic systems in a strongly socialist direction. And I will try to convince you that the arguments support this conclusion.

On the other hand, this book is still meant as a general introduction to the contemporary arguments concerning socialism and capitalism. If this were simply a polemic in favor of socialism, then I would present those arguments for socialism that I think *work*, and I would aim to defeat prominent arguments for capitalism and against socialism. I would not bother to present arguments for socialism that, in my opinion, are dubious, even if they have currency among socialists. In fact, I will examine a broad array of arguments for and against socialism, and I will make an effort to cover some of those that have historically (or more recently) been given for socialism, even when I don't think those arguments are successful. In this respect, the book is more neutral.

Nonetheless, this book is not an introduction to socialism in a broader or more historical sense: I will not be taking you back to the writings of Karl Marx or the earlier utopian socialists, and I will not be providing anything like a history of socialist movements or even of socialist thought. Not that there is anything wrong with such historical introductions, and I can recommend a number of them if that's where your interest lies (see the "Suggested Readings" section at the end of the book). But this book is about the *reasons*

Socialism. Scott R. Sehon, Oxford University Press. © Oxford University Press 2024.
DOI: 10.1093/oso/9780197753330.003.0001

4   INTRODUCTION

for adopting socialist policies now, in our current political context; it is an introduction to the logic of the arguments for and against socialism. The arguments I present and analyze will draw on considerations and evidence from a number of fields: contemporary politics, economics, anthropology, psychology, and my own field of philosophy. Nonetheless, the book is still an introduction, not a specialized work of scholarship.

Argument *Ad Hominem*

This book is for people willing to go beyond slogans and dig deeply into the *arguments*, both for and against socialism. I'll try to make a case for socialism by convincing you that certain arguments for it are *sound* and that the arguments typically raised against it are *unsound*. I'll say more in Chapter 2 about what I mean by "argument" and by the technical terms "sound" and "unsound."

Analyzing arguments is not always easy. A. E. Housman is widely cited as having written the following: "A moment's thought would have shown him. But a moment is a long time, and thought is a painful process." I'm often reminded of this quotation when I hear people talking about political issues. Especially in the United States but also in the United Kingdom and the rest of Europe, we live in polarized worlds, where your chosen political camp conveniently tells you what to think about almost everything. Questioning that orthodoxy can lead to accusations of betrayal or fear of being canceled. When people do happen to run across evidence or arguments for the other side's position, they tend to dismiss them without engaging in any serious way. Perhaps they think, "I'm sure I could find a different article making my side's point, so I don't need to think about this." Or perhaps they just attack the source of the argument: if the source is not from their side, then it is biased, stupid, or evil.

This latter reaction, of attacking the source of an argument, even has a name: argument *ad hominem*. Despite having taught logic classes for decades, I'm not actually a big fan of classifying bad arguments into different types of fallacies and especially not of the tendency to refer to them by Latin names. But "*ad hominem*" is a useful phrase. Translated literally, it means "to the man" or "to the person," but, in the context of arguments, it means this: responding to an argument by making claims about the person who made the argument rather than the argument itself.

I should note that there are times when dismissing the source of an argument is not really a fallacy and makes reasonable sense. I have a friend in Germany who is a font of misinformation and half-truths concerning climate change, 9/11, and other topics; Gerhard never met a conspiracy theory he didn't like. If Gerhard tells me about a good *Hausbrauerei* in Freiburg, I will believe him, but when he presents data in favor of climate change denial, I have learned to be suspicious of his alleged facts.

But when someone makes an explicit argument and appeals only to facts that you accept or can confirm, then it makes far less sense for you to reject the argument simply because the person presenting it is not in your political camp. I can, of course, understand the attraction of *ad hominem* attacks: if you don't know how to refute an argument, but you do know how to make accusations about the person making the argument, then it is tempting to let the latter substitute for the former. In principle, however, we should be able to evaluate arguments irrespective of the source. If an argument is a good one, then it doesn't matter whether it was produced by Albert Einstein or monkeys randomly hitting the keys of a typewriter. (For the record, I will note that Einstein was a socialist. I'm not sure about the monkeys.)

Within political debates, especially in the United States, *ad hominem* attacks often come in the form of conservatives dismissing ideas or arguments because they come from the "liberal elite," where this latter term typically refers to those espousing liberal views who are upper middle-class people with degrees from fancy private universities and who are thought to be out of touch with *real* people—you know, those Americans who work hard, own guns, and drink Bud Light. I say this because I know that some people will have a tendency to reject anything that I say in this book on the grounds that I am part of that hated liberal elite. And I am. For nearly 30 years I have been a philosophy professor at a prestigious East Coast liberal arts college, teaching logic and all kinds of other philosophical material. I have a BA from Harvard and a PhD from Princeton. Although I think I work hard, I don't have any firearms, and I drink artisanal craft beer and hard-to-find imported German pilseners.

However, for those who would hold all of that against me, I might also mention a few further aspects of my background. I grew up in the deeply red state of Kansas. The last Democrat to receive Kansas's electoral votes was Lyndon Johnson in 1964, and I was way too young to remember that election. My roots are middle class. My parents could only afford to send me to Harvard because Harvard offered significant financial aid. My grandfather

6   INTRODUCTION

and many members of my extended family were (and some still are) farmers. Throughout high school, I had a job working for minimum wage at a local janitorial supply company. My summers were otherwise occupied playing baseball and fishing in my grandfather's farm ponds. I was never very good at either; my older brother was the far better fisherman, and my younger brother the far better baseball player. My lack of talent in baseball was undoubtedly a disappointment to my father, a conservative Republican who made his living as a baseball talent scout. In the offseason, Dad would pick up extra money by refereeing high school football games and occasional basketball games. I absorbed some liberal political perspective from my mother and my grandfather as a kid, but Kansas was not a particularly hospitable place for such views.

So, between my current position and my background, you have ammunition for two very different sorts of *ad hominem* attacks on me. You could dismiss anything I say because I am an eggheaded, East Coast intellectual. Or you could dismiss anything I say because I am an unsophisticated hick from Kansas. Or you could simply read the arguments, check the references for facts, and make up your own mind. I promise I will not exercise my philosopher-Jedi mind tricks on you. (I don't actually have any such tricks. I sometimes wish I did, but then I would undoubtedly get distracted with long hours of thinking through the ethical issues of when, if at all, it is okay to use such mind control. I might also contemplate using it on myself when that seemed advantageous. Then I would start worrying about whether my past self has already done so. Actually, the more I think about it, the more I am sure it is a good thing that I have no such abilities.)

What Is an Argument?

What exactly does it mean to consider the *arguments* for and against socialism? What is an argument? One might start with a famous treatment of the issue from the iconic British comedy group Monty Python. In their sketch, a man (played by Michael Palin) walks into an office where you can pay to have an argument. He gives his money to buy a five-minute argument from a character played by John Cleese, who immediately begins to contradict everything Palin says. The Palin character complains, "An argument is not the same as contradiction." Cleese answers, "It can be." Palin replies: "No

LOGIC AND ARGUMENTS 7

it can't. An argument is a connected series of statements to establish a definite proposition."[1]

The word "argument" can clearly be used in different senses. One might agree with the John Cleese character that in *one* sense of the term, mere contradiction is an argument. In another sense of the term, perhaps an old married couple hurling unrelated insults can also be said to be having an argument. In the context of a moral or political debate, simple gainsaying and exchanging insults might or might not have a place, but it is not an application of reason and logic. The sense of the word "argument" that I have in mind is very close to that proposed by the Michael Palin character in the skit: "An argument is a connected series of statements to establish a definite proposition." Specifically, I will take an argument to be a series of premises—claims assumed to be true—along with a conclusion that is said to follow logically from those premises.

Here is a very simple example of an argument: all people are mortal; Alexandria Ocasio-Cortez is a person; therefore, Alexandria Ocasio-Cortez is mortal. The argument has two premises, each of which is, I am pretty sure, true; and the conclusion follows logically from the premises. I will often lay out arguments in very explicit form as follows:

Ocasio-Cortez

(1) All people are mortal. [P]
(2) Alexandria Ocasio-Cortez is a person. [P]
(3) Alexandria Ocasio-Cortez is mortal. [1,2]

The "[P]" at the end of steps (1) and (2) indicates that those claims are assumed as premises for the sake of this argument. The "[1,2]" at the end of step (3) indicates that this line is taken to follow logically from lines (1) and (2). Laying out arguments in numbered step form has some very clear advantages: we can see exactly what is assumed to be true, and we can see exactly what is being claimed to follow logically from those premises.

The latter idea—of one statement *following logically* from one or more other statements—is critical. When I say that I am providing a *logical* introduction to socialism, I mean "logical" in a very specific sense. When one hears the term "logical," one might conjure up images of *Star Trek*'s Mr.

---

[1] The full skit is available at https://www.youtube.com/watch?v=xpAvcGcEc0k.

8 INTRODUCTION

Spock, calmly and coolly reasoning, as if the ideal is to drain any emotion from one's reasoning. That's not what I have in mind. In the specific sense in which I am using the concept, "logical" is a term that applies (or fails to apply) to the argument itself, irrespective of the emotional state of the person presenting the argument. One could very calmly and coolly reason in a grotesquely fallacious manner, or one could scream out a perfectly valid syllogism even in the throes of passion.

In the argument I have denoted as *Ocasio-Cortez*, statements (1) and (2) logically imply (3) in the following sense: given the assumed truth of any two statements of the same form as (1) and (2), the statement of the corresponding form of (3) would *have* to be true. The fact that (3) follows logically from (1) and (2) has nothing to do with the nature of mortality or Alexandria Ocasio-Cortez; any two statements of the same form would imply the corresponding third statement. It is not possible that (1) and (2) could be true while (3) is false, and we can see this simply by looking at the *form* rather than the specific *content* of the statements. For example:

Scholz

(1) All German politicians are human beings. [P]
(2) Olaf Scholz is a German politician. [P]
(3) Olaf Scholz is a human being. [1,2]

Here is another argument of the same logical form:

Mets Fans

(1) All Mets fans are long-suffering. [P]
(2) Scott is a Mets fan. [P]
(3) Scott is long-suffering. [1,2]

The arguments *Ocasio-Cortez*, *Scholz*, and *Mets Fans* have the same form. In completely abstract form it is this:

(1) Anything that is A is B. [P]
(2) x is A. [P]
(3) x is B. [1,2]

And this form of argument is valid, meaning precisely that any conclusion of the form of (3) logically follows from the premises of the form of (1) and (2). For example, even those inclined to doubt the conclusion of *Scholz* have to admit that the conclusion does follow from the premises; if the premises are true, then the conclusion *must* be true.

Indeed, an argument can be valid (in the sense just defined) and thus perfectly logical, even if we know that one or more of the premises is false. For example:

Beards

(1) All socialists have beards. [P]
(2) Karl Marx is a socialist. [P]
(3) Karl Marx has a beard. [1,2]

This argument follows the same form, and if the premises are true, then the conclusion would have to be true. So it counts as valid. Moreover, the conclusion is in fact true. However, the first premise of the argument is clearly false—Alexandra Kollontai and Rosa Luxemburg were socialists without beards. So, although *Beards* is valid, it is not *sound*, where we define "sound" to mean a valid argument whose premises are true.

There are only two ways in which an argument could fail to be sound: either one or more of its premises could be false, or one or more of its claimed inferences could be logically fallacious. For example:

Vaudeville

(1) If Karl Marx was a vaudeville comedian, then he was an entertainer. [P]
(2) Karl Marx was not a vaudeville comedian. [P]
(3) Karl Marx was not an entertainer. [1,2]

Both premises of *Vaudeville* are true, as is the conclusion (though I rather like the image of Karl Marx tap-dancing). But the argument is nonetheless invalid, because the premises do not logically imply the truth of the conclusion. Here is a parallel argument to make the fallacy clearer:

10   INTRODUCTION

No Clouds

(1) If it is raining, then there are clouds in the sky. [P]
(2) It is not raining. [P]
(3) There are no clouds in the sky. [1,2]

Premise (1) is true: if it is raining, then there are clouds. But we also know that there can be cloudy days with no rain; so (1) and (2) must not actually imply that there are no clouds in the sky. Both *No Clouds* and *Vaudeville* fail to be valid arguments. Of course, the mere fact that an argument is invalid does not show that its conclusion is false. Perhaps there are no clouds in the sky, and it is true that Karl Marx was no entertainer; but the arguments above do not establish those propositions.

In *Vaudeville* and *No Clouds*, there was an identifiable fallacy. In abstract terms, those arguments both had this form:

(1) If p, then q. [P]
(2) Not-p. [P]
(3) Not-q. [1,2]

And both examples show that this form of argument is indeed fallacious, in the sense that it is possible for the premises to be true while the conclusion is false. This particular type of fallacy even has a name: *denying the antecedent*. However, I will typically not be concerned with naming fallacies or with specifying the abstract logical form of arguments using variables. Most informal arguments, if they are invalid, have a relatively simple problem: the premises don't imply the conclusion because the argument fails to include a needed implicit premise.

A Sample: Socialism and Starvation

I'll give you an example of the sort of argumentative analysis we can do with these tools. One tactic you often see against socialism in the comments section of a social media post: whenever someone says something good about socialism, just bring up starving people in Venezuela. A cartoon by A. F. Branco illustrates the idea.[2] On the left side of the drawing one sees a scraggly young

---

[2] You can see the cartoon at A. F. Branco, "Venezuela Crisis | Political Cartoon | A.F. Branco," *Comically Incorrect*, June 1, 2016. https://comicallyincorrect.com/wp-content/uploads/2016/05/Ven-Bern-600-LA.jpg.

white man with bad posture, six whiskers on his chin, and a sign saying, "Feel the Bern"; the young man's dialogue bubble reads, "DUDE!" Next to him is a middle-aged man wearing ragged and dirty clothes with "Venezuela" written on his shirt. The man holds a sign saying, "Hungry Please Help!" and he says in answer to the Bernie Bro: "BEEN THERE DONE THAT." The implicit idea is that Bernie Sanders's socialist ideas have been tried in Venezuela, and they led to widespread hunger, or, at least, food insecurity. If we try to see some sort of argument against socialism embodied in the cartoon, we could start by reconstructing it this way:

Socialism and Starvation 1.0

(1) Venezuela has a socialist economic system and Venezuela has rampant food insecurity. [P]
(2) Socialist governments should be rejected. [1]

However, this argument is clearly not valid; (2) does not follow logically from (1), for the argument does not contain a premise making any sort of connection between food insecurity and the claim that socialism should be rejected. Branco would need to fill in the gap in some way to make the conclusion logically follow from the premises. For example, one might rerun the argument with an intermediate premise:

Socialism and Starvation 2.0

(1) Venezuela has a socialist economic system, and Venezuela has rampant food insecurity. [P]
(2) If there are countries with an economic system of type X that have rampant food insecurity, then economic systems of type X should be rejected. [P]
(3) Socialist economic systems should be rejected. [1,2]

Now the conclusion indeed follows logically. Premise (2) is a universal proposition about any sort of system of government, claiming that if some countries with that system of government have rampant food insecurity, then that system should be rejected. That premise, combined with (1), would indeed logically imply that socialist governments should be rejected.

12 INTRODUCTION

Let's set aside the question of whether premise (1) is actually true, whether Venezuela is socialist. Even if we granted Branco that point, he has a different problem: premise (2) of his argument can be used against capitalism, for we need merely note that there are countries with capitalist economic systems that also have food insecurity. For example, the country of Botswana is widely regarded as capitalist,[3] but it has food insecurity issues. According to the Global Food Insecurity Index, run by the British publication *The Economist*, 22% of the population is undernourished, meaning that they do not receive the minimum number of calories required for an average person.[4] In fact, even in the United States, over 10% of households are deemed "food insecure" by the US Department of Agriculture, where by this they mean that these households did not always have "enough food for an active, healthy life for all household members."[5] Perhaps we could agree not to count the United States as an instance of *rampant food insecurity*, since 10% of *households* not *always* having enough food for an *active, healthy* life is not as bad as having more than one in four individuals be undernourished. So, to show the problem for Branco's argument, we will go with Botswana:

Capitalism and Starvation

(1) Botswana has a capitalist economic system and Botswana has rampant food insecurity. [P]
(2) If there are countries with an economic system of type X that have rampant food insecurity, then economic systems of type X should be rejected. [P]
(3) Capitalist economic systems should be rejected. [1,2]

The cartoonist Branco, and other defenders of capitalism, can protest that Botswana and Venezuela are different sorts of cases. There certainly are many differences between Botswana and Venezuela. Botswana is in

---

[3] See, for example, Marian Tupy, "Botswana's Success Is Remarkable—and It's Down to Capitalism," cato.org, August 21, 2020, https://www.cato.org/commentary/botswanas-success-rem arkable-its-down-capitalism (accessed March 18, 2023). The Heritage Index of Economic Freedom ranks Botswana as "moderately free," giving it a higher ranking in this regard than various European countries, including Belgium, Portugal, Spain, Hungary, France, and Italy: https://www.heritage.org/index/ranking.

[4] "Global Food Security Index (GFSI)," n.d., https://impact.economist.com/sustainability/project/food-security-index/explore-countries/botswana (accessed March 18, 2023).

[5] "USDA ERS—Key Statistics & Graphics," n.d., https://www.ers.usda.gov/topics/food-nutrition-assistance/food-security-in-the-u-s/key-statistics-graphics/ (accessed March 18, 2023).

LOGIC AND ARGUMENTS   13

Africa and Venezuela is not; Botswana's name starts with a "B" whereas "Venezuela" starts with a "V." My point: there are *always* differences between any two distinct things. But the differences between these two countries are utterly irrelevant to evaluating *Capitalism and Starvation*. Premise (1) of *Capitalism and Starvation* is true. The two premises of the argument do logically imply the conclusion that capitalist economic systems should be rejected. If defenders of capitalism want to reject that conclusion, they must deny premise (2); they have no other choice. But premise (2) of *Capitalism and Starvation* is exactly the same as Branco's own premise in *Socialism and Starvation 2.0*. Is he going to deny the premise when it appears in *Capitalism and Starvation* but affirm it when the very same claim is made in *Socialism and Starvation*? That would be simply inconsistent and logically contradictory.

So Branco will probably want a different intermediate premise—some other way of connecting the existence of starvation in Venezuela to the claim that socialism should be rejected. One might complain that Botswana is but one minor example of a capitalist country and point out that it is surely not enough to say (as does premise (2) in both arguments) that the mere existence of an example or two of a country with an economic system of type X having widespread hunger does not mean that the economic system is to blame. Branco might, for example, revamp (2) as follows:

(2)   If *all* countries with an economic system of type X have rampant food insecurity, then economic systems of type X should be rejected.

But now, to make *Socialism and Starvation* still be valid, he needs to change premise (1) as well, and have it claim that *all* socialist countries have rampant food insecurity:

Socialism and Starvation 3.0

(1) All countries with socialist economic systems have rampant food insecurity. [P]
(2) If all countries with an economic system of type X have rampant food insecurity, then economic systems of type X should be rejected. [P]
(3) Socialist economic systems should be rejected. [1,2]

---

14   INTRODUCTION

This version is valid (the conclusion follows logically from the premises), but now mere mention of Venezuela and its problems does not support premise (1). We would need to know which countries count as socialist and then investigate the existence of food insecurity in each of them. Indeed, premise (1) seems obviously false: even ignoring controversial cases for the moment (e.g., whether the Nordic countries count as socialist), I need merely point out that Cuba (which Branco presumably counts as socialist) does not have rampant food insecurity (the International Food Policy Research Institute said that Cuba's Global Hunger Index was "very low").[6]

So, to sum up the situation so far, all three versions of *Socialism and Starvation* fail. Here were the results:

Version: Problem:

1.0   Clearly not valid.

2.0   Premise (2) would also imply that capitalism should be rejected as shown by *Capitalism and Starvation*; so the conservative will want to reject (2).

3.0   Premise (1) is obviously false.

One thing Branco or other antisocialists might try: take the plausible premises from each version of the argument and put them together this way:

Socialism and Starvation 4.0

(1) Venezuela has a socialist economic system, and Venezuela has rampant food insecurity. [P]

(2) If all countries with an economic system of type X have rampant food insecurity, then economic systems of type X should be rejected. [P]

(3) Socialist economic systems should be rejected. [1,2]

Now both premises (1) and (2) are plausible. But the conclusion no longer follows; version 4.0 is logically invalid: premise (2) allows us to say that if *all* socialist countries have rampant food insecurity, then we should reject

---

[6] Global Hunger Index (GHI)—Peer-Reviewed Annual Publication Designed to Comprehensively Measure and Track Hunger at the Global, Regional, and Country Levels, "Cuba," n.d., https://www.globalhungerindex.org/cuba.html (accessed March 18, 2023).

socialism; but premise (1) only gives a single example, rather than even attempting to claim that this is a feature of all socialist countries.

So, when Branco and other conservatives think they can refute socialism just by making quick references to Venezuela, what *do* they have in mind? What *is* the argument? What are they thinking? I honestly don't know. One might suggest that they are illegitimately sliding back and forth between the versions: when one points out the problem with 2.0, they move to 3.0; when they see the problem with 3.0, they move to 4.0; when one points out the logical problem with 4.0, they slide back to 2.0; and around they go.

To be clear, I have not in this chapter presented any sort of argument *for* socialism, nor have I by any means refuted all possible arguments *against* socialism. A more serious effort could, for example, try to marshal systematic evidence that the more socialist a system is, the more food insecurity results. But that would be an entirely different argument. Venezuela would merely be one data point, as would Botswana. Later in the book, I will be looking at evidence in a systematic fashion like this, attempting to make the case that socialism actually leads to *better* health and well-being outcomes. The point here is that some antisocialists think that they can refute socialism without bothering with any careful analysis of that sort, that they need merely point to Venezuela. They may think they gained rhetorical points and somehow scored a "gotcha," but mere reference to Venezuela provides no coherent argument against socialism (even apart from the question of whether Venezuela counts as socialist).

A Look Ahead

Not all arguments concerning socialism are so, well, cartoonish. Before diving into the much more substantive arguments for and against socialism, I will take you through a brief introduction to some basic ideas in moral philosophy that are directly relevant to evaluating socialism and capitalism as ideologies in Chapter 3. That chapter will also present two parallel arguments: the *Master Argument for Socialism* and the *Master Argument for Capitalism*. The rest of the book will be devoted to analyzing the reasons for and against those arguments, with a great many subarguments discussed along the way.

Before getting into those arguments, you might have a rather fundamental question: What exactly *is* socialism? In fact, you *should* be uncertain about that. Readers who start with a strongly fixed idea of the nature of socialism may well misinterpret or misunderstand the claims made by this book.

16 INTRODUCTION

Different people use the word "socialism" (and "capitalism") in rather different ways, and if we are to make progress in analyzing relevant arguments, we will have to be very clear and explicit about the meanings of our terms (see Chapter 2).

While I do hope to convince you of the wisdom of socialism, I also have three broader goals. First, I hope you will come away with a better understanding of the reasons and arguments concerning this issue. If you are opposed to socialism, then, even if you don't change your mind by the end of the book, I hope you will at least better comprehend the reasons many find it plausible. You will learn, I hope, that some of the traditional arguments against socialism crumble rather quickly under close analysis; other arguments against socialism or for capitalism are more serious but rely on substantive assumptions that might have escaped your notice. If you come to the book already in favor of socialism, then I trust that there is value in exploring more analytically the reasons you might have for your belief. You might, for example, conclude that some of your reasons for being a socialist are less compelling than you thought, and that the best reasons for socialism lie elsewhere. You might even come away with a better understanding of why so many people oppose socialism, even if I also endeavor to explain why their reasons are ultimately wrong.

My second goal goes further than understanding some of the specific reasons for and against socialism: I hope to help you to see *how* to think critically about the things people say about capitalism and socialism. In our hyperpolarized world, political debate often seems to produce more heat than light. If more people applied the tools of reason and analytical thought, political debate might become more civil and more productive. Applying those tools is not easy, but I hope to provide you with both implicit and explicit lessons in how to do that.

Finally, third, I'll admit to one more hope that I have in writing this book: that some will come to see that there is a certain beauty to a carefully constructed argument, and that there is something rewarding and even fun about uncovering and truly understanding the structure of a piece of reasoning.

Key Takeaways

- This book is an introduction to contemporary *arguments* for and against socialism. I hope you will learn something about the substance of these arguments and that you will also gain insight into how to use the tools of logic and analytical reasoning.

- An argument is not just contradiction, nor is it just shouting at or insulting each other. An argument is a connected series of premises leading to a conclusion.
- Conservatives sometimes bring up Venezuela as a quick refutation of socialism, but there is no obvious way of interpreting their argument that makes it sound: on some readings the argument is logically fallacious; on other readings, one of the premises is obviously false.
- Yes, I'm from Kansas; but I've never seen a tornado, and I've never been able to get back home by clicking my heels three times.

2

Defining "Socialism"

Don't Argue about Words

Everyone has their own pet peeves. For me, I hate it when people misuse the phrase "begs the question"—i.e., when they use "begs the question" just to mean the same thing as "elicits the question" or "invites the question." For example, one might hear that "the election results beg the question of why blue-collar workers are voting against their own economic interests." By contrast, the *correct* use of "begs the question" (at least if you ask a philosopher) is when one asserts that an argument is circular, that it presupposes the very thing in question. For example, consider the following argument: "I know that what the Bible says is true, because the Bible says that it is the word of God." Whether or not the Bible is true, this is a lousy argument, for the argument claims that the Bible must be the word of God *on the grounds* that the Bible *says* that it is the word of God; the argument thus simply assumes that what the Bible says (that it is the word of God) is *true*. But that was the very point that the speaker's argument was meant to establish. Philosophers accuse each other of begging the question in this sense, and it is a useful phrase, for which there is no equally pithy substitute. By contrast, if one wants to say that a particular claim or occurrence invites a further question, then we could simply say that "the election results *invite the question* of why blue-collar workers are voting against their own economic interests."

However, when I am done being annoyed by such nonphilosophical uses of "begs the question," I also tend to step back and acknowledge that I can't really claim that the philosophically purist usage of "begs the question" is the only correct one. There is no God-given oracle that determines the one, true correct usage of a word or phrase. Newspapers and books are filled with the supposedly incorrect use of "begs the question"; one hears it repeatedly on network news broadcasts. The actual meaning of a word or phrase is given by its everyday usage; neither I nor anyone else is in a position to claim that widespread usage is wrong. I will probably continue to groan about the "incorrect" use of "begs the question" until the day I die, but I also know that

Socialism. Scott R. Sehon, Oxford University Press. © Oxford University Press 2024.
DOI: 10.1093/oso/9780197753330.003.0002

I am the one who is wrong, insofar as I claim that my preferred usage is the only correct one. It is generally pointless to argue about the meanings of words or to claim that someone's use of a word is wrong, my own sense of linguistic travesty notwithstanding.

It is important to keep this lesson in mind when it comes to the even more fraught term, "socialism." As with any other word, so long as someone is clear and consistent in how they use the term, then we can argue about substance, rather than bickering about whether their use of the word conforms with ours. Of course, one breeds confusion if one uses a word in a way that is widely out of step with common usage; it would be odd to write a book nominally about socialism, and then to proceed to define "socialism" as whatever is contained in the Republican Party platform.

It All Comes in Degrees

The problem with the word "socialism" is that there is no widely agreed upon common usage. We could start, of course, with a dictionary. Here is what the *Oxford English Dictionary* says about the term:

> A theory or system of social organization based on state or collective ownership and regulation of the means of production, distribution, and exchange for the common benefit of all members of society; advocacy or practice of such a system, esp. as a political movement. Now also: any of various systems of liberal social democracy which retain a commitment to social justice and social reform, or feature some degree of state intervention in the running of the economy.[1]

This definition starts by mentioning two features that are associated with socialist forms of political and economic organization: first, the state or collective *ownership and regulation* of the means of production and, second, that this ownership and regulation is done for the purpose of the *common benefit* of all members of society. The second of these could be put in terms of the equality of the distribution or redistribution of wealth: if economic productivity is done for the benefit of *all*, then this presumably means that members

---

[1] "Socialism, n.," OED Online, July 2023, Oxford University Press, https://doi.org/10.1093/OED/5225057167 (accessed October 8, 2023).

20 INTRODUCTION

of the society benefit from it in approximately equal ways. In the first sentence of the definition, the suggestion seems to be that a society would have to have nearly complete collective ownership and regulation and that the distribution of resources would have to be nearly equal before a society would count as socialist. The second sentence of the definition softens this stance by requiring that there must be *some degree* of ownership and regulation ("some degree of state intervention in the running of the economy"), and that there is some "commitment to social justice," suggesting some degree of egalitarian distribution of resources.

We could summarize this by suggesting that there are two principal criteria associated with the word "socialism":

(i) Collective ownership and control of the means of production
(ii) Equality of distribution or redistribution of wealth

As acknowledged by the second part of the OED definition, these criteria admit of degrees. In principle, a system could have *complete* collective ownership and control of the economic forces in society; or there could be completely private ownership of the means of production, and an absolutely free market with no intervention whatsoever by the collective or the state. Or, as is the case with any actual governmental system, one could have some degree of collective ownership and control somewhere between these extremes. Similarly, a government could in principle arrange things such that every single citizen had exactly the same degree of wealth and income; or there could in principle be a system where one individual owns everything, and the rest of the citizens are penniless. Or any degree in between.

Here is how I will use the term "socialism": a system is socialist to the extent that it has more of each of these two features—more collective ownership and control and more egalitarian distribution of wealth. I suggest that it is probably best not to get too hung up on defining some precise degree of each that would be required before we count a system as socialist. But it is worth some discussion of each of the criteria.

First, with respect to the first criterion, it is important to distinguish between the *means of production* and *personal property*. My wife sometimes jokes that she is a socialist about bath towels—they are common property and any one of them can be grabbed off any rack as one exits the shower. By contrast, while I don't have monogrammed towels that I think of as mine forever, once I have used a bath towel, I tend to prefer that only I use it, at least until it goes back through the laundry. Whatever one thinks of this familial dispute, it is not really in any sense about socialism: towels are not *productive property*, for nothing of economic value is created by their use. The factory that made the towels, on the other hand, is part of the means of production. As philosopher Sam Arnold puts it, the means of production include "a society's *instruments of production*, its land, buildings, factories, tools, and machinery; consider also its *raw materials*, its oil and timber and minerals and so on."[2] However, focusing on factories and raw materials gives a bit of a 19th-century feel to the term "means of production." I would also include the infrastructure that goes into today's more service-focused economy: things like stores, delivery centers, computers, the internet, and schools. Even with this broader definition, and even if one ruled out *any* private ownership of the means of production, socialism does not mean that there is no personal property. (It's still my towel, dammit!)

Under capitalism, the means of production are typically privately owned and controlled. There are not many large businesses in the United States that are owned by the workers, though there are a few, for example Publix Super Markets.[3] However, there are numerous examples of state ownership. In Pennsylvania, the state government owns a vast network of retail alcohol stores that sell wine and spirits. They have a monopoly on most wine and spirit sales in the state, and all of the profits generated from their retail stores are funneled into the state budget for use on education, infrastructure, and other services that benefit citizens. In the case of Publix Super Markets, the collective that owns the company consists of the workers themselves; in the case of retail wine and liquor stores in Pennsylvania, the collective is the residents of the state of Pennsylvania. Other examples of collective ownership are the Cabot Creamery, owned by 800 farm families in New England and New York or the Cheese Board Collective, a worker-owned co-op in Berkeley, California, since 1971.

The first criterion specifies both collective *ownership* and *control* of the means of production. These two facets are at least somewhat independent of each other. True, in the paradigm case of ownership, an owner both controls the operation and reaps any financial rewards. But these could come apart. One could set things up such that a manager has complete authority over

---

[2] Sam Arnold, "Socialism | Internet Encyclopedia of Philosophy," n.d., https://iep.utm.edu/socia lis/ (accessed March 18, 2023).

[3] "The Employee Ownership 100: America's Largest Majority Employee-Owned Companies | NCEO," n.d., https://www.nceo.org/articles/employee-ownership-100 (accessed March 18, 2023).

22   INTRODUCTION

how a factory is run but does so for a straight salary that bears no relationship to the profitability of the company. One could also be a completely silent partner in a firm or factory—reaping the financial benefits and taking the financial risks, while exerting no control in the day-to-day operations of the business. For example, the state of Alaska has a sovereign wealth fund from petroleum revenues that is worth over $60 billion.[4] The country of Norway has a far larger sovereign wealth fund, with more than $1 trillion in assets. Such funds amount to partial ownership of the means of production by the collective—either the citizens of Alaska or the citizens of Norway.

When one hears "collective ownership of the means of production," one might first imagine the general model of the Soviet bloc countries: the government owned the factories and other resources for producing goods and services, and thus completely controlled both how they were run and where any proceeds went. There was virtually complete government ownership of the means of production. On the other hand, few would claim that the Soviet Union was anything like a genuine democracy. There were elections to legislative bodies, but typically with only one candidate per office, a candidate approved by the Communist Party. Citizens could register dissent by not voting, but there was no prospect of electing even a single member to the legislative bodies who disagreed strongly with Communist Party leadership.[5] More powerful elements within the Soviet government—the Central Committee, the Politburo, and the general secretary of the Party—were chosen by means even further removed from votes of the people. Arrangements were varied in other countries within the Soviet bloc, but none of them had open, multiparty elections for positions of real power. Of course, the governments in the Soviet bloc countries *claimed* to be acting on behalf of the people, and they would have claimed to be the nearly perfect embodiment of *collective ownership* of the means of production. But *claiming* to be the people's representative is rather empty without genuine democracy. Even if we accept, for the sake of argument, that the government of the USSR worked to ensure that it was the people as a whole who reaped the benefits of the means of production, given the lack of multiparty democracy, it was simply not the case that the people (the collective) controlled the operation.

---

[4] James Brooks, "Alaska Permanent Fund Grows Despite State Spending of Billions on Services and Dividend," *Anchorage Daily News*, September 9, 2019, https://www.adn.com/alaska-news/2019/09/08/permanent-fund-grows-in-first-year-of-new-system-despite-spending-billions-on-state-servi ces-and-dividend/.

[5] Rasma Karklins, "Soviet Elections Revisited: Voter Abstention in Noncompetitive Voting," *American Political Science Review*, vol. 80, no. 2 (June 1986): 449–470.

The astute reader might notice that the original OED definition of "socialism" with which I began included the possibility of "*state* or collective" ownership of the means of production, which might be taken to mean that, for the purposes of its definition, it matters little that the Soviet bloc countries were not democratic. As I said at the outset, don't argue about words. It's fine to count the Soviet bloc countries as socialist in one sense of the word. However, since the Soviet variety of socialism has few advocates (and I am not one of them), I will at least insist on a distinction between a form of socialism in which the means of production are, to some degree, *collectively*, i.e., *democratically*, owned or controlled. I will return to that later in the chapter.

Beyond examples of state ownership, we also know that governments can impose regulatory control over aspects of the economy while not actually owning the businesses affected. For example, the government can have safety regulations requiring seatbelts in cars and building codes that demand that new structures built in California be able to withstand earthquakes. In the opposite direction lies a less regulated economy, with little or no government intervention. In a more truly free market system, we would rely on the market to pressure car manufacturers into having safety devices like seatbelts, and we would leave it up to those who buy buildings to decide whether they want to save a few dollars and risk having the building collapse at the next tremor—perhaps they would be willing to take that gamble, especially if they don't plan on being in the building themselves.

No major country or society has anything like a *perfectly free market* economy in which the government plays no role. For starters, throughout the world governments provide legal systems by means of which contracts can be enforced and a system of liability in the case of failure to meet those contracts. This legal system is not some optional thing that parties can agree to if they so choose; if you make an agreement with me and fail to comply, I cannot just take matters into my own hands (the legal system will punish such vigilante justice), and I can sue you in court regardless of whether you think such courts are legitimate. More ambitiously yet, governments around the world set up systems of patent and copyright protection—which, again, are not some optional service to which you may choose to subscribe but are backed by the full coercive authority of the state.

Another example of government interference in the economy to which few on the right seem to object: through government-enacted legislation, we created the possibility of a *corporation*. This is nominally a collection of people pooling their money together for a specific economic purpose, but

24 INTRODUCTION

with the following feature: if the corporation goes bankrupt or causes great harm, the individuals who reap the dividends from profits are not individually liable for the losses faced by the corporation beyond the amount they invested. Moreover, as we have seen in the economic crisis of 2008 as well as the economic fallout of the pandemic in 2020 and 2021, governments will often go to extreme lengths to bail out large corporations on the brink of insolvency. This means that the individual investors get all the profits; however, not only are they not liable for losses beyond their investment, but they will often even have the government save them from loss of that initial stake. Corporations create a curious system: individuals get the rewards, but the rest of society is there to bail them out in case things go bad. These odd entities (Nathan Robinson refers to them as "psychopathic androids")[6] are also deemed to have free speech rights under the First Amendment in the United States.

Criterion (ii) in the definition was the equality or inequality of the distribution of wealth. If the government simply owns and operates factories or businesses, then it can control the distribution of wealth directly through salaries that it pays people. However, in any system where collective ownership and control of the means of production is far from complete, redistribution of resources will typically take other forms. The most direct method of redistributing resources is to take taxes paid by some people and give that money directly to people who are less well off. This method, in the form of a negative income tax, was advocated strongly by economist Milton Friedman,[7] and the United States has a small program to that effect in its Earned Income Tax Credit.

Apart from directly redistributing money in this fashion, government programs can be designed to help people in other ways. The United Kingdom has the National Health Service. The United States has programs like food stamps (officially, the Supplemental Nutrition Assistance Program, or SNAP), Medicaid, provision of free school lunches to children from low-income families, etc. Moreover, taxes in nearly all developed countries are graduated or progressive, meaning that those with higher incomes pay a higher percentage of that income in taxes. (Or, at least that's what the marginal tax rates would seem to specify; rich people often have a variety of ways of avoiding paying those higher rates. According to the Institute on Taxation

---

[6] Nathan Robinson, *Why You Should Be a Socialist* (New York: St. Martin's Press, 2019).
[7] Milton Friedman, *Capitalism and Freedom* (Chicago: University of Chicago Press, 1962), 191.

and Economic Policy, the top 1% of income earners in the United States pay a total effective tax rate of 30.4%, which is actually a tad *lower* than the tax rate paid by many with lower incomes.)[8] Progressive tax rates appear to be redistributive, insofar as they allow poorer people to pay a smaller percentage of their income for the same government services than do rich people; on other hand, to the extent that rich people benefit from government services more than poor people, taxes would not be redistributive.

According to criterion (ii), a system counts as more socialist to the extent that it moves in the direction of distributing resources in an equal manner. The extreme version of this would be each person having exactly the same wealth and income—or, perhaps, each person having exactly the amount of wealth and income that they need for their particular situation. (Hence Marx's [1875] slogan, "From each according to his ability, to each according to his needs.")

The two criteria are, at least in principle, independent of one another. One could have complete state ownership of the means of production but distribute wealth in a radically unequal way; or one could have virtually complete private ownership of the means of production and have very little regulation but nonetheless impose heavy redistribution via taxes and government spending. No country has ever had complete collective ownership of all means of production, or has completely controlled the economy, or has mandated completely equal distribution of wealth. On the other hand, all countries have had some of each of these three features. Some might prefer to have black-and-white, cut-and-dried categorizations: "*That's* a socialist country" and "*That's* a capitalist country." We could stipulate definitions of "socialism" and "capitalism" such that things would be black and white in this way, but, I claim, that would just obscure the extent to which the relevant considerations come in degrees.

The Classical View

A classical view of socialism, perhaps reflected in the first sentence of the OED definition, is that these things are *not* matters of degree: socialism marks a complete break with capitalist modes of production and ideas. For

---

[8] ITEP, "Who Pays Taxes in America in 2018?," n.d., https://itep.org/who-pays-taxes-in-america-in-2018/ (accessed March 18, 2023).

26 INTRODUCTION

example, Pablo Gilabert and Martin O'Neill say: "socialism, unlike capitalism, requires that the bulk of the means of production workers use to yield goods and services be under the effective control of workers themselves, rather than in the hands of the members of a different, capitalist class under whose direction they must toil."[9] Or compare Alan Maass in *The Case for Socialism*: "The elementary point of socialism will be to take profit out of the equation. Therefore, the resources of society could be commonly owned and controlled by everyone, with decisions made democratically according to what's needed and wanted, not how much money can be made."[10] Or Micah Uetricht and Megan Day: "Ultimately, our vision for socialism is this: we want to eliminate private ownership of the means of production. We want the principal productive assets of society to be owned in common and run democratically by workers."[11]

On this sort of view, while socialism may involve some degree of control of the economy and redistribution, a socialist system *must* have a very high degree of collective ownership. According to these purists, a state with a heavily regulated market economy with high degrees of redistribution might be called a "social democracy," but it would not count as *socialist* so long as any significant portion of the natural resources and productive capacities remained in private hands, or if any substantial inequality (not related to differing needs) remained. If we simply redistribute some of the profits under capitalism in a more egalitarian way, we haven't changed the mindset; to do that we need a reorientation away from profit. Or so the proponents of the classical view argue.

On the face of things, this looks to be a mere semantic dispute of the sort that I began the chapter by urging us to avoid: never argue about words. The classical socialists have a linguistically purist position, rather like my own philosopher's inclination regarding the term "begs the question." And, just as I admitted that common usage was out of step with the purist insistence on "begs the question," one could also point out that the classical definition of "socialism" is out of step with common usage. For example, in the United States, Bernie Sanders refers to himself as a democratic socialist, and he is widely referred to as a socialist by commentators on both left and right; yet

---

[9] Pablo Gilabert and Martin O'Neill, "Socialism," *The Stanford Encyclopedia of Philosophy* (Fall 2019 ed.), ed. Edward N. Zalta, https://plato.stanford.edu/archives/fall2019/entries/socialism/.

[10] Alan Maass, *The Case for Socialism*, 3rd ed. (Chicago: Haymarket Books, 2010), 77.

[11] Micah Uetricht and Meagan Day, *Bigger Than Bernie: How We Can Win Democratic Socialism in Our Time* (New York: Verso, 2021), 147.

Sanders says explicitly, "I don't believe government should own the means of production,"[12] and the policies he advocates call for a relatively modest increase in collective ownership. On the purist sense of the term, both Sanders's supporters and his critics, as well as Sanders himself, are making a simple and egregious linguistic mistake when they refer to Sanders as a democratic *socialist*.

In the more academic realm, economist Thomas Piketty defends what he calls "democratic socialism," where this does not look like what the linguistic purists insist upon. Piketty notes socialist movements have historically "been constructed around . . . state ownership of the means of production and centralized planning," but he rejects this model.[13] Instead, Piketty defends higher degrees of fiscal progressivity in taxation (thereby leading to far less inequality of distribution of resources) while also advocating for much greater collective control over vast sectors of economic activity, "notably in health care and education, but also in culture, transportation, energy, and so on."[14] He explicitly notes that this comes in degrees and says that "no one can decide in advance how far such a process" should go, i.e., "how and to what extent they will be collectively financed (perhaps someday 60 or 70 percent of the national income, or even more)."[15]

You can insist that Piketty, Sanders, and much of our political culture are simply misusing the term "socialism" by seeing it as coming in degrees and by going beyond the classical model of nearly complete collective ownership of the means of production. However, if, on your preferred use of a term, almost everyone else is misusing the term, then perhaps you should at best see yourself as making a linguistic proposal, rather than being able to truly say that your usage is somehow the correct one. It matters not that the purist usage of "socialism" was or was not once commonly accepted or goes back to Marx. After all, the word "awful" at one time meant "inspiring awe," such that one could say that a piece of art was *awful* and mean it as a high compliment; anyone who insists that this is therefore *really* what "awful" means

---

[12] Andrew Prokop, "Read Bernie Sanders's Speech on Democratic Socialism in the United States," *Vox*, November 19, 2015, https://www.vox.com/2015/11/19/9762028/bernie-sanders-democratic-socialism.

[13] Thomas Piketty, *A Brief History of Equality* (Cambridge, MA: Harvard University Press, 2022), 155.

[14] Piketty, *Brief History of Equality*, 156.

[15] Piketty, *Brief History of Equality*, 156–157.

28   INTRODUCTION

today simply doesn't understand how language works; and they are likely to dish out some unintended insults.

However, underlying the apparently semantic dispute about how to use a word *might* be a more substantive argumentative point. I propose using the word "socialism" such that it simply comes in degrees and claim that we need not find and label some tipping point before which we have capitalism and after which we have socialism. But beyond issues of historical antecedents, a socialist might say that the *reasons* or *arguments* for adopting socialism do point to some sort of important tipping point. This might happen in one of two ways. First, given a particular tipping point, the arguments and evidence might unequivocally suggest that we should move at least that far if not beyond—that any reason for moving in the socialist direction would be a reason for moving to at least the tipping point. If that is the case, then we might as well say that socialism includes anything after the tipping point but not anything before it. The argumentative situation might be even more extreme: there could be arguments or reasons for moving to the tipping point, but where these arguments don't suggest that moving a few steps in that direction is a good thing by itself. The idea would be that capitalism is gravely wrong unless you change it drastically and go beyond the tipping point. For example, one might claim that capitalist modes of production intrinsically involve a completely unacceptable exploitation of workers, and it doesn't really help to exploit workers a little less, for any degree of exploitation is morally wrong. (I will explore this sort of argument in Chapter 5.) If there are such arguments against capitalism and for socialism, then it would indeed make sense to refuse the label "socialism" to anything less than the proper amount of collective ownership.

However, I think we would unduly constrain things if we were to presuppose at the outset that the arguments for socialism are of this sort. The two criteria that I list above *do* come in degrees. We should not prejudge the issue of whether the arguments for socialism themselves strongly imply a decisive tipping point concerning these degrees. Indeed, in contrast to certain elements of the socialist tradition, I will ultimately suggest that the arguments do not work this way; I will contend that the best arguments for socialism suggest moving in the socialist direction to some significant degree, but that there is no antecedently clear dividing point concerning how far we should move; I will claim that this depends in part on empirical matters and might vary with the circumstances. And I will claim that each step in this direction is a good thing. As Bhaskar Sunkara says in his book, *The Socialist Manifesto*, "class struggle

DEFINING "SOCIALISM" 29

social-democracy . . . isn't the foe of democratic socialism—the road to the latter runs through the former."[16]

So, in the end, my preference for defining "socialism" as a matter of degree will come down to the substantive nature of the arguments for and against socialism. Here, of course, I could be wrong, and the more classically inclined socialists might be correct. But I will still maintain this about the linguistic point: we should not prejudge those substantive issues by artificially stipulating that a socialist system must have x degree of collective control of the means of production or y degree of egalitarian distribution of resources.

Some Rough Distinctions

Despite having just spent several pages making the case for seeing socialism and capitalism as coming in degrees and denying that there is any crucial tipping point, I will nonetheless make a rough-and-ready distinction between several sorts of political and economic systems. First there is one what might call *US-style capitalism:*

- Some government ownership of the means of production, some regulation and control of the economy, and some redistribution, but relatively little of these things.

It is important to make the banal observation that even the United States does have some degree of the features defining socialism. Regarding ownership of the means of production, local governments largely run primary and secondary education, and state governments operate some tertiary education; local governments typically operate police departments, fire departments, public works, and public libraries. Local and state governments also often provide funding for sports arenas (to which privately owned teams sell expensive tickets). The federal government builds major infrastructure like roads and bridges, provides a postal service, runs national defense, and helps air travel by running airport security. In Washington, DC, the federal government even runs museums and other cultural institutions. In general, the US federal government employed 2.1 million workers in 2018, and the

---

[16] Bhaskar Sunkara, *The Socialist Manifesto: The Case for Radical Politics in an Era of Extreme Inequality* (New York: Basic Books, 2019), 222.

30 INTRODUCTION

services many of those workers provide rightly count as part of the means of production.[17] Even where the government does not own the means of production, there are regulations and other controls on economic transactions. Finally, regarding criterion (ii), there is some redistribution via programs like Medicare, Medicaid, Obamacare, food stamps, welfare, Social Security, the Veteran's Authority, etc., and we have a moderately progressive income tax, though it is much less progressive than it used to be (under Dwight Eisenhower, not generally regarded as a left-wing radical, the top marginal tax rate in the United States was 91%; as of this writing, it is 37%).[18]

So if we think of socialism as coming in degrees along the two scales, the United States will still be, to some degree, socialist. Nonetheless, it is reasonable enough to say that the United States counts as *not* socialist, because it falls relatively low on both. Of course, there are conservatives and libertarians who would like far less collective control and far less redistribution, but I think we can still count the United States as basically capitalist.

Toward the opposite extreme, we could imagine the following, which one could refer to as *classic socialism*:

- Systems with a *very* high degree of state ownership of the means of production and a planned economy, with *very* low levels of income and wealth inequality.

If we imagine the two criteria as a two-dimensional graph, we could plot the United States and this version of socialism as in Figure 2.1. Of course, any such depiction has the risk of portraying the situation much more precisely than is actually feasible. I do not have up my sleeve any simple numeric scale on which we could accurately measure the degree of collective ownership and regulation of an economy. Even measuring the level of egalitarian distribution is far from trivial. There are all-purpose calculated numbers like the Gini coefficient by which countries are often rated in terms of their levels of either income or wealth inequality. Using such numbers, one can see that the United States is much more unequal than, for example, the countries of Western Europe. However, the complex calculations involved in the Gini coefficient do not yield numbers that are intuitively very meaningful, and there

---

[17] "Federal Workforce Statistics Sources: OPM and OMB," Congressional Research Service, June 24, 2021, p. 1, https://sgp.fas.org/crs/misc/R43590.pdf.

[18] Tax Policy Center, "Historical Highest Marginal Income Tax Rates," February 9, 2022, https://www.taxpolicycenter.org/statistics/historical-highest-marginal-income-tax-rates.

DEFINING "SOCIALISM" 31

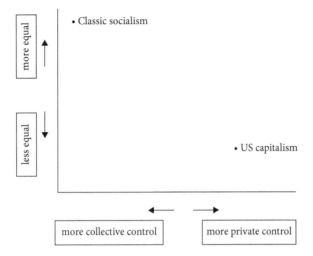

Figure 2.1

are problems with thinking of it as an all-purpose representation of levels of inequality.[19] Moreover, if what we want to know is the degree to which a political and economic system is arranged so as to distribute resources in an egalitarian fashion, snapshots of the currently existing levels of inequality are a start, but do not by any means tell the whole story. Nonetheless, we know that there are degrees of collective control and degrees to which a system distributes resources equally, and we can form educated, rough ideas about where particular systems would fall in the chart.

If we temporarily overlooked the fact that Soviet-style ownership and control of the means of production was not truly *collective* (because it was far from a genuine democracy), then we could attempt to place the USSR on this rough chart as well. Though it certainly never achieved that Marxist ideal of redistributing to each according to need, there was a substantial amount of egalitarian redistribution. The nondemocratic *state* did own and control very large portions of the means of production, though even here small private enterprises were allowed, and there was always a not insignificant black market. So we could include on the graph a dot for *state socialism* of this sort, and it would be in the upper left-hand corner of the graph, albeit not as far as

---

[19] See Thomas Piketty, *A Brief History of Equality* (Harvard University Press, 2022). See also Evelyn Lamb, "Ask Gini: How to Measure Inequality," *Scientific American*, November 12, 2012.

32 INTRODUCTION

the dot for classic socialism. (And with the ever-present caveat that the control was not really collective.)

In the graph presented in Figure 2.1, there is a great deal of space between what I have called classic socialism and US capitalism. Without attempting any precision in the matter, I will refer to anything significantly further left and up from the dot representing the United States as "democratic socialism." This means that classic socialism certainly counts as democratic socialism, but that much else will besides.

When it makes a difference in the arguments discussed later in the book, I will sometimes use a shorthand to distinguish between these varieties of socialism. The Soviet model of state socialism, including its nondemocratic aspects, I will refer to as *S-socialism*. I will use the term *D-socialism* for democratic socialism, representing the area significantly further left and up from US capitalism.

Scandinavia and Democratic Socialism

In making these characterizations, I have not mentioned any currently existing economic systems beyond that of the United States. However, I will use "D-socialism" to include the Nordic countries (Denmark, Norway, Sweden, and Finland); that is to say, I will count them as democratic socialist states.

This is controversial. Although American politicians who identify as democratic socialists, like Bernie Sanders and Alexandria Ocasio-Cortez, point to the Nordic countries as examples of the general ideas they are talking about, there are others who insist that this is all wrong, and that the Scandinavian countries are not actually socialist in any reasonable sense. As one example, a 2018 article in *Forbes* has the title "Sorry Bernie Bros but Nordic Countries Are Not Socialist."[20] Rand Paul in his book called *The Case against Socialism* has an entire part of the book labeled "Capitalism Makes Scandinavia Great." Some on the left echo this sentiment. Micah Uetricht and Meagan Day, in a book with the subtitle "How We Go from the Sanders Campaign to Democratic Socialism," say that the Nordic countries "are often called 'socialist' or 'democratic socialist,'" but they say that "this isn't quite right." By their accounting, the Nordic countries count as "social

---

[20] Jeffrey Dorfman, "Sorry Bernie Bros but Nordic Countries Are Not Socialist," *Forbes*, July 8, 2018, https://www.forbes.com/sites/jeffreydorfman/2018/07/08/sorry-bernie-bros-but-nordic-countries-are-not-socialist/?sh=77a6a6874ad3.

Table 2.1 Percentage of National Wealth Owned by Government

Denmark	11%
Finland	32%
Norway	56%
Sweden	24%
United States	−3%

democracies: capitalist societies with a strong social safety net and high progressive taxation."[21]

When these various authors on both sides of the spectrum deny that the Nordic countries are socialist, this largely has to do with the semantic issue over what counts as socialism; I don't intend to reopen that issue. Instead, it is worth looking briefly at how the Nordic countries stack up on the two criteria by means of which I have defined "socialism." That question is still important to the arguments of this book, for in Chapters 7–8 I will be pointing to evidence of how socialism works successfully, in part, by looking at how things are going in the Nordic countries.

First consider collective ownership of the means of production. I know of no data source that would give anything like a complete measure of this, in part because we would have to decide exactly what counted as part of the means of production and what counted as collective ownership. Collective ownership need not be restricted to government ownership, and not everything that is owned by government is properly thought of as part of the means of production. But we can start to get some idea by looking at where we do have data: we can measure the degree to which national wealth is owned by the government, and we have numbers on this from the World Inequality Database (Table 2.1).[22]

---

[21] Uetricht and Day, *Bigger Than Bernie*, 141–142.

[22] WID—Wealth and Income Database, "Home—WID—World Inequality Database," WID—World Inequality Database, https://wid.world/. I will note that Senator Paul refers to the same source when he attempts to refute the idea that the Scandinavian countries are socialist: "As far as private ownership, Giancarlo Sopo reports that even using Thomas Piketty's World Inequality Report (WIR) data, '90 percent of Scandinavia's combined wealth is privately owned' " (p. 79). However, the Senator errs badly here. Giancarlo Sopo did indeed draw that conclusion from the World Inequality Data in an August 17, 2018, article; however, the article as it now appears on the web includes an update from 12 days later on August 29, 2018, in which it admits that "the data was actually faulty." Thus Senator Paul cites data whose own source admits the data to be faulty. Perhaps this was an honest mistake on the Senator's part; perhaps he checked that website during the 12 days when it was up without the correction, and somehow never checked again prior to publishing his own book in October 2019. It is

34 INTRODUCTION

If one puts together the four Nordic countries, the total of nationally owned wealth is 34%. The United States comes in negative because our national debt actually outweighs the positive wealth owned by the government. (One reason that Norway's percentage is so much higher than the others: Norway has two separate government pension funds, mostly from petroleum revenues. Naturally, this is not just wealth that is sitting there as gold or piles of currency; the funds are invested. That is to say, they are used to buy shares in the means of production. And the shares are considerable. At the time of this writing, the two funds have a value of almost $1.3 trillion, which comes to nearly $250,000 for each Norwegian citizen.)[23]

As I said, I would not take these numbers to be anything like a perfect measure of the degree to which there is collective ownership of the means of production. And the fact that national debt counts against national wealth complicates the picture. The United States obviously does have much property and other assets, even if it also owes more than that to those who hold its debt. (To complicate the picture even further, a large amount of the debt is in fact owned by Americans.) Nonetheless, the data paint a picture of Scandinavian governments with a significantly greater share of the means of production than is true in the United States.

The second part of the first criterion was collective *control* of the economy. This is even harder to measure in any precise or uncontroversial way. Governments do all kinds of things that affect markets and the economy. The things that seem most obvious to conservatives are regulations, taxes, and fees. Governments also directly affect the markets through monetary policies, including setting key interest rates. As we well know from the economic crisis of 2008–2009 and the pandemic of 2020, governments can also bail out struggling companies. But beyond these surface-level features, governments also enforce contracts, hand out copyrights and patents, set up bankruptcy laws, and regulate (or fail to regulate) monopolies through antitrust legislation.

---

interesting, though, that many of his other sources are from 2019, including another reference to *The Federalist* in March 2019, so it is not as if his book was already in production. The other hypothesis is that Senator Paul knew full well that the data had been deemed faulty by his own source, but decided to go with it anyway.

[23] To be precise as of the end of 2022: $233,000 per citizen. Data on fund values from Norges Bank Investment Management, "The Fund | Norges Bank Investment Management," n.d., https://www.nbim.no/ (accessed March 19, 2023).

Table 2.2 General Government Spending as Percentage of GDP

Denmark	54.5%
Finland	56.5%
Norway	49.3%
Sweden	49.3%
United States	37.9%

Table 2.3 Percentage of Workforce in Public Sector

Denmark	28.0%
Finland	24.3%
Norway	30.3%
Sweden	28.8%
United States	15.2%

One thing we can easily enough measure is simply the *size* of government—its overall expenditures in proportion to the size of the country's economy as measured by gross domestic product. Those numbers are shown in Table 2.2.[24] Among all 37 countries that are members of the Organization for Economic Cooperation and Development (OECD), the average is 42.9%; so the Scandinavian countries are about 22% above this average and the United States is about 12% below it. In general, relative to GDP, government spending in the Scandinavian countries is 38% higher than in the United States. Naturally, size of government is far from a perfect measure for degree of control of the economy, but it is some indication. And the indication is that government plays a significantly larger role in Scandinavia than in the United States.

Another measure of the degree of government involvement in the economy would be the percentage of the workforce that is in the public sector. If a country employs more of its workforce in the government, then that presumably means that the government is playing more of an active role in the overall economy—if nothing else, it is directly paying more of the workers. Table 2.3 gives the numbers from 2017 on the percentage of the

---

[24] "General Government Spending," OECD Data, https://data.oecd.org/gga/general-government-spending.htm (accessed February 4, 2022).

36 INTRODUCTION

Table 2.4 Distribution of Income

	Top 1%	Top 10%	Bottom 50%
Denmark	10.7%	31.0%	23.7%
Finland	10.1%	33.1%	22.5%
Norway	9.4%	30.1%	26.0%
Sweden	9.0%	29.8%	24.7%
Nordic countries average	9.8%	31.0%	24.2%
United States	20.5%	46.8%	12.7%

workforce employed in the public sector in the United States as opposed to the Scandinavian countries:[25]

Averaging the Nordic countries together, they employ over 80% more of the workforce in government than does the United States, thus indicating that they have a much higher collective role in the economy than the United States.

The second criterion was the degree to which there was equality in distribution or redistribution of resources. Here we have clearer data, at least as regards income. We can first look at how income is distributed in the Nordic countries as opposed to the United States (Table 2.4).[26] As the chart shows, in the United States, the top 1% of earners rake in over 20% of the total income, while the bottom *half* of earners only get 12.7% of the total income. While there is inequality in the Nordic countries too, it is far less: on average, the top 1% take in about 10% of the income and the bottom half still takes in at least about a quarter of the income. If we look at the top 1% and the bottom 50% as benchmarks, we could say that inequality of income is approximately twice as extreme in the United States as in the Nordic countries.

It would be good to look at the distribution of wealth in addition to that of income. Unfortunately, as the "World Inequality Report" states, the data on wealth inequality are "much sparser than for income inequality." Wealth is, of course, different from income. One might earn $50K in income per year, but essentially have no assets to show for it; or one might have a modest salary but have inherited vast swaths of real estate or have a huge trust fund.

---

[25] Government at a Glance 2019, OECD, 2019, https://doi.org/10.1787/888934031997.
[26] Data from World Inequality Database (https://wid.world) from the most recent year available for each country (2019 for the United States; 2017 for the Nordic countries).

Accordingly, one might expect that wealth inequalities will be even more extreme than income inequalities.

Wealth inequality in the United States certainly is extreme. According to the WID database, the wealthiest 1% of the US population owns 37% of the wealth; the bottom 50% barely owns any, possessing less than one-half of 1% of the wealth. There appear to be no data of this sort for all of the Nordic countries, though the OECD reports that in Denmark, Finland, and Norway, the top 1% owns an average of 19% of the wealth—thus again indicating that at least in these Nordic countries the wealth inequality is about half of that we see in the United States.

The OECD also reports another measure that is interesting, the ratio between mean and median wealth in those countries. The *mean* is just the average income, where you add up the entire wealth and divide by the number of people. The median wealth would be arrived at by ranking from top to bottom the wealthiest to the poorest people, and then choosing the middle one—the one such that half the people are wealthier and half the people are poorer. A mean or average can be driven to very high ranges by some anomalously high numbers. The median is less susceptible to these extremes, since there is a limit to how poor one can be; adding one person of zero net worth will not skew an average nearly so much.

Illustration of mean vs. median.

Imagine Yankee Stadium filled to capacity, with 47,309 cheering fans. Suppose those fans have an average net worth of $50,000, which is something close to the median net worth of individuals in America. Now Elon Musk and Mark Zuckerberg, with a combined net worth of about $350 billion, enter the ballpark. Suddenly, the *average* net worth of the fans has soared from $50,000 to $7,500,000, although no individual is a penny richer since entering the ballpark (indeed, if they bought a beer and a hot dog, they would be about $15 poorer). By contrast, *median* net worth of the fans would go up barely at all. If we arranged all the fans in order of net worth, the median before the entrance of the Musk and Zuckerberg would be the wealth of the 23,654th of the fans. After the arrival of Musk and Zuckerberg, the median would move up one notch to the wealth of the 23,653rd fan—a minor difference.

Accordingly, one could take the ratio between mean and median as an indication of the degree to which wealth is unequally distributed. Table 2.5 shows

38 INTRODUCTION

Table 2.5 Mean to Median Wealth Ratio

Denmark	4.7
Finland	1.8
Norway	2.0
Nordic countries average	2.8
United States	8.2

those numbers (without Sweden because the OECD reports no numbers for Sweden). In the United States, the ratio between mean and median wealth is almost three times as much as the average in the Nordic countries on which we have the data, meaning that there are way more super-rich people at the top skewing the average upward, relative to the median. Again, the lesson is clear: there is much greater inequality of wealth in the United States than in the Nordic countries.

Key Takeaways

- As I use the term, a socialist system tends toward more of the following:
  (i) Collective ownership and control of the means of production
  (ii) Equality of distribution or redistribution of wealth
- According to a more classical definition, socialism requires largely complete collective ownership of the means of production, and it is wrong to say that socialism comes in degrees. The arguments for socialism *might* make this a reasonable proposal, but we should not prejudge those arguments by defining socialism in this way.
- Soviet-style state socialism (S-socialism) involved a fair amount of egalitarian distribution, but actually failed badly on criterion (i), for the lack of democracy meant that there was not truly *collective* ownership and control.
- Democratic socialist (D-socialist) states are, on this account, systems where there is a fairly significant degree of both (i) and (ii)—much more than, say, in the United States.
- The Nordic countries count as D-socialist by this criterion.
- One should not argue about words. (But *please* don't use "begs the question" simply to mean the same as "invites the question.")

3

Moral Philosophy Background and the Master Arguments

The Fundamental Question

We can make a distinction between socialism as a political and economic system—defined as coming in degrees along the two axes—and socialism as the *advocacy* for such a political and economic system. Thus, a socialist favors socialism as a political and economic system. We can, of course, make the same distinction for the word "capitalism." In asking whether socialism or capitalism is correct, we are asking which, if either, system we should advocate. In other words, we can pose the fundamental question as follows: How ought we to structure our political and economic system?

The first thing to note about this question is that it is a *moral* question. It is a question about what *ought* to be the case. Some readers, perhaps especially some of those on the political left, will be uncomfortable with such moral language. It is one thing to say that there are facts about what happened where and when, or facts about evolution, vaccines, or climate change. But facts about what we *ought* to do? About how society *should* be organized? It is popular in some liberal circles to be suspicious of such language, perhaps saying that concepts like *morality* are "socially constructed." One might claim that these concepts, at best, are valid only within a particular cultural framework; or, at worst, one might say that talk of moral values is itself a tool of the patriarchal, neoliberal, capitalist system that needs to be overthrown.

I find such skepticism about morality and rights understandable but deeply misguided. However, I will not fully argue for that here, since that would take us too far astray. But I will note if we were to genuinely avoid the moral question of how we ought to structure our society, then it is not clear what other question we might be asking when we talk about political matters. We can of course ask purely historical questions, e.g., questions about the conditions under which different systems have been implemented. Or we could ask empirical questions about the future, e.g.: What sort of political

Socialism. Scott R. Sehon, Oxford University Press. © Oxford University Press 2024.
DOI: 10.1093/oso/9780197753330.003.0003

40 INTRODUCTION

and economic system will country X have in 2050? But advocacy of socialism can surely not just mean either of these sorts of questions; one can easily imagine a rational socialist and a rational capitalist (yes, I believe that there are instances of both kinds) agreeing on the history and even agreeing on tentative predictions about the future. Questions about history or what will happen in the future are not what typically divide socialists and capitalists. (There is one strand in Marxist thought according to which the downfall of capitalism and the rise of socialism is historically inevitable, and this *is* an empirical claim. But one can surely be a socialist without accepting the historical inevitability of socialism.)

One might also ask questions about the psychological motivations of socialists and capitalists: Why do socialists want socialism? Why do capitalists want capitalism? But, again, one could imagine a socialist and a capitalist largely agreeing on these matters. Psychological questions about the typical advocate of either capitalism or socialism clearly do not exhaust the debate between socialists and capitalists.

One might also ask this question: What political and economic system is in my best interests? But this, too, cannot be the question that divides socialists and capitalists, for one can easily imagine a person who honestly believes that capitalism is in her own best interest but who nonetheless favors socialism. There also seem to be opponents of redistribution and collective control who themselves might well benefit from more of each.

Any question about the sort of political and economic system we *should* adopt is fundamentally a moral question. The typical socialist will have to admit that, at root, what motivates socialism is a deeply moral sense of concern for our fellow human beings. At least according to some socialists, socialism ultimately is the sense of injustice one feels when thinking about the fact that some are inheriting billions of dollars when others are working multiple minimum wage jobs in a desperate struggle to keep their children fed and housed.[1] Socialism fundamentally promotes the ideal that we are in this together, and that we should care about the well-being of each person. I think it is very hard to be a skeptic about moral truth and nonetheless be really committed to socialist ideals.

---

[1] See, for example, Robinson, *Why You Should Be a Socialist.*

Socialists will sometimes accuse capitalists of not having any similar moral commitment, of celebrating pure selfishness and of the idea that each person should be expected to do nothing other than what is in their immediate economic self-interest. For example, Uetricht and Day argue that "Capitalism, especially in its neoliberal form in recent decades, has dismantled any sense that we all belong to such a common project with the rest of humanity."[2] However, most defenders of capitalism will certainly deny that they are in favor of selfishness. They will say that the best system for everyone, including those currently in the bottom rungs of the well-being ladder, is a free market capitalism that builds immense wealth that is ultimately enjoyed by all, even if there are great inequalities. It's not that they don't care about the poor, they will say; it's that capitalism is the best system even for the poor and downtrodden.

A Moral Framework

Once we acknowledge that the fundamental question is moral, then we need to think about how to approach it. One obvious approach would simply be to ask which system, capitalism or socialism, is the best for overall human welfare or human well-being. This would be the approach of utilitarianism, according to which the right action under any given set of circumstances is the one that maximizes overall utility. Whatever else one thinks of this view, the utilitarian surely is right about this much: promoting human well-being is good, and, all things being equal, a political system that better promotes human well-being seems to be the better choice. Of course, one might well dispute that all things are equal. One might claim that well-being is not always enough: the mere fact that a policy makes more people happy, or even leads to greater well-being overall, does not show that we should accept the policy. It could be that there are *rights* involved, rights that ought not to be violated irrespective of general judgments about what would make people happier.

---

[2] Uetricht and Day, *Bigger Than Bernie*, 163–164.

42 INTRODUCTION

Taking these points into account, a socialist might propose the following very general argument:

Master Argument for Socialism

(1) Socialism better promotes human well-being than extant alternative styles of governance. [P]
(2) Socialism does not violate moral rights of individuals. [P]
(3) Given two styles of governance, if the first better promotes human well-being than the second and does not violate moral rights of individuals, then it should be chosen over the second. [P]
(4) Socialism should be chosen over extant alternative styles of governance. [1,2,3]

On the other hand, one might also offer a perfectly parallel argument for capitalism:

Master Argument for Capitalism

(1) Capitalism better promotes human well-being than extant alternative styles of governance. [P]
(2) Capitalism does not violate moral rights of individuals. [P]
(3) Given two styles of governance, if the first better promotes human well-being than the second and does not violate moral rights of individuals, then it should be chosen over the second. [P]
(4) Capitalism should be chosen over extant alternative styles of governance. [1,2,3]

Much of the rest of this book will essentially be devoted to evaluating these arguments. Before proceeding to that, we will first investigate some key questions about the meaning of the premises: What does it mean to better promote human well-being, and what does it mean for rights to be violated? The *Master Arguments* embody a very broadly utilitarian approach to questions of political justice, tempered by allowing the possibility that there are rights that can take precedence over utility calculations. Both aspects require some discussion and clarification.

Promoting Well-Being

As an all-encompassing moral theory, utilitarianism is subject to many questions and objections. Since philosophers like Jeremy Bentham and John Stuart Mill codified the ideas into a philosophical theory in the 18th and 19th centuries, philosophers have debated all aspects of the view, with many questions still not fully resolved.[3] I will mention a number of these issues, only to set aside most of them as irrelevant to the concerns of this book. Other questions are more relevant in the sense that they might seem to yield objections to the premise that is affirmed in both versions of the *Master Argument*:

(3) Given two styles of governance, if the first better promotes human well-being than the second and does not violate moral rights of individuals, then it should be chosen over the second.

This premise is put specifically in terms of *human* well-being, but I don't mean to suggest that I am utterly indifferent to the claims of the well-being of other sentient individuals, whether they be animals or space aliens. I will in fact put the discussion in terms of humans, but I don't think the argument would change significantly if we included the interests of animals. There would be a problem for my phrasing of the *Master Argument* if, for example, one thought that socialism might be best for humans, but that capitalism is far better for animals. But that seems highly implausible to me, so I won't worry about it. (I suppose that one could also worry about whether our adoption of socialism or capitalism will affect the interests of space aliens, but I'll leave that aside too. I'll note, however, that in the *Star Trek* universe where there are many nonhuman species, the implied governmental structure is apparently quite socialist, and the nonhuman species seem fine with that. There is the exception of the Ferengi, who appear to view profit as the only worthwhile goal; but that also makes them, at best, a strange curiosity to the others; at worst, it makes them quite villainous.)

Even when it comes to measuring the well-being of humans, there are all kinds of complications. What exactly do we mean by "well-being" if not just pleasant sensations? Is it a matter of having more of your desires or preferences satisfied? Does it mean having a more *meaningful* life, even if

---

[3] For a couple of good introductory texts on different approaches to justices see Will Kymlicka, *Contemporary Political Philosophy: An Introduction*, 2nd ed. (New York: Oxford University Press, 2001) and Michael Sandel, *Justice: What's the Right Thing to Do?* (New York: Farrar, Strauss and Giroux, 2009).

44 INTRODUCTION

it has less pleasure and fewer fulfilled preferences? Also: Is the right action the one that leads to the most happiness, or is the right action the one that follows a general *rule* that normally leads to the most happiness, even if it does not do so in this particular case? Are we looking to maximize the sum total of well-being, or are we looking at a per capita basis?[4]

I do not plan any effort to settle these sorts of disputes about the nature of well-being for the simple reason that it seems unlikely that they will affect the debate between socialism and capitalism. As we will see in Parts III and IV, there is a lively debate one can have concerning whether socialism or capitalism better promotes human well-being, but I don't think anything in that debate will hinge on these details about how we count well-being. We would need to decide these debates about the nature of well-being if there were considerations or arguments that indicated that, for example, that one way of counting well-being worked well for socialism but that a different way worked better for capitalism. The reader is invited to keep an eye out for such differences, but I doubt they will find anything.

Objection 1: We Can't Measure Well-Being

On the other hand, one might have more thoroughgoing doubts about the whole project of basing questions of justice, even in part, on the promotion of well-being. First, one might make the relatively obvious observation that it is difficult to measure well-being. For example, many countries around the world had to make decisions about what restrictions to impose on ordinary life in light of the coronavirus pandemic. One such difficult decision involved whether to have children continue to attend public schools in person. Making education remote had clear costs for children, particularly when this was more difficult for some families than others. Children's education and socialization suffered, in ways that were hard to predict or quantify. On the other hand, there was a hard-to-determine probability that we reduced the spread of the disease by closing schools, and thereby reduced the number of people who became seriously ill or died. This was not an easy balance to draw, in part because it involved our best guess at certain probabilities, but

---

[4] For a glimpse into all of the different variations on utilitarianism, see Walter Sinnot Armstrong, "Consequentialism," *The Stanford Encyclopedia of Philosophy*, ed. Edward N. Zalta (Summer 2019 ed.), https://plato.stanford.edu/archives/sum2019/entries/consequentialism/.

also because it was hard to know how to compare the value of a child's education and psychological well-being with the health (or life) of an older person.

As difficult as it is to make such decisions, I am not much impressed by this as a general objection to the approach of aiming for policies that better promote human well-being, nor specifically as an objection to premise (3) of the *Master Arguments*. While it is tempting to say that there is no common currency by means of which we can compare different sorts of values (e.g., a child's education vs. the risk of serious illness), life forces us into making such comparisons all the time. That is perhaps clearest when it is your own life. When faced with a decision involving competing values, you don't simply throw your hands in the air and make no decision at all—after all, that would itself be a decision. We recognize that such decisions are difficult and sometimes involve high degrees of uncertainty, but that's just the way life is. We would not want a moral theory that makes decisions artificially easier than they really are.

Objection 2: Antidepressants and Brainwashing

A second objection to premise (3): What if we could make everyone happier by putting antidepressants into the drinking water? Should we do that? Presumably not, but why not? As a fictional example, we could consider Aldous Huxley's novel *Brave New World*. The people in Huxley's world have distinct castes—alphas, betas, gammas, deltas, etc. To keep them content with their lot, the government employs several techniques, including a form of brainwashing called "hypnopaedia" as well as an antidepressant drug known as "soma." On the face of things, such a scenario seems to be a counterexample to approaches to justice based on well-being. In terms of the *Master Arguments*, the point would be that this appears to show that premise (3) is false, insofar as the political and economic system of *Brave New World* might seem to be one in which human well-being is promoted but which is nonetheless unjust.

I will consider this issue by first mentioning an example far from questions of capitalism and socialism. When you cook rice in certain ways, you can get a crusted, toasted layer of rice at the bottom of the pan. (The Spanish know it as *socarrat*, Persians as *tahdig*, Koreans *nurungji*, Senegalese *xoon*, and Dominicans *con con*.) For most of us who are familiar with this, the "bottom part" is the best part of the rice, and it must be divided equally among the family, though perhaps the cook is entitled to a bit more—or at least so the cooks in my family usually claim. However, a relative of mine used to tell her

46   INTRODUCTION

children, as she was spooning that part onto her plate alone, "Oh, you don't want that part; it's burned." With the situation thus explained, the children were perfectly happy, in one sense of the term, with their part of the rice, and of course the mom was quite happy with hers. But even though the children were content, we might think that there is something unfair about the situation. The contentment of the children rested on false information, namely that they would not like the bottom part and that their mother was doing them a favor by taking all of it. The general point: when evaluating the right thing to do, we look beyond superficial levels of contentment; at bare minimum, we count it as relevant if a person's preferences and happiness *would have* changed if they had more, or more accurate, information.

Let's now return to *Brave New World*. The hypnopaedia consists of a voice that plays while the children sleep and inculcates in them the belief that they are happy with their caste. For example, children destined for the beta class are told things like this:

> Alpha children wear grey. They work much harder than we do, because they're so frightfully clever. I'm really awfully glad I'm a Beta, because I don't work so hard. And then we are much better than the Gammas and Deltas. Gammas are stupid. They all wear green, and Delta children wear khaki.[5]

The aim is to condition people to "like their unescapable social destiny." If hypnopaedia fails to achieve the desired result, the powers that be simply use the drug, soma.

While it may be that the betas in Huxley's novel *report* high degrees of well-being, one could question these reports. Or, to avoid arguing about the meaning of the word "well-being," I can just stipulate that the notion of *well-being* involved in premise (3) is more than a contented state in which one fails to report any dissatisfaction. As with the children who were misinformed about the yumminess of the crispy bottom part of the rice, the betas and all the rest are being systematically deceived, even brainwashed, into thinking that their lot in life is the best. When I suggest in premise (3) that a system of governance should lead to greater happiness, I mean an *informed* state of happiness, not one that results only from deception, misinformation, or involuntary subjection to drugs. Since the alleged happiness of the people in *Brave New World* results from such things, it is not a counterexample to premise (3).

---

[5] Aldous Huxley, *Brave New World* (London: Chatto & Windus, 1932).

Moreover, one might defend premise (3) of the *Master Arguments* by saying that *even if* the people in the hypothetical scenario are happier than those in our current system, we might conclude that the people in the *Brave New World* situation have had their rights violated. Since premise (3) stated that we should choose one style of governance over another if it leads to greater well-being *and* does not violate rights, then this would mean that the *Brave New World* scenario is not a counterexample.

An opponent of the *Master Argument* might try to come up with new counterexamples to (3)—different hypothetical cases that show that well-being is not enough, even if rights are not violated. Fending off such counterexamples might involve specifying many more details than I do in premise (3), or at least saying much more about exactly what is intended by the key terms "well-being" and "rights." Indeed, ultimately what we would want would be a complete theory of justice—a theory that can rank all systems of governance in accord with how just or desirable they are. You will be happy to know that I won't be attempting that; nor will I engage deeply with the philosophical literature that does approach this project. Instead, I will just say that premise (3) looks reasonable, and that even if a full theory of justice would require something much more detailed and precise, those details will be largely irrelevant to making basic judgments about realistic systems of government like D-socialism and US-style capitalism.

The Distribution of Well-Being

Premise (3) of the *Master Argument* is far from advocating a straightforward version of utilitarianism, for the premise states that we should accept the style of government that best promotes well-being *unless* there are violations of rights involved. That's a nonutilitarian thought, for a strict utilitarian would not allow for exceptions concerning rights; they would claim that moral correctness always comes down to well-being, and that if violating an alleged right makes people happier, then we should do it. I'll talk more about rights in the next section, but first I will mention another aspect of the premise, as I intend it, that perhaps takes it even further from a traditional version of utilitarianism.

Traditional utilitarians like Bentham and Mill did not concern themselves much with the *distribution* of happiness or well-being. As noted above, there have long been questions about whether we should be maximizing the sum total of happiness versus whether we should be maximizing per capita

48   INTRODUCTION

happiness. Those two possibilities could come apart in a number of ways, depending on the level of population. As argued by Derek Parfit, if we are to maximize the sum total of happiness, then instead of a global population of several billion people with very good lives, we should instead aim for a much higher number of people each of whom has a barely tolerable life, for if the much higher number is high enough, it will have a greater total of happiness than will the world with a few billion happy people.[6]

However, questions about the distribution of happiness go far beyond scenarios involving different levels of population. To illustrate with a completely abstract scenario, let's assume we can cleanly measure well-being in terms of a unit that we will call, following philosophical tradition, *utiles*. Suppose that utiles come in a scale of 1 to 50, where 1 is utter misery, 10 is enough well-being for a basically good life, and 50 is a life that is wildly high in well-being. Now suppose that we are considering two different policies that will affect seven people, or seven groups of people, and will lead to the following levels of well-being as measure in utiles:

Person	Policy 1	Policy 2
A	6	1
B	8	1
C	10	1
D	12	1
E	14	1
F	16	30
G	18	50

In terms of either average well-being or total well-being, Policy 2 comes out slightly better: a total of 85 utiles versus 84 utiles. But we might dispute the claim that Policy 2 would be the best policy to enact, for having a couple of people (or groups) be wildly happy does not seem to compensate for letting the bulk of the population be utterly miserable. Even at the cost of a lower average happiness, I think most of us would see Policy 1 as the more just one to pursue.

The utilitarian might suggest in reply that we should use *median* rather than *average* as the relevant measure. The median value for Policy 1 is 12, but the median value for Policy 2 is 1, so this would accord with our intuitions about

---

[6] Derek Parfit, *Reasons and Persons* (New York: Oxford University Press, 1986).

the case. However, we can concoct another case that makes this new proposal still seem wrong:

Person	Policy 1	Policy 3
A	6	1
B	8	1
C	10	1
D	12	13
E	14	13
F	16	14
G	18	42

Now both the median and the average utiles for Policy 3 are higher than that of Policy 1, but we still might prefer Policy 1. Philosopher John Rawls suggests that we think about such scenarios by imagining that we are choosing from behind a *veil of ignorance*: we are going to enter one of the situations, but we don't know to which group of people we will belong.[7] Who would choose Policy 3 behind the veil? Even though there is a sense in which Policy 3 maximizes human well-being, we recoil at the idea that three groups of people would have utterly miserable lives essentially so that one person can have an amazingly high degree of well-being.

This is not to say that we would require that everyone simply be equal in terms of their well-being. Suppose we had this choice:

Person	Policy 1	Policy 4
A	6	6
B	8	6
C	10	6
D	12	6
E	14	6
F	16	6
G	18	6

[7] John Rawls, *A Theory of Justice* (Cambridge, MA: Belknap Press, 1971).

If these are genuinely our choices, it would seem rather odd to drag everyone down to a somewhat unhappy existence just to avoid there being any inequality of outcome.

But, if, when promoting general well-being, we are not simply maximizing happiness (whether judged by sum total, average, or median) and we are not simply insisting that everyone be equal, then what would be our ideal aim? Rawls proposed that any social and economic inequalities must be to the benefit of the least-advantaged members of society, and we might propose something similar when it comes to promoting well-being more generally.

I will take no official position on these questions. I will assume that, in either version of the *Master Argument*, when we assume that one political system "better promotes human well-being," we mean that it does so in the fairest way possible, where this includes the possibility that the best way of promoting human well-being is *not* that we simply create the most of it that we can, even if it is very badly distributed. This qualification might well mean that the premises of the *Master Argument* have strayed even further from anything recognizable as utilitarianism. That's fine, for I make no claim to being a utilitarian.

I said above that some of the other disputes about measuring human well-being seemed unlikely to affect any substantive argument concerning socialism versus capitalism. These last considerations about the distribution of well-being might be different. Since capitalism allows much more inequality of resource distribution than socialism, it is conceivable that capitalism better promotes human well-being *if* we mean the sum total of well-being or the average, but that socialism better promotes human well-being if we take a more measured and egalitarian approach to what we mean by "better promotes human well-being." I will ultimately argue that moving in a socialist direction better promotes human well-being regardless of the position we take on these questions. But we would do well to keep the point in mind as we proceed.

Rights

Controversies about Rights

While I have been talking about promoting human well-being, it is not to be taken for granted that this is the only aim we should care about when considering a political and economic system. One might think that one system or the other systematically violates rights of individuals, irrespective of questions involving human well-being. This concern is reflected in the third premise of both *Master Arguments*, which, again, was this:

(3) Given two styles of governance, if the first better promotes human well-being than the second and does not violate moral rights of individuals, then it should be chosen over the second.

Accordingly, for either version of the *Master Argument* to be sound, one also needs the premise that one's favored system does not violate moral rights.

Both the claim that socialism does not violate rights and the claim that capitalism does not violate rights are controversial. It is a commonplace to hear that socialism involves giving up our "God-given rights," as claimed by an official White House statement under the Trump administration.[8] Senator Rand Paul takes it to be obvious that socialists "promote the will of the collective over the rights of the individual."[9] Socialists are likewise rather quick to accuse capitalism of being unfairly exploitative, thereby suggesting that capitalism allows a form of theft that amounts to violating rights of workers. To take one example, Danny Katch writes: "capitalism is a fundamentally unjust and exploitative system" and "All bosses—not just the mean ones—exploit their workers, by which I mean all bosses keep for themselves some of the value produced by workers. This theft is how businesses make profits."[10] Of course, it is not enough simply to assert that either socialism or capitalism violates rights. Surely one should also, at the very least, be able to state *which* alleged right or rights are supposedly violated and to support that these are genuine rights.

All kinds of things get claimed as rights these days. Some people seem to think that, even during a pandemic, they have the specific right to walk around Walmart without a mask on. Perhaps the alleged right not to wear a mask stems from a general right to be stupid. John Kerry, while serving

---

[8] The White House, "National Day for the Victims of Communism—the White House," November 7, 2017, https://trumpwhitehouse.archives.gov/briefings-statements/national-day-victims-communism/.

[9] Rand Paul, *The Case against Socialism* (New York: Broadside Books, 2019), 145.

[10] Danny Katch, *Socialism . . . Seriously: A Brief Guide to Human Liberation* (Chicago: Haymarket Books, 2015), 42.

52   INTRODUCTION

as secretary of state, proclaimed that Americans had just such a right.[11] (As an educator, I find that idea troubling. Am I violating my students' rights when I teach them logic?) In France, there was a lawsuit about the rights of a rooster named Maurice. A retired couple who owned a vacation home on the French island of Oléron sued the owners of Maurice to make him stop crowing, claiming that this was ruining their holidays. The vacationers lost and Maurice won. At least according to the *New York Times* reporting of the case, "The judge found that the rooster, being a rooster, had a *right* to crow in his rural habitat."[12]

Some claimed rights are much more disturbing to contemplate. Evidently some "incels" (involuntary celibates) claim the *right* to have sex, and they do not mean a right to do with themselves as they wish in the privacy of their own home. They mean a right to have sex with women, a "right that is being violated by those who refuse to have sex with them," whether that person is willing or not.[13] I mention this horrific thought only as an utterly clear example of a *false* claim to a right: I can't imagine any grounds for thinking that any man has a *right* to have sex with an unwilling woman. That would, in fact, be the definition of rape.

Other claims to rights at least seem more reasonable, for example three rights enshrined in the First Amendment to the US Constitution: the right to freedom of speech, the right to exercise one's religion, the right to peaceably assemble. Another alleged right is referred to in the very next amendment to the Constitution but is much more controversial: the right to bear arms.

Some Distinctions between Types of Rights

Having mentioned a legal document—the US Constitution—I should also be explicit about an important distinction between *legal* rights and *moral* rights. A legal right would be, as the name suggests, one that is enshrined in the law, either by statute, constitution, or by accepted legal precedent in court. As an

---

[11] His words: "In America you have a right to be stupid—if you want to be." Staff, Reuters, "Kerry Defends Liberties, Says Americans Have 'Right to Be Stupid,'" February 26, 2013, https://www.reut ers.com/article/us-usa-kerry-liberties/kerry-defends-liberties-says-americans-have-right-to-be-stu pid-idUSBRE91P0HJ20130226.

[12] Adam Nossiter, "Rooster 'Was Just Being Himself': Court Rules He Can Keep Crowing," *New York Times*, September 5, 2019, https://www.nytimes.com/2019/09/05/world/europe/france-maurice-rooster.html?action=click&module=RelatedLinks&pgtype=Article%2C. Emphasis added.

[13] Amia Srinivasan, "Does Anyone Have the Right to Sex," *London Review of Books*, vol. 40, no. 6 (March 2018): 22.

MORAL PHILOSOPHY BACKGROUND   53

example of a trivial legal right, the FDA requires that food manufacturers give their address on any food packaging label;[14] so there is a sense in which I, as a consumer, now have a legal right to know the address of the manufacturer of any processed food I buy.

Moral rights, if there are any, are essentially independent of the law, even if they are also mentioned in legal documents like the Constitution. Consider again, for example, freedom of speech. Many find it plausible that this is a moral right, and not just a matter of what is written in the First Amendment. When authoritarian communist regimes made criticism of the government illegal, it seems that they violated the moral rights of their citizens, even if there was nothing in their statutes or constitution that guaranteed freedom of speech. If the US government restricts the political speech of its citizens, then it seems that it violates both a legal and a moral right of its citizens.

By contrast with freedom of speech, I doubt that anyone would claim that I have a *moral* right to have the address of the food manufacturer printed on the label of my macaroni and cheese. I don't think we would say that manufacturers were violating the moral rights of their customers by not including their address on the package prior to the FDA instituting this requirement.

Some readers, perhaps particularly those on the left, will be uncomfortable with the idea of genuine moral rights, even if they accept the idea of legal rights. To some extent, this might stem from a much broader skepticism about the very idea that there are moral truths at all. Although I am committed to the existence of moral truths in general, this does not mean that I am committed to the existence of *rights*, and, in particular, I need take no position on whether we have a genuine right to free speech or any other specific right. The relevant question before us is that embodied in premise (2) of either version of the *Master Argument*, namely the claims that socialism and capitalism do not violate rights. *One* way of denying that a political system violates moral rights would be to argue that moral rights are a fiction, that there are no such things. I won't take that line; I at least want to leave open the possibility that there are genuine rights. But even if you think that all talk of rights is poppycock, I think it is important to look more sympathetically at the claims that socialism violates rights or that capitalism violates

---

[14] "FDA Food Labeling Requirements—FoodPackagingLabels.Net," Custom Food Packaging Labels—Printable and Adhesive, June 4, 2019, https://www.foodpackaginglabels.net/food-labeling-requirements/.

54 INTRODUCTION

rights—and to do so without attempting to make the broader claim that there are no moral rights at all.

Although it seems to be more often those on the left who deny the existence of moral rights altogether, it is also sometimes those further to the left who will make broader claims about what we might say is a *positive right* as opposed to a *negative right*. For example, Bernie Sanders and others have often claimed that healthcare is a human right,[15] and some socialists claim he should go further and likewise declare that housing is a human right. Socialists can point to documents like the Universal Declaration of Human Rights, passed by the United Nations in 1948, which says this: "Everyone has the right to a standard of living adequate for the health and well-being of himself and of his family, including food, clothing, housing and medical care and necessary social services, and the right to security in the event of unemployment, sickness, disability, widowhood, old age or other lack of livelihood in circumstances beyond his control."[16]

The sorts of rights postulated by the UN Declaration and by Sanders are of a rather different sort than a right like free speech. Let's assume for the moment that I have the right to openly criticize the governor in the state where I live (Maine). To say that I have a right to criticize the governor means, in the first instance, that there can be no law *against* criticizing the governor. The government cannot attempt to interfere or stop me from criticizing the governor; it cannot punish me for having done so. So my right to free speech is a right specifically against government interference. Similarly with the claimed right to freely exercise my religion: the government is not allowed to single out my religion and prohibit its practices. Of course, even these examples get complicated. The right to free speech does not include the right to yell "Fire!" in a crowded theater, and the right to free exercise of religion does not mean that I can practice human sacrifice. However we sort out those complications, the point is still basically clear: these rights are freedoms *from* certain sorts of government interference, especially interference in the form of legal punishment. These are, so to speak, *negative* rights, and they only apply to my relationship with the state.

By contrast, compare the idea of a right to healthcare; as stated by the World Health Organization director-general in 2017, "The right to health for

---

[15] Bernie Sanders, "Health Care Is a Right, Not a Privilege," *Huffington Post*, December 7, 2017, https://www.huffpost.com/entry/health-care-is-a-right-no_b_212770.

[16] United Nations, "Universal Declaration of Human Rights: United Nations," n.d., https://www.un.org/en/universal-declaration-human-rights/.

all people means that everyone should have access to the health services they need, when and where they need them, without suffering financial hardship."[17] If we have such a right, then this would not merely be the right not to have the government interfere or stop me from seeking and paying for medical care. Rather, the idea seems to be this: if I am sick, then I have the right to receive medical treatment, even if I cannot afford to pay the cost of it. Unlike free speech, the right to healthcare would be one where something needs to be *provided*. It would be a *positive* right, a right that I should be given something.

The existence of positive rights is even more controversial than the existence of negative rights. Rand Paul, who is an ophthalmologist in addition to being a US Senator, claims this:

> With regard to the idea whether or not you have a right to health care you have to realize what that implies. I am a physician. You have a right to come to my house and conscript me. It means you believe in slavery. You are going to enslave not only me but the janitor at my hospital, the person who cleans my office, the assistants, the nurses. . . . You are basically saying you believe in slavery.[18]

This is ridiculously hyperbolic, but it does point to some good questions about an alleged positive right like the right to healthcare. Is it a right to *free* healthcare? A right to receive healthcare for what you can afford to pay? Who, exactly, is obligated to provide this healthcare to any given individual? Senator Paul assumes the most implausible answers to these questions and concludes that the right to healthcare would amount to believing in slavery. But, of course, rather than saying that I can barge into any doctor's office (or home!) and demand free care, Sanders and others might claim that a right to healthcare implies that the *government* should set up a system whereby healthcare is accessible to all and the government pays the costs, such as with the National Health Care system in the United Kingdom.

But this position still raises delicate issues. Suppose the government sets up a healthcare system in which doctors are paid by the government, but that

---

[17] World Health Organization: WHO, "Health Is a Fundamental Human Right," December 10, 2017, https://www.who.int/news-room/commentaries/detail/health-is-a-fundamental-human-right.

[18] Quoted in Kate Nocero, "Paul: 'Right to Health Care' Is Slavery," *Politico*, May 11, 2011, https://www.politico.com/story/2011/05/paul-right-to-health-care-is-slavery-054769.

56 INTRODUCTION

the pay is relatively low, and, as a result, people stop going to medical school and there is a massive shortage of doctors. When we say that there is a right to healthcare, what exactly is the government's obligation here? If nothing else, this means that it becomes very difficult to decide exactly what it is that the government needs *to do*, lest it be violating the public's right to healthcare.

Dworkin: Rights as Trump Cards

I will come back to the question of positive rights, and the healthcare example in particular, but I think it will be helpful first to be somewhat more systematic about what it *means* to say that people *have a right* to this or that. In other words, what exactly are rights? I highly doubt that there is one uniform meaning to the word "right," but, for purposes of the *Master Argument*, I do have a specific idea in mind, which I can best explain by an analogy.

When I was growing up in Kansas, my extended family played a lot of different card games, but mostly bridge. I imagine that few readers will even be familiar with that game now (alas!); maybe a few more know Spades, essentially a much simpler version of bridge. In order to explain a useful view of the notion of rights, I will start by explaining just a little bit about Spades. Spades is typically played with four people. After some preliminaries that are irrelevant here, one person starts by putting down a card, for example, the 3 of clubs. Play proceeds clockwise, with each of the other players putting down a card as well. They must play a card of the suit that was led (in this case, clubs) unless they have no cards of that suit. If everyone plays a club, then whoever played the highest club wins that round, or "trick" as it is called. Suppose I am the last of the four to play on this round, and that when it gets to me the cards on the table are the 3, the queen, and the ace of clubs. If I have a club, I must play it, and I will not win the trick, since the ace has been played. But suppose I have no clubs left; then, I can play a spade, and any spade will beat any club. If I play the 2 of spades, I will win the trick, much to the disappointment of the person who played the ace of clubs. Spades are *trumps* in this game; by playing a spade, I played a trump card. Trump cards, so to speak, outweigh the cards played from the original suit that was led.

Rights, on one conception of the term derived from the work of philosopher Ronald Dworkin (1978), are like trump cards.[19] If we are faced with a

---

[19] Ronald Dworkin, *Taking Rights Seriously* (Cambridge, MA: Harvard University Press, 1978).

choice between two policies, and one of them, we are pretty sure, will make people happier and better off overall, then that seems like what we should do. For example, if a town is deciding between building a swimming pool or upgrading its public library, and if we somehow know that the swimming pool will bring greater happiness and life satisfaction overall to the people of the town, then it seems like the town should build the swimming pool. That is to say, the utilitarian calculation (concerning which option leads to the most happiness for the greatest number) favors the swimming pool, and for that reason, all things being equal, the town should build the swimming pool instead of upgrading the library. (Of course, the town will also need to consider the option of doing neither project and lowering property taxes by the amount that would be saved; if the extra money in people's pockets leads to more happiness than either the swimming pool or the library upgrade, then that would militate in favor of the tax cut.)

By contrast, suppose that the same little town is considering banning construction of Muslim mosques. The town council knows that their small community of Muslims is planning to build a mosque; but within the rest of the community anti-Muslim sentiment runs deep, and the presence of a mosque will make these residents unhappy. We can suppose that the addition of a mosque would increase the happiness and life satisfaction of the Muslims in the town. But suppose that the number of Muslims is small and that, because of the anti-Muslim sentiment, in total the mosque would lead to more displeasure than pleasure. If those are the facts about the preferences of the residents, then it could well be that a straightforward utilitarian calculation would come out in favor of banning the mosque. (There was, in fact, a referendum held in Switzerland in 2009, passed by 57% of the vote, that banned the construction of new mosques with minarets.)

The mosque case seems quite different from that of the swimming pool. The Muslims in town might plausibly say, "But I have a *right* to exercise my religion; you are violating that right if you ban construction of mosques simply on the grounds that you don't like my religion; I don't care if banning mosques would lead to more happiness overall." In terms of the card game analogy, it would be like this: "Your ban on mosques may be the highest card played in terms of utility, but I have a trump card, namely my right to religious freedom; the trump card wins the trick." Even if overall considerations of utility and life satisfaction in the town would lead to banning the mosque, you can't do it if doing so violates the *rights* of a person or group of person; rights trump utility.

58 INTRODUCTION

This need not mean that rights are *absolute*; we need not push the analogy to trump cards that far. Dworkin allows that the government can limit a right under three sorts of situations:

- When "the values protected by the original right are not really at stake in the marginal case, or are at stake only in some attenuated form."[20]
- When the right involves conflicts with a genuinely competing right.
- When the "cost to society would not be simply incremental, but would be of a degree far beyond the cost paid to grant the original right, a degree great enough to justify whatever assault on dignity or equality might be involved."[21]

Which Rights Do We Have?

This framework for talking about rights leaves many questions unanswered, and it does not give us a simple or algorithmic way of determining when it is okay to limit a right. More importantly, by itself this account does not tell us which rights we have. Is there a right to freely exercise your religion, as claimed in the example? How do we know which rights we have?

Dworkin himself does give some arguments and considerations about the basis on which we could determine whether something counts as a right. We might suggest that the fundamental right you have is to be treated as a free, equal, and autonomous citizen. The idea is that there would be something so deeply insulting about treating me as a less than equal citizen that this could not be justified on mere utility grounds, whether the allegedly increased well-being is for other people or for me. If the government fails to treat me as a free, equal and autonomous citizen, then it is effectively treating me as less than a full person. This in turn suggests that each of us has a sphere of personal dignity and autonomy that is, at least within certain limits, sacrosanct.

If we accept this picture, then certain traditional political liberties might indeed seem to count as genuine rights. Consider the liberty of free speech, and, in particular, the liberty to express my political views, even if (or especially if) they are critical of the government. If the government can punish me for expressing my political beliefs, then such a restriction might be seen as a

---

[20] Dworkin, *Taking Rights Seriously*, 200.
[21] Dworkin, *Taking Rights Seriously*, 200.

fundamental expression of disdain for who I am as a person. Accordingly, one might suggest the following argument:

Free Speech and Autonomy

(1) If government punishes a person's political speech, then government treats that person as less than a free, equal, and autonomous citizen. [P]
(2) If government treats a person as less than a free, equal, and autonomous citizen, then government violates that person's rights. [P]
(3) If government punishes a person's political speech, then government violates that person's rights. [1,2]

One might run a similar argument concerning freedom of religion. The central idea would be that by forbidding a particular religion, the government would be treating members of that faith as less than fully equal and autonomous citizens.

In both of these cases—freedom of speech and freedom of religion—it is not just a matter of being allowed to do what you feel like doing. In the example involving the mosque, I stipulated that, in this small town, the utilitarian calculation might well come out in favor of banning the construction of a mosque. But one might suspect that the *reason* any utilitarian calculation would come out that way would involve a certain form of prejudice or disdain: the Christian majority in the hypothetical town does not like other religions, and effectively wants to count the preferences of Muslims as less worthy than those of Christians (Dworkin does propose something like this form of reasoning concerning rights). In this way, a utilitarian calculation can be based on preferences that, by their nature, involve holding some people to be less worthy, less autonomous than others. One might make the same suggestion about restrictions on speech. In *Planned Parenthood of Southeastern Pa v. Casey*, the Supreme Court stated: "At the heart of liberty is the right to define one's own concept of existence, of meaning, of the universe, and of the mystery of human life."[22] One might take this as suggesting that being treated as an autonomous citizen requires that we give people the space to make up their own minds, especially on issues central to what it is to be a person. Restrictions in this realm cut to the heart of what it is to be a free and

---

[22] *Planned Parenthood of Southeastern Pa v. Casey*, 505 U.S. 833, 851 (1992).

60   INTRODUCTION

equal person, and, one might argue, we cannot allow one's very status as a free and equal autonomous citizen to be balanced away by considerations of overall utility. (Perhaps it is even similar with Maurice the rooster; the report was that "a rooster, being a rooster, had a right to crow," suggesting that the court thought that punishing a rooster for crowing would be treating it as less than a, well, as less than a full rooster. I'm not convinced, but for purposes of this book I will remain agnostic about rooster rights.)

It might help clarify these questions to look back at the issue of positive and negative rights, and the example of healthcare in particular. First, it is far from clear that by failing to provide people with healthcare, the government is thereby treating those citizens as less than free, equal, and autonomous citizens; so it is doubtful that one could run an argument analogous to *Free Speech and Autonomy*. Given the general conception of rights as trump cards, to say that there is a right to healthcare would be to say this: government is under a moral obligation to provide everyone with (affordable? free?) healthcare *even if* we are in circumstances such that providing healthcare reduces overall utility. How could it happen that providing healthcare could reduce overall utility? Such a situation would not be hard to imagine. If a country were extremely poor and simply did not have the resources to provide affordable healthcare, at least not without sacrificing other even more basic services (e.g., education and minimal public order), then it is hard to see that such a government would be violating the rights of its citizens by not bankrupting itself to pay for healthcare. Even in a wealthier country, one could imagine that there was a sudden environmental crisis that would lead to massive starvation if not addressed immediately with all the resources we could muster. In such circumstances, it might well be that using our resources on normal levels of healthcare would actually cause more suffering in the end than if we addressed the environmental crisis in question. Under such purely hypothetical circumstances, would we still claim that the government should, regardless of concerns about overall happiness or suffering, focus on healthcare? Frankly, that doesn't seem plausible to me. There might be a case for saying that we have a positive right to healthcare, even in the sense of rights as trumps, but I won't be making it or relying on it for the purposes of arguing for D-socialism.

To be clear, under current circumstances in countries like the United States, I think that the government *should* guarantee good healthcare to all. I say this because I am fairly confident that providing good healthcare to all

MORAL PHILOSOPHY BACKGROUND 61

will increase overall life satisfaction for more people. Even if some relatively wealthy people must forgo some of their wealth in order to raise the tax revenue required, I believe that the gain in happiness to those whose lives were made healthier will outweigh the loss of wealth at the top. But this is a fundamentally utilitarian argument: that we should provide healthcare because it will make people happier and more fulfilled, not because it is a right that must be accommodated irrespective of whether it makes people happier.

Given the looseness with which most people speak about rights, I think that there is an understandable confusion or elision between the sense of "right" in "it is the right thing to do" and "I have a *right* to X." Liberals or socialists will sometimes talk of economic rights, like a right to healthcare or housing, when all they mean (I think) is to really emphasize that it is the *right thing to do* under the circumstances to provide universal healthcare or to make sure that all citizens have housing, etc. By contrast, with certain negative rights mentioned above—e.g., freedom of speech, freedom of religion, freedom of assembly—it *might* seem more plausible that these are things that it would be wrong to sacrifice even if one could have more happiness for a greater number of people. I'm inclined to believe that, but I need not defend it here. In the present context of arguing for socialism and defending the *Master Argument for Socialism*, by assuming that these rights are real, I am only making it more difficult: if there are no genuine rights, then it would obviously be true that socialism does not violate rights, for there would be none to violate.

Key Takeaways

- According to the *Master Argument for Socialism*, we should adopt socialism because it better promotes human well-being and does not violate the rights of individuals.
- According to the *Master Argument for Capitalism*, we should adopt capitalism because it better promotes human well-being and does not violate the rights of individuals.
- There are complicated questions concerning what it means to better promote human well-being, but most of these questions can be ignored for the purpose of evaluating the two *Master Arguments*.

62   INTRODUCTION

- There are also complicated questions concerning what it means to have a moral right. I adopt a view from Ronald Dworkin, according to which rights, if we have them, serve as something like trump cards when evaluating considerations of overall well-being.
- I resent the fact that I can no longer think of trump cards without thinking of the Trump of the Donald variety.

PART II
RIGHTS-BASED ARGUMENTS

4

Does Socialism Violate Rights?

The *Master Argument for Socialism* needs the premise that socialism does not violate moral rights. Irrespective of that particular positive argument for socialism, any defender of socialism will, of course, need to deny that socialism violates rights. If it were accepted that socialism *does* violate rights, then one could run a very simple argument against it:

Socialism Violates Rights

(1) Socialism systematically violates the moral rights of individuals. [P]
(2) Any system that violates the moral rights of individuals should be rejected. [P]
(3) Socialism should be rejected. [1,2]

Using the trump-card sense of "right" specified in the previous chapter, premise (1) says that socialist forms of government restrict liberties that it would be wrong to abridge even if doing so would create greater happiness in general. It would be hard to begin to evaluate this objection to the *Master Argument* unless we know *which* alleged right socialism is said to violate. It is not much of an objection to claim, "Socialism violates rights!" if you cannot then go on to specify the right or rights that socialism violates. (And it doesn't help to add "God-given" in front of "rights.")

Socialism and Political Rights

One might start with the claim that socialism violates one of the traditional political rights: free speech, freedom of religion, freedom of assembly, or perhaps freedom to travel. As noted in the previous chapter, I am inclined to think that there are some genuine rights of this sort, particularly insofar as such rights are grounded in a more general right to be treated as a free, equal, and autonomous citizen. (I will note again that nothing in the argument

Socialism. Scott R. Sehon, Oxford University Press. © Oxford University Press 2024.
DOI: 10.1093/oso/9780197753330.003.0004

66 RIGHTS-BASED ARGUMENTS

for socialism depends upon this claim.) But, even granting that there are genuine political rights in the trump-card sense, why think that socialism violates these rights?

Conservatives might point out that Soviet bloc countries, China, Cuba, and others that have labeled themselves as socialist, have a particularly bad track record concerning political rights. They could then propose something like this argument:

Socialism Violates Political Rights 1.0

(1) Countries based on a socialist ideology consistently violate political rights. [P]
(2) If countries based on a particular ideology consistently violate political rights, then that ideology should be rejected. [P]
(3) Socialism should be rejected. [1,2]

There is a great deal of truth to the claim that the Soviet bloc countries and others violated political rights. Speech was significantly restricted, as was travel; freedom of religion was usually technically allowed, but the exercise of religion was uncomfortable and intensely scrutinized.

But this history is not enough to support premise (1) of *Socialism Violates Political Rights*, or at least not if the argument is meant to be used against socialism as defined in this book or by contemporary proponents. In Chapter 2, I defined socialism as coming in degrees in two different scales: collective ownership and control of the means of production and egalitarian distribution of resources. The Soviet bloc countries were examples of what I termed *S-socialism*, where they had high degrees of both, although, as noted in that chapter, one might well argue that these countries did not have *collective* ownership of the means of production or control of the economy, for the fundamentally undemocratic nature of these states meant that the control was more dictatorial than collective. Whatever one thinks of the Soviet bloc countries, there are other countries that move much further than the United States in the socialist direction on those scales, namely the Nordic countries and, to a somewhat lesser extent, other northern European countries. I referred to this model as *D-socialist*. The problem for *Socialism Violates Political Rights 1.0* is that the Nordic countries show no sign of consistently violating political rights. That is to say, once we take into account D-socialist countries, premise (1) of *Socialism Violates Political Rights* loses all plausibility.

The proponent of *Socialism Violates Political Rights* might make a change to accommodate this:

Socialism Violates Political Rights 2.0

(1) Countries based on a S-socialist ideology consistently violate political rights. [P]
(2) If countries based on a particular ideology consistently violate political rights, then that ideology should be rejected. [P]
(3) D-socialism should be rejected. [1,2]

The newly revised premise (1) is at least more plausible. But now the argument is simply invalid, for the conclusion in (3) no longer logically follows from premises (1) and (2): premise (1) makes an empirical claim about S-socialist states, but then step (3) attempts to infer something about D-socialism. Unless one falsely claims that S-socialism and D-socialism are the same ideology, then that simply doesn't follow.

You might try a different sort of argument about socialism and rights by claiming that it is somehow intrinsic to any form of socialist ideology (even D-socialist) that political rights must be restricted. Matthew Harwood argues for this, noting that contemporary democratic socialists *claim* that socialism would *strengthen* political rights. But he says that this is false, for the socialist goal of ending capitalism requires "ruthless intervention in politics and culture." He asks rhetorically,

> Say a democratic socialist like Ocasio-Cortez does one day achieve the presidency of the United States and her party takes Congress. Could democratic socialists abide a free press, one where papers like *The Wall Street Journal* and magazines like *Reason* criticize the party for its economic illiberalism? Could writers and artists critical of the regime work without fear of political repression and surveillance? I think not, if the socialists are serious about their project.[1]

At first glance, the argument seems to be this:

---

[1] Matthew Harwood, "Civil Liberties and Socialism Don't Mix," *Reason: Free Minds and Free Markets*, October 18, 2018, https://reason.com/2018/10/18/civil-liberties-and-socialism-dont-mix/.

68 RIGHTS-BASED ARGUMENTS

Socialists Will Restrict Speech 1.0

(1) Socialists oppose capitalism. [P]
(2) Anyone who opposes an ideology will, if they are in power, restrict the speech of proponents of that ideology. [P]
(3) Socialists will, if they are in power, restrict the speech of proponents of capitalism. [1,2]

One could then add a couple of steps claiming that if socialists will restrict speech in this way, then socialism should be rejected. But if Harwood really believes premise (2), then he would be likewise committed to the following argument:

Capitalists Will Restrict Speech

(1) Capitalists oppose socialism. [P]
(2) Anyone who opposes an ideology will, if they are in power, restrict the speech of proponents of that ideology. [P]
(3) Capitalists will, if they are in power, restrict the speech of proponents of socialism. [1,2]

Premise (1) is clearly true, and premise (2) is exactly the same as that in *Socialists Will Restrict Speech*, so it seems that Harwood would be committed to the conclusion that capitalists will restrict speech as well. And then, by the same token, capitalism should be rejected as well, given Harwood's own apparent premises.

Perhaps Harwood would revise *Socialists Will Restrict Speech* to avoid that parallel:

Socialists Will Restrict Speech 2.0

(1) Socialists oppose capitalism. [P]
(2) Anyone whose ideology intrinsically allows restricting speech will, if they are in power, restrict the speech of any ideology they oppose. [P]
(3) Socialism is an ideology that intrinsically allows restricting speech. [P]

> (4) Socialists will, if they are in power, restrict the speech of proponents of capitalism. [1,2,3]

Harwood might then claim that the parallel version of this will not work against capitalism, because capitalism is not an ideology that intrinsically allows restrictions on speech. But now his argument simply *assumes* that socialism intrinsically allows restrictions on speech, when that was the conclusion for which he was supposed to be arguing! *Socialists Will Restrict Speech 2.0* simply begs the question.

Perhaps Harwood has a different idea: that socialism in particular could not survive in a society with political freedoms. Then the argument would look like this, where we make the background hypothetical that socialists are already in power:

Socialists Will Restrict Speech 3.0

(1) Socialists will want to stay in power. [P]
(2) Anyone who wants to stay in power will do whatever is necessary to stay in power. [P]
(3) Socialists will do whatever is necessary to stay in power. [1,2]
(4) For socialists to stay in power, it is necessary that they restrict speech of opponents. [P]
(5) Socialists will restrict speech of opponents. [3,4]

Harwood might then claim that the parallel argument against capitalism cannot succeed, for he would deny the analogy to premise (4)—he would deny that it is necessary to restrict speech for *capitalists* to stay in power.

But then this just pushes the question back to why Harwood thinks that it would be difficult for the socialist to stay in power without restricting political rights, whereas the capitalists can do so. Perhaps the thought is something like this: truly awful political and economic systems can only stay in power if they restrict speech, and socialism is a truly awful political and economic system. Accordingly, we could have a revised version of the argument that includes a subargument for premise (4):

Socialists Will Restrict Speech 3.1

(1) Socialists will want to stay in power. [P]

70 RIGHTS-BASED ARGUMENTS

> (2) Anyone who wants to stay in power will do whatever is necessary to stay in power. [P]
>
> (3) Socialists will do whatever is necessary to stay in power. [1,2]
>
> (3a) For proponents of an awful system to stay in power, it is necessary that they restrict the speech of opponents. [P]
>
> (3b) Socialists are proponents of an awful system. [P]
>
> (4) For socialists to stay in power, it is necessary that they restrict speech of opponents. [3a, 3b]
>
> (5) Socialists will restrict speech of opponents. [3,4]

The argument is valid, and the opponent of socialism might well agree with all of the premises. But the argument nonetheless has a glaring flaw: it simply *assumes* in (3b) that socialism is an awful system. The whole point of the argument was to show that socialists will restrict speech, and the point of trying to show this was to show that socialism is a bad system that ought not to be adopted. But if we can simply *assume* that socialism is an awful system, then we don't need the rest of the argument. That is to say, if this is the correct reading of his argument, Harwood has simply assumed the very thing he was ultimately trying to show; the argument is, again, question-begging.

I have yet to find any stronger argument for the claim that socialism leads to violations of standard political rights. This, of course, does not mean that such arguments are not out there, but I think we can at least say that the point is not nearly so obvious as opponents of socialism take it to be.

Socialism and Economic Rights

Defenders of capitalism often speak of property rights, and it is commonly thought that capitalism, but not socialism, respects those rights. For example, Will Kenton says: "Private property rights are one of the pillars of capitalist economies."[2] However, even more so than with the political rights, it is not immediately clear what one might mean by "property rights." If it is the liberty to be able to own property, then there are a couple of further questions: What sort of property do people have the right to own? What

---

[2] Will Kenton, "Property Rights," *Investopedia*, November 24, 2020, https://www.investopedia.com/terms/p/property_rights.asp#:~:text=Property%20rights%20define%20the%20theoretical,individuals,%20businesses,%20and%20governments.

does it mean to say that you *own* a piece of property? The phrase "property rights" is sometimes suggested as a way of referring to a more catchall category of "economic rights," where these might be said to include property rights but also go beyond them, presumably including some sort of right to form contracts and perhaps the right to amass wealth on the basis of such contracts. If meant as an argument against socialism, then the critic will need to specify a particular right, R, that meets the following criteria:

- It is plausible that R is a right in the trump-card sense.
- Capitalism typically protects R.
- Socialism would violate R.

This task may be harder than the critic imagines.

If the right, R, is a right to own a certain *kind* of property, then what kind is that? Even the most ardent defender of property rights does not typically think that one has the right to own *anything*. At the time of the founding of the United States and through much of its first century, it was widely believed that property rights extended to the ability to own other human beings. Only after a massive war and amendments to the Constitution did that change. Presumably, nobody is suggesting that we go back to that degree of property rights. I also don't know of anyone actively advocating that individuals have the right to own, say, an atomic bomb. Even if we have a right to own things, everyone will exclude some things from that list.

Perhaps the thought is simply that socialists will exclude too much. One might even have an image of socialism as an enforced hippie-commune where everyone literally shares everything. Such pictures have been advocated in some texts: "All the believers were one in heart and mind. No one claimed that any of their possessions was their own, but they shared everything they had" (Acts 4:32). This biblical description of the earliest Christians notwithstanding, socialists generally agree that one can own *personal* property: I have my books, my computer, my guitar, my bath towels, etc., and nobody is suggesting that it be otherwise. On the other hand, socialists do advocate more collective ownership of *productive property*, of the means of production; the extent to which there is collective ownership of the means of production was one of the axes along which I defined the term "socialism." While it would only be the most extreme form of socialism that would prohibit all private ownership of productive property, perhaps the thought is that there is a right to such ownership that socialist systems would typically fail to adequately respect.

72 RIGHTS-BASED ARGUMENTS

Even if there are certain sorts of things that we have the right to own, this still leaves open a broader question: What does it mean to *own* something? As philosopher Sam Arnold says,

> Standardly, to own something is to enjoy a bundle of legally enforceable rights and powers over that thing. These rights and powers typically include the right to *use*, to *control*, to *transfer*, to *alter* (at the limit, even to destroy), and to *generate income from* the thing owned, as well as the right to *exclude* non-owners from interacting with the owned thing in these ways. Because these rights admit of gradations, so too does ownership, which is scalar—a matter of degree—rather than dichotomous.[3]

A conventional legal system will grant us certain powers and privileges over the things that are in our legal possession. I can, with impunity, walk on my property, park my car on the driveway, plant daisies, or take out the remnants of a garden and put rocks down instead because I hate gardening. But even the most extreme advocates of property rights will not typically say that I can do *anything* with my property. Just because I own the materials and the land does not mean that I am legally entitled to build and detonate a bomb. Current zoning regulations in my town would prohibit me from ripping down my house and putting up a 20-story building instead. Factory owners may own their factories and the land on which they sit, but we typically have in place regulations that prevent them from simply emitting toxic waste from the factory onto the adjacent ground, even if the factory owner owns that ground as well. Legal limits on what you can do with your property come in degrees. Beyond what degree would we be violating a right to property ownership?

In addition to literal ownership of property, one might take the broader category of economic rights to include the ability to make *contracts* of various sorts. Again, few people would defend an unlimited right to make contracts. For example, most would deny a person the right to sell herself into slavery. Most legal systems currently do not allow you to make a contract to sell one of your kidneys, though many libertarians will defend this as a right that we should have.[4] I don't know of any libertarians that openly defend a broader right to sell *any* organs, for example a right to sell my heart to someone who

---

[3] Sam Arnold, "Socialism," *Internet Encyclopedia of Philosophy*, n.d., https://iep.utm.edu/socialis/.

[4] For example, Jason Brennan, *Libertarianism: What Everyone Needs to Know* (New York: Oxford University Press, 2012), 92.

needs it and is willing to pay a lot. Most legal systems also allow for contracts to be rescinded when they were made under inappropriate duress or where some degree of fraud was involved. Thus, simply saying that we have economic or contract rights leaves the situation quite underspecified, since there is plenty of room for intelligent disagreement concerning what sort regulations should or should not be imposed on contracts and on privately owned property.

Here is one way to determine the proper extent of these economic liberties: do our best to ascertain which regulations and limits on contracts and property would be in the interest of people in general, including future generations. That is to say, we could approach the question of economic liberties by doing our best to do a utilitarian calculation: we would adopt those policies that maximize human well-being in the long run. Of course, there would be utilitarian reasons to be cautious about implementing regulations that affect how one can use one's property or laws by means of which one can rescind voluntarily made contracts. We want to be careful about assuming that we fully understand the downstream effects of any regulations we impose. We should take into consideration any beneficial effects of allowing people more control. We should be cautious about changing the rules midstream, since that would lead to uncertainty. All of this is perfectly consistent with a utilitarian approach. But saying that we should be cautious and careful concerning our judgments about overall utility is not the same as saying that property owners have *moral rights* (considered as trump cards) against some degree or other of government regulation. What grounds might one have for saying that there are such rights, and that socialism violates them? I'll consider two broad possibilities in the following sections.

Self-Ownership and the Nonaggression Principle

One strand of libertarian thought, stemming from Locke, starts with the idea of *self-ownership* and then draws fairly strong consequences for economic rights. The basic idea is that I *own* my body and any labor I perform with it, and that I should thus likewise fully own whatever wealth I can produce with my labor. Some libertarians then take this to imply that any "taxation of earnings from labor is on a par with forced labor."[5]

---

[5] Robert Nozick, *Anarchy, State, and Utopia* (New York: Basic Books, 1974), 169.

74 RIGHTS-BASED ARGUMENTS

This is rather extreme, even if one grants the claim that I own, in some sense, my body and my labor. We already saw that ownership seems to come in degrees. Just as nobody would claim that I am free to do *anything* I want with my own property, the mere claim that I own my body and my labor does not mean that I am free to do anything I want with it. Just as the fact that it is my car does not mean that I am allowed to drive it into a bunch of pedestrians, the fact that it is my body and my fist does not mean that I can swing it and hit your face. Nor am I free to do anything with the wealth I earn from my labor, since nobody would claim that I should be allowed to use that wealth to hire a hit man. To get to the claim that taxation is theft, one would presumably make a further assumption and run something like the following argument:

Taxation Is Theft

(1) I own the wealth produced through my labor. [P]
(2) It is theft for anyone to take something I own without my consent. [P]
(3) If the government forces me to pay taxes, then it takes something I own without my consent. [P]
(4) If the government forces me to pay taxes, it commits theft. [1,2,3]

This argument is too quick because one could simply dispute premise (2). If someone is holding a shopkeeper at gunpoint, and then if a police officer manages to grab the gun away from the perpetrator, then it would just be a bad joke for the gunman to say, "Hey, that's my gun! You can't take it!" Or suppose that I gain legal title to your car, but that I do so through coercion or fraud; then, even though I do now own your car, it would not obviously be theft for you to take it back. Of course, one might respond to the latter sort of example by protesting that I didn't *really* own your car in the appropriate sense if I acquired it through unjust means. But the need for such qualifications on the concept of *ownership* is actually my point: merely saying that I own something is too vague, since ownership is, as Sam Arnold points out, a matter of degree.

Some libertarians attempt to spell out a more detailed version of the metaphorical idea of self-ownership via something they call the "nonaggression principle" or "NAP" for short. The central idea is that we need to respect everyone's boundaries (their liberty) and that nobody is allowed to use *initiatory force*: you violate a person's rights if you use force when they have not used force against you. Loosely adapting a formulation by philosopher Roderick Long, the principle can be cast as follows:

NAP Any act of forcible interference (or threat thereof) with another individual's person or property is a violation of that person's rights, unless the act is a response to forcible interference (or threat thereof) by that person.[6]

One might then use this principle to launch an argument against socialism, claiming that socialistic redistribution violates the right against initiatory force as embodied by NAP:

NAP and Redistribution

(1) Any act of forcible interference (or threat thereof) with another individual's person or property is a violation of rights, unless the act is a response to forcible interference (or threat thereof) by that person. [P—NAP]
(2) If the government levies taxes for the purpose of redistribution, then this is an act of forcible interference with another individual's property, and it is not a response to forcible interference (or threat thereof) by that person. [P]
(3) If the government levies taxes for the purpose of redistribution, this is a violation of rights. [1,2]

Premise (2) of this argument seems to be true, and premise (1) just is the NAP; so acceptance of NAP indeed implies that taxation for the purpose of redistribution is a violation of rights.

However, while redistributive taxation policies amount to forcible interference with another's property, this point does not actually depend at all on the fact that the taxation was for this particular purpose. When the government sends me a tax bill, irrespective of the purpose for which it will use my money, it comes with a threat: it can garnish my wages or even throw me in jail. This threat is not in response to any act of forcible interference on my

---

[6] Roderick Long, "Non-aggression Principle," *Libertarian.org Encyclopedia*, August 15, 2008, https://www.libertarianism.org/topics/non-aggression-principle.

76 RIGHTS-BASED ARGUMENTS

part; I was just sitting here not paying taxes. But this implies that the tax bill is, according to NAP, a violation of my rights. In other words, we can likewise run this argument:

NAP and Taxation

(1) Any act of forcible interference (or threat thereof) with another individual's person or property is a violation of rights, unless the act is a response to forcible interference (or threat thereof) by that person. [P—(NAP)]
(2) If the government levies taxes, then this is an act of forcible interference with another individual's property, and it is not a response to forcible interference (or threat thereof) by that person. [P]
(3) If the government levies taxes, this is a violation of rights. [1,2]

This conclusion is indeed quite radical. Government, in any form with which we are familiar, requires taxation to provide services. Even if government were pared all the way down to what the libertarian wants—typically just police, courts, and national defense—we would still need to pay for these things. This consequence of NAP would indeed mean that D-socialism violates NAP, for socialism certainly involves having taxes. But it also equally means that any government of which I am aware likewise violates rights; even the level of government proposed by the most conservative politicians in the United States or Europe would violate rights.

There are indeed some libertarians and others who accept this result of NAP, namely those whom Jason Brennan calls "hard libertarians" and who basically claim that no amount of government is morally legitimate.[7] In some ways, I can admire that position. As a friend of mine put it, these libertarians are like a dog who has a bone and really doesn't want to let it go: they have sunk their teeth into NAP, like the taste, and won't give it up for anything. Their tenacity is impressive. But most of us don't mind the idea of at least a little bit of government; we don't think it is a terrible thing that we can call the police if our home is being burglarized or the fire department if it is burning; we don't think it is really *so* awful that some of us live in countries that had taxpayer-financed armies with which to respond to the Nazi attempt to conquer Europe in World War II. But, if you honestly think that

---

[7] Brennan, *Libertarianism*, 21.

it is truly a violation of rights to have government even for such purposes, then I will present no further response in this book. (Libertarians might have one more trick up their sleeves: they might continue to maintain that compulsory taxation is a violation of rights, but they might suggest that they can still avoid anarchy, for they might claim that we could have a government, or at least something like one, that does not violate NAP by imposing any taxes or regulating economic activity. In fact, this is the sort of quasi-state that is proposed by political philosopher Robert Nozick in his classic 1974 book *Anarchy, State, and Utopia*. I think that Nozick's attempt fails, but I will not go into that here.)

Even if you are willing to accept the anarchistic implications of NAP, I will argue further that the principle would have implications that libertarians would disavow, meaning that even the libertarian would have to regard NAP as false. The libertarian can modify NAP to avoid those consequences, but at a severe cost: the libertarian will then lose any argument (or at least any non-question-begging argument) for the claim that D-socialism violates the rights postulated by NAP.

Let's first start with a specific hypothetical case, a case I will adapt from one presented by Ben Burgis while making a very similar argument against a version of the nonaggression principle.[8] Suppose I steal a priceless painting from you and then give it to Bob, a friend of mine. Even if Bob knows the painting was stolen, *he* did not use or threaten force. According to NAP, this means that it would be a violation of Bob's rights if anyone were to force him to give the painting back to you, since that would be an act of forcible interference with his property without being a response to any act of forcible interference by Bob. Putting this point more generally: NAP prevents rectification of past crimes or injustices, so long as the original criminal has transferred the proceeds of his iniquity to someone else.

Even the libertarian would not welcome this result. NAP implies something absurd (that Bob has a right to the painting), and thus NAP, as formulated, is false. The libertarian could attempt to avoid the absurd consequence by modifying the principle, perhaps along the following lines:

NAP Any act of forcible interference (or threat thereof) with another individual's person or *legitimately acquired* property is a violation of rights,

---

[8] Ben Burgis, *Give Them an Argument: Logic for the Left* (Winchester, UK: Zero Books, 2018).

78   RIGHTS-BASED ARGUMENTS

unless the act is a response to forcible interference (or threat thereof) by that person.

Since the artwork Bob received was stolen, the libertarian could claim that Bob did not *legitimately* acquire the painting; thus we are allowed to use forcible interference to get it back.

However, adding "legitimately acquired" to NAP opens up a can of worms, for now we need to know what counts as *legitimate acquisition*. The defender of NAP needs to say that Bob did not legitimately acquire the painting, presumably on the grounds that there was a grave injustice *prior* to Bob's coming into possession of the painting. One possible way of spelling that out: a person's property was legitimately acquired if and only if they got it through a sequence of transfers each of which was free and uncoerced, and where this sequence goes back to an original acquisition of property that was just and fair. So, for example, if Bob proceeds to give the painting to Hannah, she would still not have legitimately acquired it.

However, if we adopt this theory of what it means to be legitimately acquired, then, perhaps somewhat surprisingly, the socialist can simply *accept* NAP, and the libertarian will not have any argument against socialism based on NAP. Here's why. First, there presumably never was some initial acquisition of property that was just, or at least we have no way of ascertaining that there was. But even if we were to suppose that this happened in the dark recesses of history, it beggars belief to claim that the current distribution resulted from a sequence of free and uncoerced transfers through the subsequent centuries. As Burgis points out,[9] capitalism emerged from feudalism, and since then the distribution of wealth throughout the world has been hugely affected by the institution of slavery. The building of the British Empire certainly had its share of brutal subjugation of its new subjects and the expropriation of their natural resources. In the United States, besides slavery and the blatant oppression of Black Americans after the eventual end of slavery, we would also need to consider the slaughter of Native Americans and theft of the land they occupied in the early days of the republic. The point is this: given humanity's history of injustice and oppression, we can conclude that almost *no* property was legitimately acquired, if legitimate acquisition requires a just initial acquisition and a series of free transactions after that. And if no property was legitimately acquired, then NAP poses no restrictions

---

[9] Burgis, *Give Them an Argument*.

on what we can do in terms of forcibly interfering with someone's property. So there can be no objection to socialism stemming from the revised NAP.

Perhaps libertarians can come up with a less stringent theory of the legitimate acquisition of property, one where they can still claim that D-socialism violates NAP. For example, they might say, "Well, it's okay if there was horrific injustice in the transfer of property, so long as that injustice seems long enough ago for us to feel comfortable in ignoring it." But as a principle of *justice*, that does not seem very plausible. In any event, it is now on the libertarian to come up with such a theory—one that does seem morally plausible. And observe: even if such a theory is in place, the dispute between the libertarian and the socialist would then have nothing to do with the revised NAP, which they can both accept. NAP, which was originally put forward as the *basis* for the libertarian position, no longer plays any real role in the argument. All the real work would be done by the yet-to-be-provided ancillary theory about what counts as legitimately acquired property.

Self-Authorship and Economic Rights

One might try to ground economic rights, including property rights, on principles other than self-ownership or the nonaggression principle. John Tomasi (2013) proposes a view of economic rights based on broader ideas of *self-authorship* and *citizenship*,[10] and if his arguments are correct, they would suffice to show that most forms of socialism would violate rights.

Tomasi's argument is addressed in the first instance to those socialist or left-leaning liberals—he refers to this as the "high liberal" tradition—who agree that the political liberties of free speech and religion are genuine rights. These high liberals claim that "economic liberties are morally less important than the other traditional rights and liberties of liberalism,"[11] and Tomasi says that this is a mistake. To illustrate, recall the argument from Chapter 3 for regarding free speech as a right in the trump-card sense:

[10] John Tomasi, *Free Market Fairness* (Princeton, NJ: Princeton University Press, 2012).
[11] Tomasi, *Free Market Fairness*, xxv.

80   RIGHTS-BASED ARGUMENTS

Free Speech and Autonomy

(1) If government punishes a person's political speech, then government treats that person as less than a free, equal, and autonomous citizen. [P]
(2) If government treats a person as less than a free, equal, and autonomous citizen, then government violates that person's rights. [P]
(3) If government punishes a person's political speech, then government violates that person's rights. [1,2]

The idea here was that certain restrictions on one's liberty are much more deeply significant than others; restricting certain liberties would cut to the heart of what it is to be a free and equal citizen, and we cannot allow a person's status as equal citizen to be balanced away by considerations of utility and overall welfare.

Tomasi argues that economic liberties are of equal importance to people, and to their ability to be the authors of their own lives. As Tomasi puts it, "Restrictions of economic liberty, no matter how lofty the social goal, impose conformity on the life stories that free citizens might otherwise compose."[12] As already noted, D-socialism would still allow a great deal of economic liberty: the liberty of owning personal property, probably some ability to own productive property (depending on the variety of socialism), the ability to make contracts and acquire some wealth. But Tomasi would not be satisfied unless these liberties were deemed as on a par with the civil liberties like freedom of speech and freedom of religion. Even if the socialist grants some degree of these economic liberties—presumably on the grounds that doing so is in interest of overall well-being—Tomasi believes that the whole package of economic liberties needs to be seen as rights, as liberties not to be bargained away on grounds of overall welfare.

To illustrate the importance that economic liberties have in the lives and self-authorship of ordinary people, Tomasi considers a hypothetical example:

[I]magine a college dropout named Amy who has an entry-level job as a pet groomer. Dreaming of owning a business of her own, Amy saves her money, builds a sterling credit rating, wins a bank loan, and finally opens her own pet shop (Amy's Pup-in-the-Tub). What does it mean to Amy to

---

[12] Tomasi, *Free Market Fairness*, 93.

walk into her own shop each morning or, when leaving after a particularly long day, to look back and read her name up on the sign?[13]

Tomasi notes more generally that "many people define themselves by the financial decisions they make for themselves and their families."[14]

We might take Tomasi to be suggesting an argument about economic liberties that is parallel to *Free Speech and Autonomy*:

Economic Liberties and Autonomy

(1) If government restricts a person's economic liberties, then government treats that person as less than a free, equal, and autonomous citizen. [P]
(2) If government treats a person as less than a free, equal, and autonomous citizen, then government violates that person's rights. [P]
(3) If government restricts a person's economic liberties, then government violates that person's rights. [1,2]

The socialist or high liberal will dispute premise (1) of this argument and protest that examples like Amy and her pet-grooming shop do not adequately support the claim that restrictions on economic liberties amount to treating Amy as less than free, equal, and autonomous. The mere fact that Amy finds owning her own business to be very important and meaningful to her does not suffice to give it the special status of a right. Lots of people find lots of things to be meaningful and important, but this does not mean that each of them is a right. Recall that the idea behind the analogous premise in *Free Speech and Autonomy* was this: censoring speech with particular content arguably amounts to an expression of disdain for those with that set of political beliefs; it arguably amounts to a way of not counting their preferences as much as we count those who agree with us, and this is to treat them as less than equal citizens. (I say "arguably" because I took the premise to be contentious even in the free speech case or in the case of freedom of religion, but it at least had some plausibility.) It is far less obvious that economic regulations on businesses—even if they went to the point of prohibiting private ownership

---

[13] Tomasi, *Free Market Fairness*, 66.
[14] Tomasi, *Free Market Fairness*, 79.

82 RIGHTS-BASED ARGUMENTS

of the means of production—would likewise amount to treating one group of citizens as less than equal members of the political community.

Tomasi's intended argument is perhaps somewhat different in form than *Economic Liberties and Autonomy*. Rather than thinking in terms of what proposed regulations imply about the equal status of affected citizens, Tomasi suggests that the basic liberties (the ones to be protected as rights) "are those liberties that must be protected if citizens are to develop their evaluative horizons, thus making them capable of truly governing themselves."[15] People, he says, "have a fundamental interest in seeing themselves as central causes of the lives they are leading."[16] Perhaps the claim, then, is this: government violates rights if it restricts any liberty the exercise of which increases a person's ability to be self-governing, being able to see themselves as central causes of their own lives. Accordingly, we might have this:

Economic Liberties and Self-Authorship 1.0

Let L be a liberty.
(1) If exercise of L increases a person's ability to be self-governing, then government violates rights if it restricts L. [P]
(2) Exercise of economic liberties increases a person's ability to be self-governing. [P]
(3) Government violates rights if it restricts economic liberties. [1,2]

There is an obvious sense in which premise (2) seems plausible: by allowing Amy to run her own business, we enhance her ability to be self-governing. For one thing, she might make enough money to become financially independent, which certainly helps her to live the life that she chooses. Being her own boss might also simply be part of her dreams. The problem is that premise (1) proves too much: lots of other liberties will likewise lead to increases in the ability to be self-governing, and we would not want to include all of them as *rights*. For example, suppose that Amy, instead of enjoying grooming other people's pets, took deep pleasure in setting up and luring people into elaborate Ponzi schemes. This liberty too might allow her to become financially independent and allow her to be her own boss. Yet we would not want to say that government violates *rights* if it makes Ponzi schemes illegal. (Of course,

---

[15] Tomasi, *Free Market Fairness*, 75.
[16] Tomasi, *Free Market Fairness*, 83.

I am not claiming any sort of direct analogy between setting up a Ponzi scheme and setting up a pet-grooming business. The point is that *if* premise (1) of *Economic Liberties and Self-authorship 1.0* is true, then, given that exercise of the liberty to run a Ponzi scheme can increase a person's ability to be self-governing, we should likewise infer that government violates rights if it makes Ponzi schemes illegal. Since that is an absurd conclusion, we must reject the original premise (1) of both arguments, and we must therefore reject the soundness of *Economic Liberties and Self-authorship 1.0*.)

Tomasi might reply that a Ponzi scheme, unlike the pet-grooming shop, infringes on the ability of *other* people to be self-governing: insofar as Amy gets people to invest their money in a fraudulent scheme, she gains her own financial independence at the cost of damaging *their* financial independence. Rather than the broader principle in (1) of *Economic Liberties and Self-authorship 1.0*, we might want to say that a given liberty is a right if its exercise increases the capacity for self-governance *and* does not infringe on the ability of others to be self-governing. As Tomasi puts it, "a basic liberty can only be restricted in order to prevent a more severe restriction of some other basic liberty."[17] This amounts to changing premise (1) in *Economic Liberties and Self-authorship 1.0*; to make a revised version of the argument still valid, we will also have to change premise (2) accordingly:

Economic Liberties and Self-Authorship 2.0

Let L be a liberty.
(1) If exercise of L increases a person's ability to be self-governing, *and if exercise of L does not lessen the ability of anyone else to be self-governing*, then government violates rights if it restricts L. [P]
(2) Exercise of economic liberties increases a person's ability to be self-governing *and exercise of economic liberties does not lessen the ability of anyone else to be self-governing*. [P]
(3) Government violates rights if it restricts economic liberties. [1,2]

It would be more difficult to come up with clear counterexamples to premise (1) of version 2.0, but now the argument has a different problem: one can simply deny premise (2). Returning to Amy, we might imagine that Amy's Pup-in-the-Tub is wildly successful and that all pet owners in town prefer it

---

[17] Tomasi, *Free Market Fairness*, 76.

84 RIGHTS-BASED ARGUMENTS

to the shop where Amy had her entry-level job as a pet groomer. That shop goes out of business and its owner loses a great deal of money and is thus less capable of self-governing. There need not be anything unfair or underhanded about this turn of events, but the point remains: the economic liberties involved in owning productive property do routinely involve effects on other people's ability to be self-governing, given the wide range of things that can affect that capacity, and this means that premise (2) is false.

The breadth of things that can affect people's ability to be self-authors comes out in a related argument that Tomasi makes: Tomasi claims that the socialist proposal of more egalitarian distribution of wealth actually undermines the ability of people to be central causes of their own lives. This might seem surprising, since you might think that helping people gain financial independence through redistribution would *help* them to do what they value and thus be self-authors. But Tomasi objects:

> [L]eft liberals typically hasten to emphasize that it requires that people be given the material means needed to pursue their goals effectively. But, as we have seen, the mere possession of material means is not sufficient: a person's self-respect is diminished if one is not (and so cannot think of oneself as) the central cause of the life one is leading. Having others secure them with "material means" could not provide liberal citizens with that form of self-respect.[18]

Tomasi suggests that significant redistribution, whereby we provide citizens with the material means they need for self-governance, we would diminish their self-respect and thereby prevent them from viewing themselves as the *central cause* of the life they are leading. Significant redistribution, on this view, denies citizens the ability to develop their moral powers and self-respect, and that we would be thereby allowing citizens to develop "in only a stunted way."[19]

If accepted, this would yield an argument to the effect that socialism (via its tendency toward egalitarian distribution of wealth) would violate rights. However, the implications of Tomasi's premises would go well beyond allowing great economic freedom and greatly curtailing redistribution of wealth. Consider Sam Walton, whose net worth was reported to be about $8

---

[18] Tomasi, *Free Market Fairness*, 82–83.
[19] Tomasi, *Free Market Fairness*, 81.

billion when he died in 1992. When he left that money to his kids, he thereby secured them with quite substantial material means. According to Tomasi, he thereby brought it about that they could not think of themselves as the "central cause" of the lives they were leading, and they would thus be able to develop "in only a stunted way." By Tomasi's premises, any rich person who gives any substantial money to his or her children violates their rights as citizens. The point would go well beyond what people bequeath to heirs but also to all sorts of financial advantages that wealthier people give to their kids. It seems odd to me that Tomasi is worried about the moral development of a person who is the recipient of government aid, but does not draw the same conclusion about the children of the rich. If it is genuinely a violation of the moral standing of a person to provide them with material security, then it seems that Tomasi should advocate incredibly steep taxes on inheritance, as well as restrictions on how much rich people can benefit their children even while still alive.

None of what I have said here implies that economic liberties are unimportant. I certainly do not mean to belittle Amy's desire to run her own pet-grooming shop. Anyone concerned with overall levels of well-being should take into account the genuine pleasure and meaning that people like Amy find in running their own business. We should also take into account the possibility that allowing the economic liberties provided by a free market would create more well-being overall, perhaps because the very possibility of running your own business and making a profit might motivate people toward the sort of economic activity that boosts the well-being of everyone. As Tomasi notes, some in the classical liberal tradition (people like F. A. Hayek or Milton Freidman) argue for free market capitalism precisely on such utilitarian grounds. I have not considered those arguments yet (see Part IV). In this chapter, we are instead merely considering the claim that there is a set of economic liberties that are *moral rights* in the trump-card sense, and that moves toward socialism violate those rights. I have not seen a successful argument for that claim.

Key Takeaways

- There is no reason to think that socialism violates political rights (freedom of speech, freedom of religion, etc.).

86 RIGHTS-BASED ARGUMENTS

- Critics of socialism claim that it violates property rights or more broadly defined economic rights. But it is not immediately clear what they count as property rights or what justification they have for claiming these as rights in the trump-card sense.
- One possible justification for a strong system of economic rights lies in the libertarian nonaggression principle, or NAP. However, the NAP as typically proposed would have wildly implausible consequences. If the NAP is revised to avoid those consequences, then it is not clear that the principle does real argumentative work against socialism.
- Another possible justification for economic rights comes from the idea of self-authorship, as proposed by John Tomasi. On one interpretation of his argument it would prove too much and would have absurd consequences; on a different interpretation of his argument, a different premise in the argument is straightforwardly false.
- I would gladly bring my dog to Amy's Pup-in-Tub, despite disagreeing that she has the sort of economic rights affirmed by libertarians.

5

Does Capitalism Violate Rights?

Extraction of Surplus Value: The Basic Idea

According to Marx, within capitalism, labor is a commodity to be bought and sold like other commodities, and it will be valued in accord with the cost of its production. At least for relatively unskilled labor, the cost of labor production is simply the cost of the laborer staying alive and well enough to come to work the next day. Thus, the cost of the labor can be paid by paying subsistence wages. However, labor is capable of producing more value than it costs: the labor creates surplus value. But this surplus value does not go to the laborer who produces it; instead, it accumulates as profit for the owners of the means of production.

To illustrate, suppose that Sarah owns a small factory that employs 10 people and makes 1,000 widgets a day. Sarah can sell those widgets for $10 each, pulling in $10,000 in revenue for the day. Her non-labor-related expenses per day are the following:

- Raw materials for widget making: $5,000
- Cost of building and equipment for widget making, including maintenance: $3,000
- Cost of distribution of the widgets: $500

Since selling the widgets gives her a revenue of $10,000, and her nonlabor costs are $8,500, this means that the labor provided each day by the 10 workers is, at least in one direct sense, *worth* $1,500 to Sarah. But if Sarah were to pay each of the ten workers $150 per day, that would leave her with no profit. So she pays less, say $75 per day. Why do the workers accept a wage that is less than their labor is worth to Sarah? The crude answer is that Sarah only needs to pay them enough to survive and come to work the next day, not the amount their labor is worth to her. The slightly less crude answer: because the labor is bought on a completely different market than the realm of widgets, Sarah pays her workers what she must in order to attract decent

Socialism. Scott R. Sehon, Oxford University Press. © Oxford University Press 2024.
DOI: 10.1093/oso/9780197753330.003.0005

88   RIGHTS-BASED ARGUMENTS

workers in her environment. If the workers require no special skills, and if there are generally more workers available than there are jobs, then wages necessary to attract workers will naturally tend toward subsistence wages.

As Sam Arnold puts it, according to Marxists:

> Workers spend the first part of their working day working, in effect, for themselves. This is the part of the day during which they produce the equivalent of their wages. Marx calls this "necessary labor time." But the working day does not stop there. Indeed, it *cannot* stop there, for if it did, there would be no "surplus product" for the capitalist to appropriate, and thus no reason for the capitalist to hire the worker in the first place. So the capitalist requires the worker to perform "surplus labor," which is just labor beyond "necessary labor": labor beyond what is required to produce value equivalent to the worker's wage. The value produced during surplus labor time, Marx calls "surplus value." Crucially, *this surplus value belongs to the capitalist rather than the worker, and is the source of all profits.*[1]

We could describe this process as the *transfer of surplus value* from the worker to the owner. But Marx used a stronger term. As Marx puts it, capitalistic property "rests on the *exploitation* of the nominally free labour of others, i.e., on wage labour."[2] Contemporary socialists often use the same word; e.g., Michah Uetricht and Meghan Day assert that capitalists are "exploiting the vast majority of people."[3] Some use stronger language yet. Danny Katch puts it this way: "Capitalism is built around organized theft— the theft of a portion of the value of what workers produce by the people who employ them."[4]

The use of words like "exploitation" and "theft" tends to conceal a substantive argumentative move, which we can bring out by appealing to a philosophical distinction between *descriptive* and *normative* language. A *normative* claim, as the word suggests, is one that involves appeal to a *norm*; a normative claim is not about what merely *is* but also about what *ought* to be the case. A descriptive claim *describes*, without any normative implications.

---

[1] Arnold, "Socialism."

[2] Karl Marx, 1867, *Capital: A Critique of Political Economy*, 1967. Available at https://www.marxists.org/archive/marx/works/1867-c1/. Emphasis added.

[3] Uetricht and Day, *Bigger Than Bernie*, lix.

[4] Katch, *Socialism . . . Seriously*, 81.

For example, we could have the following reports of the same event:

- Derek Chauvin caused George Floyd's death.
- Derek Chauvin murdered George Floyd.

The first of these describes the facts without explicitly making any value judgment; after all, it is *possible* to cause someone's death without doing anything wrong. In contrast with the first, merely descriptive, statement, the second contains the word "murdered," which implies, on most ordinary uses of the term, that Chauvin not only killed Floyd, but did so *wrongfully*.

By comparison, we could construct several versions of what happens between owners and workers under capitalism:

- Owners make profits by receiving more in value from labor than they pay the workers for that labor.
- Owners make profits by exploiting the workers.
- Owners make profits by engaging in theft of the value of the labor of the workers.

Capitalists can agree with the purely descriptive characterization in the first version. But the third characterization—of this transfer of value as *theft*—surely carries normative connotations that the capitalist would deny. The second is perhaps a bit ambiguous, since there are uses of the word "exploit" that do not imply that the exploiter is doing anything wrong (a soccer team can exploit a weakness in its opponent's defensive strategy). But when we speak of exploiting another person, this would normally carry the connotation that such exploitation was morally questionable at best.

Initial Attempts at an Argument

The point is not that we should avoid any normative words or any normative connotations. After all, the whole point of this book is to help us to answer the fundamental question: How ought we to structure our political and economic system? But we do need to be very careful and explicit about when we are using words in a normative rather than a merely descriptive sense. For example, when using words like "exploit," we could specify when we are using the word in a merely descriptive sense and when we might be allowing

90   RIGHTS-BASED ARGUMENTS

it to have normative connotations.[5] We could run an argument like the following, where we say that premise (1) is taken as a *definition* of "exploitation," as something that is *stipulated* to be true for the purpose of the argument:

Capitalism Exploits 1.0

(1) If X hires Y but receives more in value from Y's labor than she pays Y for the labor, then X exploits Y. [P]
(2) Under capitalism, the owners of the means of production make profit by hiring workers and receiving more in value from their labor than they pay the workers for the labor. [P]
(3) Under capitalism, the owners of the means of production make profit by exploiting the workers. [1,2]

And this argument is fine; the capitalist can scarcely deny it, given that (1) is to be taken as simply a stipulation on the use of the word "exploit" and that (2) seems true. Of course, not *all* capitalists make any profit at all, and perhaps there are other sources of profit as well; but the basic idea that owners generally make profit in the way specified is hard to deny.

However, having stipulated that we are using "exploits" in a purely descriptive sense, then *Capitalism Exploits 1.0* does no damage to the capitalist position. The conclusion *looks* damning to capitalism because the word "exploit" normally carries negative normative connotations. In normal usage, if we say that Sarah *exploited* Fred, we do mean to imply that Sarah did something *wrong* to Fred. However, the capitalist was forced to agree with premise (1) of *Capitalism Exploits* precisely because we said that we were simply *defining* exploitation as the extraction of surplus value: as that which happens when an employer receives more in value from an employee's labor than the employer pays for the labor. That much, so far, is just a non-normative *description* of a state of affairs; nothing about the moral rightness or wrongness can follow from this purely descriptive premise. The net result is that the capitalist could simply accept the soundness of *Capitalism Exploits 1.0* while noting that it doesn't follow that anything is wrong with capitalism.[6]

---

[5] This is the approach taken by Gilabert and O'Neill, "Socialism."
[6] I should note that Gilabert and O'Neill, "Socialism," are under no illusions on this point; they likewise make the distinction between a descriptive characterization of the notion of exploitation and a normative claim about exploitation as a practice.

One could add a premise explicitly connecting the stipulated descriptive sense of "exploit" to normative matters, and, in particular, to rights:

Capitalism Exploits 2.0

(1) If X hires Y but receives more in value from Y's labor than she pays Y for the labor, then X exploits Y. [P]
(2) Under capitalism, the owners of the means of production make profit by hiring workers and receiving more in value from their labor than they pay the workers for the labor. [P]
(3) Under capitalism, the owners of the means of production make profit by exploiting the workers. [1,2]
(4) If X exploits Y, then X violates Y's rights. [P]
(5) Under capitalism, the owners of the means of production make profit by violating the rights of the workers. [3,4]

But now the capitalist will deny premise (4), and will, with some justice, complain that *Capitalism Exploits 2.0*, while not quite being directly guilty of equivocation, heads in that direction: Premise (1) is held to be stipulatively true as a purely descriptive account of what the proponent of the argument means by "exploits." But, despite this stipulation, the use of a loaded word like "exploit" tends to give an undeserved sheen of obviousness to premise (4), for we are used to thinking of the word "exploit" as indeed meaning that if one person exploits another, then the first violates the rights of the second.

We could be clearer about the issues with words like "exploit" by being explicit, within the argument, about when we are using the word in a normative sense; we could do this by attaching the modifier "unfairly" to "exploit." We could then run this version of *Capitalism Exploits*, in which we are making a clearly normative claim (rather than a merely descriptive one) in premise (1):

Capitalism Exploits 3.0

(1) If X hires Y but receives more in value from Y's labor than she pays Y for the labor, then X *unfairly* exploits Y. [P]
(2) Under capitalism, the owners of the means of production make profit by hiring workers and receiving more in value from their labor than they pay the workers for the labor. [P]

92 RIGHTS-BASED ARGUMENTS

> (3) Under capitalism, the owners of the means of production make profit by unfairly exploiting the workers. [1,2]
> (4) If X unfairly exploits Y, then X violates Y's rights. [P]
> (5) Under capitalism, the owners of the means of production make profit by violating the rights of the workers. [3,4]

Now premise (4) looks reasonable, but the capitalist will simply deny premise (1). In this sort of context, economist John Roemer explains some possible lines of reasoning from the defender of capitalism:

> The neoclassical economist, and bourgeois thinker more generally, will object that the worker who owns no means of production himself is trading his labor power for access to the means of production owned by another. Both gain from the trade. Or, a different argument, the worker trades his labor power for access to the entrepreneurial skill of the capitalist, or the risk-loving nature of the capitalist which enables him to set up a business. In any case, the trade of labor power for access to capital or entrepreneurial skill is a quid pro quo, and should therefore not be viewed as [unfairly] exploitative; in the case of the risk-loving capitalist and risk-averse worker, the "surplus" labor is an insurance premium the worker pays to protect himself against having to take those business risks himself.[7]

The owner might well extract more in value from the worker's labor than the capitalist pays the worker; but for all that, the capitalist argues, it could be a freely made and fair deal between owner and worker, where both sides benefit—without any apparent unfair exploitation or violation of rights. So it seems that the socialist needs to say more to explain why exploitation, as technically defined and as it occurs in capitalist systems, counts as *unfair* exploitation and thus as a violation of rights.

Filling the Gap in the Argument: The Exploitation Principle

Socialists have tried to fill this gap in the argument in different ways, but I will consider some thoughts on this issue from Jonathan Wolff and

---

[7] John Roemer, *Egalitarian Perspectives* (New York: Cambridge University Press, 1996), 38.

G. A. Cohen in particular.[8] They suggest that the justice or injustice of the extraction of surplus value might depend on the circumstances in which the situation arises, and the nature of the choice for the person whose labor is providing the surplus value. Jonathan Wolff considers an example based on Aesop's fable of the grasshopper and the ants. In the fable, the ants spend the summer industriously building shelter and storing food for winter, while the grasshopper sings and enjoys herself. In Aesop's story, when winter comes and the grasshopper shows up and asks for the ants' help, they refuse, and the grasshopper presumably dies.

Wolff imagines a different ending, in which the ants offer the grasshopper a job working for them, and where the ants gain more in value from the grasshopper's efforts than they pay the grasshopper.[9] There are several salient features to note about the situation. First, assuming the grasshopper accepts the deal, both sides do benefit from the transaction: by hypothesis the ants get more value from the grasshopper's labor than they pay the grasshopper, and, of course, the grasshopper gets to stay alive rather than die of starvation in the cold. Second, we can see that the grasshopper is in a rather tough spot: at the point of hearing the ants' offer, the grasshopper doesn't have much of a choice. Her only alternative to accepting the ants' offer would be to die a miserable death. The ants, of course, know this, and this puts them in a position to make a deal that is greatly to their advantage. Their bargaining positions are quite unequal: the grasshopper can only walk away from the offer at the cost of death, whereas the downside of making no deal at all is not very significant for the ants (they would merely have to labor a bit more themselves in their comfy winter shelter). But, third, this very unequal bargaining position arose because of the previous preferences and choices of the creatures involved. We can stipulate that the grasshopper knew full well (or at least was *able* to understand and know) that her laziness and merrymaking in the summer would lead her to a desperate situation; she is responsible for her

---

[8] For other discussions of exploitation see Nancy Holmstrom, "Exploitation," *Canadian Journal of Philosophy*, vol. 7, no. 2 (1977): 353–369; Robert Goodin, "Enfranchising All Affected Interests, and Its Alternatives," *Philosophy & Public Affairs*, vol. 35, no. 1 (2007): 40–68; Jeffrey Reiman, "Exploitation, Force, and the Moral Assessment of Capitalism: Thoughts on Roemer and Cohen," *Philosophy and Public Affairs*, vol. 16, no. 1 (1987): 3–41; John Roemer, "Should Marxists Be Interested in Exploitation?," *Philosophy and Public Affairs*, vol. 14, no. 1 (1985): 30–65; John Roemer, *A Future for Socialism* (Cambridge, MA: Harvard University Press, 1994); Nicholas Vrousalis, "Exploitation: A Primer," *Philosophy Compass*, vol. 13, no. 2 (2018): e12486; Christine Sypnowich, *Equality Renewed: Justice, Flourishing and the Egalitarian Ideal* (New York: Routledge, 2016); Sam Arnold, "Socialism"; and Sam Arnold, "Capitalism, Class Conflict, and Domination," *Socialism and Democracy*, vol. 31, no. 1 (2017): 106–124.

[9] Jonathan Wolff, "Marx and Exploitation," *Journal of Ethics*, vol. 3, no. 2 (1999): 105–120.

94 RIGHTS-BASED ARGUMENTS

unfortunate plight. Similarly, the ants have a comfortable shelter and food because they worked for it. For this reason, we might agree with Wolff that there is nothing unjust about the ants' offer nor their subsequent extraction of surplus value from the labor of the grasshopper. The grasshopper's labor will be exploited, but, perhaps, not *unfairly* exploited.

By contrast, suppose that I am hiking in the wilderness, and I come across you, collapsed on the ground clutching your broken leg, where your unfortunate state was caused by a huge tree limb that just happened to fall on you at an inopportune time. We are only a couple of miles from the trailhead, and I check and ascertain that I have cell service. You have a phone too, but the tree limb crushed it along with your leg, and the phone no longer works. I could easily call for a rescue. I know that this trail is rarely used and that if I don't call, you may well die before anyone else finds you. Now suppose I offer you a deal parallel to the ants' offer to the grasshopper: "I'll call 911, but only on the condition that you agree to work for me at subsistence wages for the next month." If you were to agree to the offer and follow through on the bargain, then I would extract a substantial amount of surplus value from you, just as the ants did with the grasshopper (we can suppose that your particular talents are useful to me). But, obviously, my suggested deal is despicable, and, were I in a position to enforce it, it would clearly amount to unfair exploitation of you and your predicament.

Why is it despicable? Like the ants' offer to the grasshopper, my offer to call 911 *is* mutually beneficial: I'll gain the surplus value from your labor, and you will receive medical help and still be able to live. Also like the grasshopper case, what makes it possible that I can force such a deal is that our bargaining positions are highly unequal: I happen to have a key asset that you do not have (a functioning phone), and your life is at stake, whereas very little is at stake for me. (We might hope that my conscience would torture me the rest of my life were I really to simply walk away from you in those circumstances, but we will stipulate that I am appropriately heartless.) The difference between the two cases appears to be this: the *reason* that I have this superior bargaining position has nothing to do with virtuous, hard work on my part and lazy, stupid decisions by you. We both walked on the same trail at about the same time; you just had the incredibly bad luck of having a tree limb fall on you. This seems to be a key difference between our situation and that of the ants and grasshopper: our unequal bargaining positions arose not as the foreseeable outcome of our differing choices, but through what appears to be chance or circumstances beyond our control.

With this sort of difference in mind, Wolff (1999) suggests that extraction of surplus value becomes unfairly exploitative when one side has attained the required superior bargaining position through "illegitimate means."[10] G. A. Cohen suggests something similar. He says that exploitation, in the form of one person extracting surplus value from another's labor, is "unjust if and only if it occurs for the *wrong reason*."[11] If such extraction merely reflects differences in the preferences of the people involved, then it would be fine.

Cohen goes on to suggest that such extraction of surplus value becomes unjust when it is *forced* on the laborer and when the possibility of it being so forced is brought about by an unequal and unfair distribution of assets. "Forced" is Cohen's term,[12] but it might seem rather strong. No worker, not even the grasshopper in the example, is forced to work in the strong sense of being literally dragged into the office or the factory floor. But the grasshopper was, we might say, *coerced* or *pressured* in to accepting the ants' offer in this sense: it's not the sort of offer the grasshopper would normally have preferred (working for less than her labor was worth), but the grasshopper's only real alternative was to die in the cold. Similarly, with you and your broken leg and phone: your circumstances put me in the position where I would be able (should I desire it) to coerce you into making a deal that you otherwise would have flatly rejected.

Where we are headed: socialistically inclined philosophers like Cohen and Wolff suggest that surplus value extraction becomes unfairly exploitative when it is essentially coerced *and* the coercion is possible because of a distribution of assets that is undeserved. We might put forward the following:

Exploitation Principle
> Given two people O and W, W is unfairly exploited by O IF:
> (a) O pressures W into working for compensation that is significantly less than the value the work has for O, and O is able to do so because of the antecedent distribution of assets between O and W.
> (b) The antecedent distribution of assets between O and W was not deserved.

---

[10] Wolff, "Marx and Exploitation," 118.
[11] G. A. Cohen, *Self-Ownership, Freedom, and Equality* (New York: Cambridge University Press, 1995), 199.
[12] Cohen, *Self-Ownership, Freedom, and Equality*, 199.

96 RIGHTS-BASED ARGUMENTS

This principle would make sense of our reaction to the hiking case: if you had a working phone with you, you would be able to call for help yourself, but it is not as if I *deserved* to have a phone and you did not; it was just bad luck that yours was crushed by the falling tree limb.

Note that in saying that the distribution of assets was not *deserved*, I am not asserting that there is automatically something *unjust* about the distribution. It is not as if I, or anyone else, now owes you a smartphone. We can see the distinction here by thinking about lotteries. Everyone admits that the winner of a lottery did nothing to *morally deserve* her winning ticket; but that does not mean that, having set up a lottery and having sold tickets, we will now revoke the prize money of the winner or say that she is morally obligated to share it with all those who happened to buy losing tickets. There is a distinction we can draw between *moral desert* and entitlements we can expect based on *legitimate expectations*.[13]

In the context of the *Exploitation Principle*, the claim in (b) is not that the antecedent distribution of assets between O and W is necessarily *unfair* and that it should be corrected. That might be true, but the claim made by the principle is different: if you are in a position to pressure someone into transferring surplus value to you, and if you are in that position because of a very unequal distribution of assets, then this transfer of surplus value becomes *unfair exploitation* when the unequal distribution of assets was *undeserved*, even if the distribution of assets is not deeply unfair in and of itself. The idea is this: if the inequality is undeserved, then even if O does not *owe* W compensation, it would still be unfair for O to take advantage of the undeserved inequality to pressure W into deals that W would otherwise flatly reject. Or at least that is what the principle claims.

Final Version of the Argument

However, it will not be easy to use the *Exploitation Principle* as part of an argument against capitalism. The principle is phrased about a pair of people (the O and the W are meant to suggest "owner" and "worker"). Suppose you work for someone who owns a portion of the means of production. Depending on the circumstances, you might plausibly claim that there was

---

[13] See, e.g., Sandel, *Justice*.

DOES CAPITALISM VIOLATE RIGHTS? 97

nothing of justice in how your boss, but not you, came to have the assets you both in fact possess; your boss might not *deserve* the share of the means of production she possesses. And it may well be true that your compensation is significantly less than the value your work has for your boss. But are you coerced into working for your boss? The capitalist would certainly deny this. In a well-functioning labor market, the capitalist will claim, a diligent worker who does not like her current boss or working conditions can find another job. Of course, this doesn't work perfectly, and there can be circumstances in which individual workers are effectively tied to one job, especially if they have been forced to sign a noncompete clause that prevents them from seeking employment in the same industry. But *most* workers do have some choice in the matter; they are not, like the grasshopper, going to face imminent demise if they quit their current job.

In response, the socialist will be quick to point out that having a choice between several different subsistence wage jobs does not really help the plight of the less-skilled worker. It may well be that the typical worker is not under coercive pressure to sell her labor for less than its value to one particular boss. But if owners of the means of production are, across the board, only offering jobs that extract significant surplus value from the workers, then this leaves the typical worker in a bind: the worker owns none of the means of production, and thus has nothing significant to sell in a market economy except her labor. She must sell *something* in the market to get income to have housing and food. So she is, in effect, in a position quite similar to that of the grasshopper: if she insists on being paid the full value of her labor, and if nobody is offering that, then her choices are to allow the surplus value of her labor to be extracted or to face extremely negative consequences, including homelessness and hunger.

So we need to make the principle more general by talking about two groups or classes of people, the *Os* and the *Ws* (the owners and the workers). Then the whole argument would look something like the following. (I'll preface by saying that the argument is a mouthful, but the idea is fairly simple. Premise (1) sets out the conditions that I identified, following Wolff and Cohen in particular, as constituting unfair exploitation; premise (2) states that situation of the workers and the owners under capitalism meet these conditions; in (3) I draw the inference that the workers are unfairly exploited, and then (4) and (5) get to the conclusion that this is a violation of the rights of the workers.)

98   RIGHTS-BASED ARGUMENTS

Capitalism Exploits 4.0

(1) Given two groups of people O and W, the Ws are unfairly exploited by the Os if
   (a) The Os pressure the Ws into working for compensation that is significantly less than the value the work has for the Os, and they are able to do so because of the antecedent distribution of assets between the Os and the Ws.
   (b) The antecedent distribution of assets between the Os and the Ws was not deserved.
(2) Under capitalism, there are two groups of people, the Os and the Ws and
   (a) The Os pressure the Ws into working for compensation that is significantly less than the value the work has for the Os, and they are able to do so because of the antecedent distribution of assets between the Os and the Ws.
   (b) The antecedent distribution of assets between the Os and the Ws was not deserved.
(3) Under capitalism, the Ws are unfairly exploited by the Os. [1,2]
(4) If one group of people is unfairly exploited by another, the rights of the exploited group are violated. [P]
(5) Under capitalism, the rights of the workers are violated by the owners of the means of production. [3,4]

Evaluating Premise (2) of *Capitalism Exploits*: Is the Distribution Undeserved?

Capitalist Objection: "I built this!"

By way of evaluating the argument, let's start with premise (2). It seems reasonably clear that condition (a) is met: under capitalism, if owners are to make profit, they must receive more in value from their laborers than they pay them; the fact that the typical laborer has nothing to sell in the market apart from her labor means that she is indeed pressured into accepting this deal from one employer or another. The key issue will be (2b): was the distribution of assets between the owners and workers deserved?

Many an owner under capitalism will surely protest: "I worked very hard to put myself in the position of being able to run this business! I built this! If I can do it, anyone can! I deserve it!" One might question how hard many capitalists actually worked to achieve their position, but let's first start with a logical point, for the refrain "If I can do it, anyone can do it" needs to be examined more closely. There is a fallacy involved here, one sometimes known as the *fallacy of composition*, whereby one infers that if one element of a whole has a particular property, then the complete collection of elements has that property. Philosopher Ben Burgis gives an example that shows the fallacy: "None of the molecules that make up the Brooklyn Bridge are visible to the naked eye, so the Brooklyn Bridge itself isn't visible to the naked eye."[14] As applied to the exclamation of the proud capitalist, the point is this: just because *you* were able, through hard work, to become an owner rather than a worker does not mean that *everyone* is able to become an owner rather than a worker. The point here is not that some will have more obstacles in their path than others, though that is certainly true. The point, as Burgis explains, is more basic: "Not every cheerleader can be on top of the pyramid. If everyone at the bottom of capitalism's economic hierarchy was somehow able to simultaneously move up in that hierarchy, no one would be left to harvest crops or drive food to grocery stores."[15]

Nonetheless, there might seem something appealing about the owner's claim. Even if capitalists grant that it is impossible for *everyone* to become a wealthy owner of the means of production, they might insist that it is possible for *any particular person* to do so. That is to say: no, not everyone can win, but if it is a fair race, then there is no injustice, and the results are deserved. But that still leaves us with the remaining question: When is the race fair? When are differences in the distribution of assets *deserved*?

When Is It Undeserved?

If we want to answer the general question about when assets are deserved, it can help to look at cases where it seems intuitively clear to us that the difference in assets was *not* deserved. In the hiking example, it seemed

---

[14] Burgis, *Give Them an Argument.*
[15] Burgis, *Give Them an Argument*, 38.

100 RIGHTS-BASED ARGUMENTS

relevant that it was through no obvious fault of your own that you were lying there with a broken leg and a smashed phone; this came about because of circumstances over which you had *little or no control.* Or we might compare an economic system that we all agree to be unfair. Under feudalism, the nobility owned all of the land; they allowed the serfs to grow food on the land, so long as the serfs delivered to the nobility a prescribed amount of the food grown. The antecedent distribution of assets seems obviously undeserved in that case at least in part because the nobility acquired possession of the land merely due to being born into the right families, and the serfs, not being born into noble families, had no prospect of becoming an owner of land. That is to say, the antecedent distribution of assets came about in a way that systematically depends on factors over which the people involved had little or no control. So we might suggest the following principle:

Undeserved Assets Principle
An unequal distribution of assets is not deserved if the distribution systematically depends on factors over which the people involved have little or no control.

Something seems right about this. The general idea would be that there is at least the prospect of a fairness issue if large inequalities stem from factors that are arbitrary from a moral point of view. It is one thing if some people have far less wealth as a result of the fact that they made a conscious decision not to put in much effort. It is another thing if some people have far less wealth because of, say, the color of their skin, their gender, or, as in feudalism, the family into which they were born. If this principle is plausible, then the question becomes: What factors influence wealth but are factors over which the people involved have little or no control? And how prevalent are these factors under capitalism?

Luck, Innate Talent, and Diligence

If you receive something by *pure luck*, then that is pretty much the definition of receiving something in a way that depends on factors over which you had little or no control. How much luck is involved in the distribution of assets under capitalism? Well, for starters, a great portion of wealth in both Europe and the United States is simply inherited, 60% by some estimates.[16] If you inherited the business from your father, you can hardly say that it was the product of hard work or that you built it, even if you did *also* work hard. Inherited wealth would be the paradigm case of something one *did* nothing to earn, unless the suggestion from the hypothetical owner is the employees should have done a better job of choosing their parents. Moreover, having wealthy parents gives substantial advantage to economic well-being well beyond the eventual literal inheritance of one's parents' wealth. Capitalism was a great advance over feudalism precisely because it opened the *possibility* of property ownership and wealth in ways that did not strictly depend on factors of one's birth, but it is still true that a very significant proportion of wealth distribution depends precisely on who your parents were, something over which you had no control whatsoever.

However, the effect of luck goes far beyond the family you were born into. Consider Clayton Kershaw, who made over $20 million in 2021 as a baseball pitcher for the Los Angeles Dodgers. Kershaw came from modest upbringings but was still lucky enough to have had the right coaches and mentors at the right time. But we can also think about Kershaw's luck on a grander scale. Kershaw's particular talent is, in essence, this: he can throw a small sphere in a way that makes it very hard for others to hit that sphere with wooden club-like implements. The skill Kershaw has, and it is considerable, is highly valued in United States in the 21st century. But that same skill would have been far less valuable in, say, 17th-century France. So, besides the luck involved in having the right coaches and training, Kershaw is immensely lucky that the particular time and culture in which he lives places significant value on his particular talent of small sphere throwing.

Or consider Mark Zuckerberg, whose wealth makes Kershaw's salary seem like a pittance. Zuckerberg was not born into an incredibly rich family. But he was still lucky enough to have a father who taught him elementary programming when he was quite young and who hired a computer programmer to tutor him privately. Zuckerberg, like Kershaw, is enormously talented by all accounts. But that doesn't mean that there was little role for luck, as Zuckerberg himself is the first to admit: "You don't get to be successful like this just by being hard working or having a good idea. . . . You have to

---

[16] Facundo Alvarado, Bertrand Garbinti, and Thomas Piketty, "On the Share of Inheritance in Aggregate Wealth: Europe and the USA, 1900–2010," *Economica*, vol. 84, issue 334 (2017): 239–260.

102 RIGHTS-BASED ARGUMENTS

get lucky in today's society in order for that to happen."[17] As with Kershaw, Zuckerberg's luck goes beyond having met the right people at the right moments, or Facebook having been launched at a moment when people were particularly receptive to it; much more generally, Zuckerberg's aptitude for programming would have been less useful in a time and place where there were no computers.

Admitting the role of luck is not to deny that people like Kershaw and Zuckerberg also do have an immense amount of innate talent. But this admitted fact doesn't really help in saying that they *deserve* the wealth they have, for innate talent, being innate, is likewise a factor over which they had no control! So if, as seems natural, the *reason* that feudalism is unjust is that it allows massive inequality on the basis of factors over which you have no control, then we should likewise admit that there is nothing of justice in allowing massive inequalities that result from differences in innate talent and luck. It is at least fair to say that you do not *deserve* your talents or your luck. John Rawls pushes the point even further and notes that some people are born with much more of an inclination to work diligently than others, and that diligence can itself be affected both by genetic endowment and by your family and social circumstances.[18] So even your diligence can be seen as largely a matter of something that is effectively beyond your control.

We may feel that we have made immense progress over the days of feudalism, when one's family of birth played such an enormous role in determining one's life chances. But, besides the fact that your family still plays a huge role in determining your chances of success, you have no more control over your innate talents and luck than you do over the choice of which parents you will have, and even a propensity to hard work may be a matter over which you have little control.

"But, but, I deserve it!"

None of this implies that it is always wrong to reward talent, luck, and, especially, diligence. It is, for example, plausible to suppose that we will increase human well-being overall if we provide special incentives for those

[17] Catherine Clifford, "Billionaire Mark Zuckerberg: Success Like Mine Only Happens with Luck, and That's a Huge Problem We Need to Fix," CNBC, July 24, 2017, https://www.cnbc.com/2017/07/24/billionaire-mark-zuckerberg-success-like-mine-only-happens-with-luck.html.

[18] Rawls, *A Theory of Justice*, section 12.

with great talent to work hard. (It is far from clear to me that Zuckerberg's highly rewarded talents have actually made the world a better place for the rest of us; and, as much as I love baseball, I'm not sure how much Kershaw's pitching talent has really improved human well-being in proportion to his enormous salary, though Dodgers fans might disagree. But there are many other talented and hard-working people who have indeed made our lives much better.) In the context of *Capitalism Exploits 4.0*, the point is more limited: once we recognize that we have no control over the circumstances into which we were born, our innate talents, the luck we have along the way, and even our innate propensity for diligence, then it seems quite clear that, very few of those who own the means of production gained this bargaining position over the mere laborers in some way that was genuinely deserved. At least for the vast majority of cases, the owners of the means of production achieved this status in ways that systematically depend on factors over which they had little or no control.

Michael Sandel, a professor at Harvard, brings up these points with his undergraduate students in the context of teaching the work of John Rawls. Sandel reports that his students "strenuously object" to the very suggestion that they do not deserve the fruits of their talents and diligence: "They argue that their achievements, including their admission to Harvard, reflect their own hard work, not morally arbitrary factors beyond their control."[19] I have seen similar reactions in my own students. It is difficult to shake the idea that you are fully responsible at least for your diligence and hard work, and it is also true that it is hard to disentangle the results of hard work from the results of innate talent and luck.

One thing to keep in mind here: even if we agree that all of these factors are morally arbitrary, this does not by itself imply that we will immediately revoke admission to elite colleges nor that we should immediately strip all individuals of advantages they have accrued through these factors. In the present context of premise (2) of *Capitalism Exploits 4.0*, the question is just whether you *deserve* the advantages you thereby accrued, and thus whether it is fair to use those advantages to exploit the labor of others to thereby gain even further advantage.

Even with this point granted, I can understand the frustration of Sandel's students (and mine) at the thought that there is no moral desert involved even with gains attained because of your diligence and hard work. I think we

---

[19] Sandel, *Justice.*

104   RIGHTS-BASED ARGUMENTS

can leave that question aside, for it seems quite plausible that even if we factor out the financial gains owners received purely from their hard work, the vast majority of the owners achieved that position *largely* through factors that are clearly morally arbitrary, like inheritance, innate talent, and sheer luck. That's all we need for premise (2).

Thus, there is a good case to be made for premise (2) in *Capitalism Exploits 4.0*: the distribution of assets that allows the owners to extract surplus value from the laborers was, generally speaking, not deserved. We have little more reason to think that the owners deserve their strategic advantage over the laborers than we have reason to think that the nobility deserved their position under feudalism.

Evaluating Premise (1) of *Capitalism Exploits:* Is It Unfair?

However, we still might question premise (1) of the argument, *Capitalism Exploits 4.0*:

(1) Given two groups of people O and W, the Ws are unfairly exploited by the Os if
  (a) The Os pressure the Ws into working for compensation that is significantly less than the value the work has for the Os, and they are able to do so because of the antecedent distribution of assets between the Os and the Ws.
  (b) The antecedent distribution of assets between the Os and the Ws was not deserved.

The question is this: Does the extraction of surplus value become *unfair* exploitation when the workers are pressured into this situation by circumstances that are undeserved? Given that the argument assumes in premise (4) that unfair exploitation is a violation of rights, the essential question is this: Does it violate the moral *rights* of the workers if they are pressured into selling their labor for less than it is worth to the buyer, given that the pressure becomes possible by virtue of an undeserved difference in wealth? There does seem to be something prima facie plausible about this claim; after all, many socialists take it to be simple and obvious that exploitation is unfair.

Under the moral framework that I have proposed for consideration of such issues, whenever there is a claimed violation of rights, the question is this: Is this something that would be wrong to do *even if* we could increase overall human well-being by doing it? Is this a trump card when it comes to considerations of better promoting human well-being? Keep in mind that it is controversial whether we have *any* rights in this fairly strong sense. The traditional examples of rights include the right to free speech and the right to freely exercise one's religion. You *might* agree that it would be wrong to restrict someone's political speech or ability to worship *even if* some such restrictions would make people happier overall, for one might think that telling people that their point of view is not allowed to be heard or that their religious practices should be forbidden is to treat those people as *less worthy* than the rest of us; it is to attack their dignity as a person; it is to treat them as less than equals. Again, I take no official position on these questions, though I do find such claims to be plausible when it comes to free speech and freedom of religion.

In accord with the conception of rights as trumps, we can test the claim that exploitation (as characterized in premise (1) of the argument) amounts to a violation of rights by assuming the following hypothetical, purely for the sake of argument:

> If we were to set things up such that surplus value could not be extracted by people with undeserved wealth, then people would be worse off in general, including the workers.

This is a thought experiment, not an empirical claim; we are just going to consider the extraction of surplus value (by people with undeserved wealth) *on the assumption* that allowing this kind of extraction makes people better off in general. But it is worth noting that that it is not a completely crazy thought experiment; it could be true that allowing such extraction of surplus value makes everyone better off. How might that be? Well, the capitalist tells us that labor markets and private ownership of the means of production, with the concomitant profit incentive, spurs the development of good ideas. The old slogan has it that necessity is the mother of invention. There may be something to that, but the capitalist adds a related thought: the prospect of getting rich is the mother of entrepreneurship and economic growth. Entrepreneurship and economic growth, in turn, lead to improved well-being. The capitalist might even admit that Marx was right about something: without the extraction of surplus value from laborers, profit would basically disappear. But the capitalist then adds that if you get rid of profit as

106 RIGHTS-BASED ARGUMENTS

an incentive, the good ideas and hard work that spur growth will likewise disappear, and we will all be worse off because there will be less wealth overall. One might think that the supposition of the thought experiment is dubious, hoping that we can harness other motivations to make people think inventively and work hard, but such doubts are irrelevant to the thought experiment. If our concern is to test the idea that exploitation is a violation of *rights*, we need to grant, just for the sake of argument, the claim that such exploitation, made possible by undeserved wealth, does lead to greater human well-being. We then ask whether it would *still* be wrong to have a system like this.

One way of attempting to answer this question is to adapt John Rawls's approach by asking which of two societies we would prefer to be born into, granted that we do not know what our position in those societies will be.[20] On the supposition of the thought experiment, we will have two choices:

> *Society 1*: There is coerced extraction of surplus value, made possible by the fact that some people, undeservedly, own the means of production and others do not. But overall well-being is high, including the well-being of the workers.
>
> *Society 2*: There is no coerced extraction of surplus value on the basis of undeserved wealth. Any surplus value extraction is either the result of deserved differences in circumstances or the value extracted goes back to the benefit of all rather than wealth of those doing the extraction. *But* overall well-being is somewhat lower than in Society 1.

One inclined to a strict utilitarian position (according to which there are no rights that trump utility considerations) would choose Society 1: it maximizes utility; nuff said. But you might think that we should choose Society 2, despite the somewhat lower level of overall well-being. You might, for example, think that, irrespective of how well-off people are, there is a certain violation of a person's *dignity* involved in being pressured into being paid less than their labor is worth by virtue of undeserved differences in wealth—that if we allow undeserved differences in wealth to create that sort of coercion, based on factors beyond anyone's control, we are violating the right of the workers to be treated as equals. Or you might think otherwise: lots of things are undeserved in life, and building a society in which people are better off in general

---

[20] Rawls, *A Theory of Justice*, section 24.

on the basis of undeserved factors is worth doing; it need not involve any assault on the dignity of the workers.

Depending on which answer you give—which of the two societies you think is the right one to choose behind a veil of ignorance—you will take different positions on the plausibility of premise (1) of *Capitalism Exploits 4.0*, and thus different positions on the ultimate question of whether capitalism violates rights. That is to say, you will take different positions on the questions of whether the extraction of surplus value under capitalism amounts to *unfair* exploitation.

In my self-appointed role as analyzer of arguments, it seems that I should take a position on this question. However, I am honestly not sure what to say, and I think that this is a question on which intelligent and well-informed people could rationally disagree. Where does this leave us? Many in the socialist tradition have implicitly thought that we could run something like this argument against capitalism:

Capitalism Violates Rights

(1) Capitalism systematically violates the moral rights of individuals. [P]
(2) Any system that violates the moral rights of individuals should be rejected. [P]
(3) Capitalism should be rejected. [1,2]

If such an argument is sound, then this also connects with the question of the definition of "socialism" explored in Chapter 2. Recall that on the classical conception of socialism, anything short of full collective ownership of the means of production doesn't count as socialism; on the classical conception, it is *not* a matter of degree. That view would make good sense if *Capitalism Violates Rights* is sound: if the very nature of capitalism means that rights are violated, then we need a fundamental break, and it makes good sense to save the term "socialism" for systems that make that break.

However, suppose I am right that the best attempt to claim that capitalism violates rights is embodied by *Capitalism Exploits 4.0*, and suppose that it remains unclear whether *Capitalism Exploits 4.0* is sound. Then we do not have any compelling case for the claim that capitalism systematically violates the moral rights of individuals, and we have no case for the soundness of

108 RIGHTS-BASED ARGUMENTS

Capitalism Violates Rights. This in turn means that we no longer have any particularly compelling grounds for stipulating that "socialism" can only refer to a system that fundamentally breaks with capitalist modes of production; we can just allow that it comes in degrees.

On the more substantive issue of whether capitalism or socialism is correct (i.e., the question of which direction we should move and to what degree), the situation is this: I have argued in Chapter 4 that socialism does not violate rights, and I have not found a clearly successful argument for the claim that capitalism violates rights. If neither system violates rights, then this does not mean that we can choose either one, depending on our arbitrary preference. Rather, the issue now simply becomes the question of which system best promotes human well-being. Premise (3) of both the *Master Argument for Socialism* and the *Master Argument for Capitalism* went like this:

(3) Given two styles of governance, if the first better promotes human well-being than the second and does not violate moral rights of individuals, then it should be chosen over the second.

If, as I have suggested, there are, in the end, no compelling claims to be made about rights, then we merely need to figure out which system better promotes human well-being. This is now a fundamentally empirical matter, unlike the question of rights, which was fundamentally normative and not empirical.

I just said that we *merely* need to figure out the answer to this empirical question, but that dramatically understates the difficulty of the task, for it is not as if we can do some simple lab experiment that will give us a decisive answer. We will need to sift through data and various arguments that have been or can be proposed concerning that data. That is the topic of Parts III and IV.

Key Takeaways

- Owners of the means of production extract surplus value from workers when they pay workers less for their labor than the labor is worth to the owner.
- Many socialists have taken such extraction of surplus value to be an obvious instance of unfair exploitation and thus a presumed violation of the rights of workers.

DOES CAPITALISM VIOLATE RIGHTS? 109

- Others have suggested that whether the exploitation is *unfair* depends on the circumstances and whether, in particular, the distribution of assets that makes the exploitation possible was *deserved*.
- We can construct a clear argument for the claim that capitalist extraction of surplus value is indeed a violation of the moral rights of the workers, but it is unclear, at least to my mind, whether such an argument is sound.
- Without a clearly sound argument concerning the normative questions about rights, we will have to examine empirical questions about which system better promotes well-being.
- Even philosophers don't take firm positions on every question.

PART III
SOCIALISM AND HUMAN WELL-BEING

6

The Progress Argument

Empirical Evidence and the Master Arguments

Here again is the *Master Argument for Socialism*:

Master Argument for Socialism

(1) Socialism better promotes human well-being than extant alternative styles of governance. [P]
(2) Socialism does not violate moral rights of individuals. [P]
(3) Given two styles of governance, if the first better promotes human well-being than the second and does not violate rights of individuals, then it should be chosen over the second. [P]
(4) Socialism should be chosen over extant alternative styles of governance. [1,2,3]

And there was a parallel *Master Argument for Capitalism*. In the previous section, I have explored arguments for the claim that either socialism or capitalism violates rights. I saw no reason for thinking that D-socialism violates rights; I was more ambivalent about the claim that capitalism violates rights. Now we turn to questions about human well-being. The *Master Argument for Socialism* starts with the assertion that socialism leads to greater human well-being, while the corresponding argument for capitalism starts with the analogous premise about capitalism.

We have before us an essentially empirical question: Which sort of political and economic system leads to more human well-being? When faced with a broad empirical question of that sort, you can make a distinction between two broad types of evidence we might bring to bear:

(i) General reasons for expecting that one system or the other should typically lead to greater well-being

Socialism. Scott R. Sehon, Oxford University Press. © Oxford University Press 2024.
DOI: 10.1093/oso/9780197753330.003.0006

114 SOCIALISM AND HUMAN WELL-BEING

(ii) Broad-based empirical data showing that one system or the other better increases human well-being

We can illustrate the difference by thinking about evidence in the field of medicine. When the coronavirus pandemic emerged in the spring of 2020, researchers started working as quickly as they could to produce a vaccine. How do we know whether a vaccine will work? How do we know that it will be both safe and that it will be effective in preventing the disease (or at least effective in preventing serious illness as a result of the disease)? Researchers presumably began with reasons of type (i): based on past experience with vaccines and viruses, they would have reasons for thinking that a certain combination of ingredients should lead to a safe and effective vaccine against Covid. But, for medicines and vaccines, we will normally attempt to go beyond that sort of general evidence. Once they get a vaccine that they think is likely to work, the researchers will perform randomized, double-blind controlled studies. This is evidence of type (ii), and it can be sought out irrespective of the existence of general reasons. We divide subjects randomly into two groups, give the candidate vaccine to one group of subjects, and we give a placebo to a control group, and then we just see which group does better.

Our question in this book is not whether a particular vaccine will help to prevent dire effects from a particular disease, but the much broader question: Which form of political and economic organization leads to the greatest human well-being? Double-blind, randomized controlled trials are, of course, out of the question here. Nonetheless, we can still look at broad-based empirical data, noting empirical correlations between, say, capitalistic societies and human well-being. We can also look at evidence of the first sort: reasons for thinking that societies that are more capitalist, e.g., with freer markets, would be *expected* to lead to greater human well-being overall. In this chapter, I will look at evidence of type (ii) brought forward by capitalists: broad empirical data that seems to suggest that capitalism leads to better overall well-being.

To many conservatives, it seems obvious that the broad empirical data points in favor of capitalism, for they think that capitalism and free markets lie behind what they see as humanity's great success story: the massive *increase* in human well-being that has occurred over the last few centuries. If capitalism is responsible for a great alleviation of human suffering, then how could it possibly be that socialism will lead to greater human happiness?

However, I will argue in this chapter that the procapitalist narrative is, at least as typically defended, rather dubious. If I am right about this, it would not show that premise (1) of the *Master Argument for Socialism* is correct nor even that the analogous premise in the *Master Argument for Capitalism* is false. We will just know that a certain oft-rehearsed narrative in favor of capitalism is dubious.

Humanity's Spectacular Progress

Steven Pinker is one of the prime proponents of this sort of defense of capitalism, and thus one of the first who would dissent from the premise that socialism leads to greater human well-being. Pinker is a psychologist by training but has written two popular books that aim (in part) to show that things have, in general, been getting better and better: *The Better Angels of Our Nature* and *Enlightenment Now*.[1] The latter of these two has as one of its main theses the claim that "The world has made spectacular progress in every single measure of human well-being."[2]

Some liberals are inclined to deny this claim about human well-being, while conservatives are more likely to tout it and celebrate it. Both tendencies make a certain sort of sense given the respective general attitudes of a liberal or a conservative. Insofar as we take the term "conservative" somewhat literally, it indicates a tendency to favor the status quo, the system that got us where we are. Insofar as liberals are the opposite of conservatives, they presumably want to change the system. So it seems that conservatives have a vested interest in claiming that our existing system has done very well and does not need changing, and liberals will be more likely to point out the failings of the current system so as to justify changing it. However, besides being an misportrayal of the contemporary meanings of the terms "conservative" and "liberal," I think that this way of looking at things is simplistic. In particular, I think those who oppose the conservative views should resist the temptation to deny that there has been incredible progress on human well-being in recent centuries. Pinker and company are, so far as I can tell, *right* about the claim of progress, and it is always a mistake to attempt to

---

[1] Steven Pinker, *The Better Angels of Our Nature: Why Violence Has Declined* (New York: Viking Books, 2011) and *Enlightenment Now: The Case for Reason, Science, Humanism, and Progress* (New York: Penguin Books, 2018).

[2] Pinker, *Enlightenment Now*, 52.

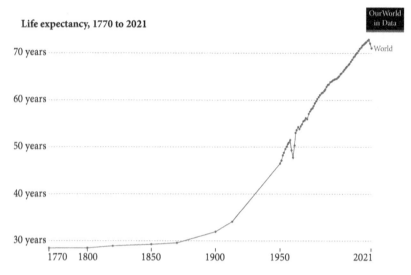

Figure 6.1

stubbornly deny facts. Pinker specifically argues that we have improved greatly in life expectancy, health, food supply and sustenance, wealth, and in diminishing inequality. We could look at all of these factors, but let's focus on life expectancy and wealth.

Pinker is correct that there have been huge increases in life expectancy for human beings over the last two centuries. Figure 6.1 is a chart of gains in overall life expectancy.[3]

Note that life expectancy was incredibly low prior to the late 19th century, and that there was no particular trend during that time. Then around 1870 or so, there was a sharp and pretty steady increase, and we now have over twice the life expectancy that people had prior to 1850. Different sources will vary on the details, but the overall trend is clear. *More* life does not necessarily mean *better* life, but surely it is a significant indication. Would you rather have a life expectancy of 75 or 28?

Now let's look at wealth. Pinker points to sources indicating that gross domestic product (GDP) per capita has skyrocketed since around 1800. This

---

[3] Max Roser, Esteban Ortiz-Ospina and Hannah Ritchie, "Life Expectancy," OurWorldInData.org, n.d. https://ourworldindata.org/life-expectancy (accessed April 7, 2023).

THE PROGRESS ARGUMENT 117

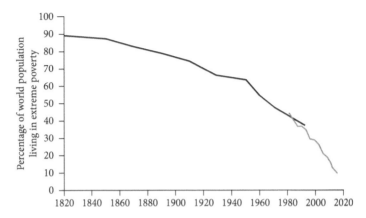

Figure 6.2

is not merely a matter of a few people at the top becoming millionaires and billionaires: the percentage of the world's people living in extreme poverty has dropped from nearly 90% in 1820 to around 10% today. Figure 6.2 is a key chart introduced by Pinker.[4] You can quibble about this sort of chart and note that we don't have very good data concerning wealth, GDP, and poverty back in the 1800s, but I think Pinker is right about the gist of the story: humanity's living conditions have improved greatly over the last couple of centuries. And we should admit that this is excellent news. Of course, a general decline in poverty should not make us complacent about the poverty that remains, but if fewer people are living in gut-wrenching poverty, then it is foolish not to admit that this is a good thing.

Capitalism as the Explanation?

Pinker and many others take a further step beyond pointing to such increases in human well-being: they *attribute* this success story to capitalism. For example, writing for the Foundation for Economic Education, Robert Murphy, looking at an almost identical chart, says: "Of course, there is more work to be done on this front, but the spread of market institutions (sometimes

---

[4] Pinker, *Enlightenment Now*, 84. He in turn gives his sources as follows: "Sources: Our World in Data, Roser & Ortiz-Ospina 2017, based on data from Bourguignon & Morrisson 2002 (1820–1992), averaging their 'Extreme poverty' and 'Poverty' percentages for commensurability with data on 'Extreme poverty' for 1981–2015 from the World Bank 2016g."

SOCIALISM AND HUMAN WELL-BEING

disparaged as "neo-liberalism" and "globalization") have gone hand-in-hand with rapid and unprecedented increases in human welfare, even for the poorest among us."[5] Luka Ladan makes a similar claim in an article titled "Capitalism Remains the Best Way to Combat Extreme Poverty."[6] Rand Paul baldly asserts, "Wealth creation is dependent on the economic system. Capitalism creates wealth. Socialism does not."[7] Jason Brenner asserts, "The wealth we now enjoy wasn't just moved around by government transfers. It was created by market economies."[8] Pinker is more careful, but he also writes that one major explanation for the great increase in material well-being across the world is the growth of market economies and "the decline of communism (together with intrusive socialism)."[9]

What exactly is the argument here? Looking at some broad-based empirical data, Pinker and the others note that the rise of capitalism is correlated with the rise in human well-being; they then seem to infer that human well-being will decrease if we move away from capitalism:

Capitalism and Progress 1.0

(1) Human well-being has increased spectacularly while capitalism has increased. [P]
(2) Without capitalism, human well-being will decrease. [1]

The premise of this argument is true. But the argument is not valid; the conclusion does not follow from the premise. Here is a parallel argument to make the fallacy obvious:

Putin and MLB Salaries

(1) Major league baseball salaries have increased spectacularly while Putin has ruled Russia. [P]
(2) Without Putin ruling Russia, baseball salaries will decrease. [1]

---

[5] Robert Murphy, "Extreme Poverty Rates Plummet under Capitalism," Foundation for Economic Education, May 30, 2018, https://fee.org/articles/extreme-poverty-rates-plummet-under-capitalism/.

[6] Luka Ladan, "Capitalism Remains the Best Way to Combat Extreme Poverty Both in America and Abroad," *Catalyst*, June 14, 2019, https://catalyst.independent.org/2019/06/14/capitalism-remains-the-best-way-to-combat-extreme-poverty.

[7] Paul, *The Case against Socialism*, 56.

[8] Brennan, *Libertarianism*, 134.

[9] Pinker, *Enlightenment Now*, 90.

It is true that since Putin ascended to power in Russia in 1999 major league baseball salaries have skyrocketed. But baseball players aren't worried that their salaries will decrease if Putin dies.

At bare minimum, the capitalist needs to claim not merely that there has been a correlation between increasing human well-being and the rise of capitalism, but that capitalism *explains* the increase in human well-being, making the argument look like this:

Capitalism and Progress 2.0

(1) Capitalism *explains* the spectacular increases in human well-being. [P]
(2) Without capitalism, human well-being will decrease. [1]

However, even if we were to grant that capitalism explains the observed increases in well-being (more on that below), this version of the argument would still be invalid, and would need an intermediate premise:

Capitalism and Progress 3.0

(1) Capitalism *explains* the spectacular increases in human well-being. [P]
(2) If X explains the increase in Y, then without X, there will be a decrease in Y. [P]
(3) Without capitalism, human well-being will decrease. [1,2]

This argument is valid, and it has some intuitive appeal. If pushing the accelerator and adding more gas made my car move faster, then I might well conclude that if I stop pushing the accelerator the car will slow down; the capitalist thinks that adding free markets was like pushing the accelerator on economic well-being, and that human well-being in general followed along.

However, premise (2) is clearly not a universal truth. Even the car example shows it to be false in some circumstances, which are unfortunately familiar to those who live in northern climates: if I remove my foot from the accelerator just as my car hits a patch of black ice, the car will scarcely slow down (and that's just the beginning of my problems). Pushing the accelerator got the car up to its current speed, but, in accord with Newton's laws of motion, the car's speed will only decrease if some further force is added, e.g., the

120 SOCIALISM AND HUMAN WELL-BEING

friction normally provided by the road's surface. Or a different example not involving motion: suppose that there was a small fire in a corner of a house, and that someone has been adding gasoline to it. That the person poured gasoline on the fire explains why the fire then grew so large. However, once the house is thoroughly engulfed in flames, it is not true that the flames will decrease if the person stops pouring the gasoline. It's often hard to get fires started and sustained, and thus the use of an accelerant. But once they get going, if they have enough flammable fuel (even without an accelerant), the fire will continue to grow, or at least not abate.

One might claim that the introduction of capitalism and free markets functioned analogously to an accelerant in a fire: perhaps it did help to spark tremendous economic growth in comparison with existing economic structures, while it still might be that we can now introduce a great deal of redistribution and collective control of the means of production without inhibiting the growth that has already begun. To show that this is wrong, and that withdrawing from capitalism will decrease well-being, it is not enough to show that the rise of capitalism explains the rise of economic growth and well-being. Moreover, even if capitalism explains the rise in well-being over the last century or so, it could still be the case that continuing with capitalism will now *decrease* well-being. How so? One might speculate that the circumstances have changed in important ways. It could be that capitalism increased well-being *by* creating economic growth, and it did that, in large part, via mechanisms that involved burning huge amounts of fossil fuels. Fossil fuel consumption is now causing highly significant changes in the climate, which threaten to have hugely negative effects on human well-being as we proceed deeper into the 21st century. So if unrestrained capitalism will lead to continued burning of fossil fuels, then it could well be that capitalism fueled (pardon the pun) the economic growth and well-being in the 20th century but that its continuation will now harm human well-being. (More on that possibility below when I discuss climate change in Chapter 12.) This would be another way in which premise (2) of *Capitalism and Progress 2.0* could turn out to be false.

Correlation versus Causation and the Capitalist Argument

Even apart from these questions about premise (2) of *Capitalism and Progress 3.0*, premise (1) should not be taken as obvious. What we know is that the rise of capitalism did happen at roughly the same time as a rapid increase in human well-being. But we should know better than to immediately infer causation from correlation. Putin's rise to power was likewise correlated with an increase in baseball salaries, but we don't think that there is any causation or explanatory relationship involved.

In abstract terms, if A is correlated with B, we cannot simply conclude that A caused B, for there are several other possibilities:

(a) Perhaps the causation went in the other direction and B caused A. (For example, the time most people tend to wake up is roughly correlated with the time of sunrise. But we would not say that our waking causes the sun to rise.)

(b) Perhaps there is a third factor that caused both A and B. (For example, the spring of 2020 saw a great increase in both Netflix viewership and sales of hand sanitizer. But neither caused the other; the correlation was brought about as secondary effects of a common cause, namely the coronavirus pandemic.)

(c) Perhaps the correlation is merely accidental; something else explains B and the occurrence of A at the same time is just a coincidence. (The Putin and baseball example is a case in point. Here is another: in the United States since the 1980s both the marriage rate and the number of people who smoke cigarettes has declined fairly steadily, but these trends were presumably unrelated; we would explain each through separate factors.)

In the medical realm, it is precisely because of worries about hastily inferring causation from correlation that we insist on controlled trials. When we take experimental subjects and randomly divide them into a test group and a control group, we thereby go a long way toward ruling out the above sorts of alternative explanations for a correlation.

We can also do observational studies, where subjects are not randomly put into test and control groups. But there are drawbacks to such studies. For example, you could do an observational study where you keep track of people's health, and then also keep track of whether they drink expensive scotch or not. And you might find that there is a strong correlation between those people who drink expensive scotch on occasion and people who have generally good health outcomes. But this would likely be a case with a correlation that is caused by a third factor: the people who drink expensive scotch

122   SOCIALISM AND HUMAN WELL-BEING

are likely to be wealthier, which might lead them to have better medical care in general. So it was not the scotch; it was the high level of wealth that enabled both the scotch purchases and the best healthcare. A controlled trial would have subjects split into random groups (so neither would be richer than the other), and the test group would be *given* scotch, while the control group received some sort of placebo version. If the results still held up (which seems rather unlikely), then this would rule out wealth as the common underlying factor.

In the case of capitalism and the global increase in wealth, we have, in effect, an observational rather than a controlled study. That much is not the fault of the conservatives; it would be impractical at best to take a huge number of subjects, divide them randomly into two fully functioning societies, and then have one operate in accord with capitalist principles while making the other one socialist. But even if we cannot perform a truly controlled study of capitalism versus socialism, we do still need to be very careful and cautious when making inferences from the observational correlations put forward by Pinker and the others. Before we could conclude that capitalism *explains* the increase in wealth, we need to think about the three possibilities just listed. Neither (a) nor (b) seems tremendously likely: though it might be possible, there is little reason to assume that greater wealth caused the rise of capitalism, and there is no obvious candidate for something that caused both the rise of capitalism and the increase in wealth.

But possibility (c) is not so easily ruled out. Capitalism's staunch proponents think the correlation is so strong that causation must be inferred. You can see this in the Robert Murphy quotation above, but economist Milton Friedman is even more explicit, for he claims that "the *only* cases in recorded history" where "the masses have escaped" from "grinding poverty" are precisely "where they have had capitalism and largely free trade." Friedman goes on to say that "the record of history is absolutely crystal clear that there is no alternative way so far discovered of improving the lot of the ordinary people that can hold a candle to the productive activities that are unleashed by a free enterprise system."[10]

---

[10] Friedman made the quoted comments in an interview with Phil Donahue in 1979, an interview that is available on YouTube: "Milton Friedman and the 'Greed' Question," YouTube.com, https://www.youtube.com/watch?v=TZDXvgUxAgQ. See also Milton and Rose Friedman, *Free to Choose: A Personal Statement* (New York: Harcourt, 1980), 54–55.

THE PROGRESS ARGUMENT   123

Testing the Capitalist Hypothesis: Data from 20th-Century Communism

Friedman's implicit idea here is a good one: since not all countries have had fully capitalist economic systems during that time, we can look at the noncapitalist countries as a way of testing the claim that capitalism was the explanatory factor for the increases in well-being. Friedman claims that it is only countries that have had capitalism that have escaped "grinding poverty." But is that true? We can test this by looking at precisely those countries that the conservatives tend to think of when they imagine socialism, namely the Soviet bloc countries and China. The Soviet Union was socialist from 1917 to 1991, and its Eastern European satellites went that way after World War II. China officially became communist in 1949. While I have said in Chapter 2 that these countries are dubious examples of socialism (since their authoritarian features mean that the means of production were not genuinely under collective control), it is also true that they were not, by any means, traditionally capitalist. If it is truly capitalism that explains increases in well-being in the world in general, then we would surely expect that these communist countries would be an exception to the worldwide trends during the relevant time periods.

Let's first look at life expectancy, gains in which were so highly touted by Pinker as evidence of the effectiveness of capitalism (Table 6.1).[11] As the chart shows, at the end of the Cold War in 1990, life expectancy in the United States and UK did exceed that of the Soviet Union by about seven years and that of China by about eight years. But if you look at the earlier dates on the chart, you can see that the USSR and China began their period of communist rule with vastly shorter life spans than those in the West. A baby born in 1920 in the USSR could only expect to live to about 21, whereas a baby born in the West could expect to live into their late fifties. Similarly, when China began its communist rule, the gap between it and the West was about 25 years. Both countries managed to make tremendous progress in closing that gap over the decades of state control of the economy. In the 70 years between 1920 and 1990, life expectancy in the United States and UK increased by about 20 years, in the Soviet Union it increased by almost 50 years. Those data don't

---

[11] Data from Max Roser, Esteban Otiz-Ospina, and Hanna Ritchie, "Life Expectancy," Our World in Data, October 2019, https://ourworldindata.org/life-expectancy.

124 SOCIALISM AND HUMAN WELL-BEING

Table 6.1 Life Expectancy from Birth

	United States	UK	USSR	China
1920	55.4	57.3	20.5	
1950	68.1	68.6	57.2	43.7
1970	70.7	71.9	67.7	56.6
1990	75.4	75.7	68.5	68.0
2000	76.8	77.9	65.3	71.9

make much sense on the conservative hypothesis that capitalism *explains* increases in life expectancy.

Also take note of the final line of the table. Three of the countries continued with modest improvements in life expectancy in the last decade of the 20th century, but life expectancy *fell* by over three years in the Soviet Union. If the end of the Cold War (the Berlin Wall fell in 1989, the USSR ceased to exist as a communist country in 1991) signified the "end of history" and the "unabashed victory of economic and political liberalism," as claimed by Francis Fukuyama,[12] and if the capitalist economic system was obviously so superior, then why did life expectancy in the USSR *drop* when market economies were introduced with Western help?

The first premise of *Capitalism and Progress 2.0* does not look any better when we look at the growth of wealth. If it is truly capitalism that is responsible for increases in wealth, one would expect that these communist countries would be an exception to the worldwide trend toward greater growth during the relevant time periods. Table 6.2 collects data from Maddison, *The World Economy*, put out by the OECD.[13] It lists GDP per capita at various key times in the United States; the former USSR; the Eastern European countries that were part of the Soviet bloc (the chart includes figures from former Yugoslavia, which was nonaligned but still socialist); and China.[14] Let's walk through some of this data. Four years prior to the 1917 revolution, Russian GDP per capita was only 28% of that of the United States, at $1,148 versus $5,301. GDP skyrocketed in the United States to $23,214 per capita in 1990.

---

[12] Francis Fukuyama, "The End of History?," *National Interest*, no. 16, (Summer 1989).

[13] Angus Maddison, *The World Economy*, Development Centre of the Organisation for Economic Co-operation and Development. Available at https://www.stat.berkeley.edu/~aldous/157/Papers/world_economy.pdf.

[14] Maddison, *The World Economy*, data for the United States, USSR, and Eastern Europe at p. 185; data for China at p. 215.

THE PROGRESS ARGUMENT   125

Table 6.2 GDP Per Capita (1990 International Dollars)

	United States	USSR	Eastern Europe	China	USSR % of United States	Eastern Europe % of United States	China % of United States
1913	5,301	1,488			28%		
1950	9,561	2,834	2,120	439	30%	22%	4.6%
1973	16,689	6,058	4,985	839	36%	30%	5.0%
1990	23,214	6,871	5,437	1858	30%	23%	8.0%

But it also went up dramatically in the USSR; GDP per capita growth in the Soviet Union kept pace with that of the United States, ending at $6,871 or 30% of the US figure, when it was at 28% of the US in 1913.

Another way of looking at this: between the years 1913 and 1990, GDP per capita in the United States increased by 438%. However, despite not being capitalist, GDP per capita in the Soviet Union increased even more: 462%. The story is similar in the Eastern European communist countries. Between 1950 and 1990, GDP per capita in the United States increased by 143%. But in the Eastern European countries the rate was even higher: 156%. China's GDP per capita began even lower, at only 4.6% that of the United States. There were various market-oriented reforms beginning in the late 1970s that complicate the question of whether to call China communist or capitalist, but even before those reforms, the table shows that China's growth kept pace with that of the United States.

These numbers make little sense on the hypothesis that capitalism gets the explanatory credit for the worldwide increase in wealth. If, as Pinker claims, it is the decline of communism that is responsible for the increase in well-being, then surely the communist countries would not have kept pace with the growth of wealth in the West; but they did, so it seems that Pinker is wrong. And Friedman's explicit claim that capitalism provides "the only cases in recorded history" of successful growth from poverty is falsified by data from the very countries he most liked to bash.

Or consider the graph in Figure 6.3, which represents the GDP per capita in the United States and the USSR from 1950 to 1998.[15]

---

[15] Maddison, *The World Economy*, 133.

126 SOCIALISM AND HUMAN WELL-BEING

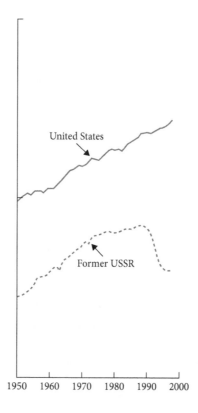

Figure 6.3

The Soviet Union was always poorer than the United States, but its wealth grew at approximately the same rate, until 1991: precisely when the Soviet Union collapsed and ceased to be communist. Instead, with Western help, Russia introduced free markets, which was immediately followed by a steep *decline* in wealth as measured by GDP. In fact, across the Soviet bloc countries, the immediate effect of the transition from communism to capitalism was an economic disaster greater and more long-lasting than the Great Depression in the United States.[16] How could that be if capitalism is the principal driver behind worldwide wealth production?

One might well question the numbers given above; historical GDP data from the communist bloc countries are not easy to know with any great deal of certainty, and perhaps even the life expectancy numbers are less clear than

---

[16] Kristen Ghodsee and Mitchel Orenstein, *Taking Stock of Shock: Social Consequences of the 1989 Revolutions* (New York: Oxford University Press, 2021).

in the West. But even if one takes the specific numbers with a grain of salt, the general picture is clear: life improved in those countries a great deal from the time before they adopted state socialism. It is true that, at the time of the collapse of the Soviet Union, the economic situation was far less good than in Western Europe or the United States, and one might mistakenly infer from that fact that capitalism produces far more economic progress; but that would be a mistaken inference for the obvious reason that the countries in question were, prior to the introduction of state socialism, far poorer than the United States or the countries of Western Europe. If one runner finishes a race far ahead of another, one would be inclined to assume that she is faster than the one who lagged behind; but if you also knew that the claimed winner had a huge head start, then you would withdraw that inference. The same applies here.

The capitalist might assert that the GDP numbers from the state socialist countries are misleading for another reason; the capitalist might insist that it was the elements of capitalism within those countries (black markets and the like) that allowed for such growth as they managed. And one might point out that they were, in at least some cases, able to profit from interactions with capitalist countries. Even if there is something to these considerations, note that this means there is a great shift in the argumentative dynamic: instead of pointing to what the capitalists thought was an *obvious* empirical case in favor of capitalism, the capitalist is now struggling to *explain away* data that seem to indicate that capitalism had no particular economic advantage in the 20th century. From the standpoint of evaluating the Master Arguments, the key point is just this: despite the claims by numerous conservatives, it is far from obvious that the economic data point strongly in favor of capitalism as the system that better promotes human well-being.

Moreover, data concerning well-being go beyond statistics about growth and life expectancy. Ethnographic and survey data contradict any straightforward claim that well-being was substantially lower under the state socialist regimes in Eastern Europe.[17] After the collapse of communism and the subsequent dismantling of social safety nets, ordinary citizens grew increasingly less critical of their state socialist pasts. A 2009 poll in eight east European countries asked if the economic situation for ordinary people was "better,

---

[17] This paragraph draws on Kristen Ghodsee and Scott Sehon, "Anti-Anti-Communism," *Aeon*, March 22, 2018, https://aeon.co/essays/the-merits-of-taking-an-anti-anti-communism-stance. Though I coauthored the article, I should note that these ethnographic data about the Eastern Bloc are far more her specialty than mine.

128 SOCIALISM AND HUMAN WELL-BEING

worse or about the same as it was under communism." The results: 72% of Hungarians, and 62% of both Ukrainians and Bulgarians believed that most people were *worse* off after 1989. In no country did more than 47% of those surveyed agree that their lives improved after the advent of free markets.[18] Subsequent polls and qualitative research across Russia and Eastern Europe confirm the persistence of these sentiments.[19]

Here's a specific piece of information about life in the state socialist countries that might surprise you: in a provocative book entitled *Why Women Have Better Sex under Socialism and Other Arguments for Economic Independence*, anthropologist Kristen Ghodsee has documented that people had better intimate relationships and better sex under socialism, even in otherwise repressive regimes like East Germany.[20] The basic explanation: where women have jobs and a better guaranteed social safety net, their relationships can be chosen on the basis of love and mutual attraction, rather than hoping to find a good breadwinner who may or may not be your heart's desire. (Ghodsee emphasizes *women* having better sex, and some of the data from Germany are in that vein, e.g., East German women having more satisfying sex and more orgasms than their West German counterparts. But I'm going to go out on a limb here and suggest that if women are having better sex, then it is better for their male (or female) partners as well.)

I'd like to reiterate at this point that I am not trying to defend the state socialism of the 20th century; those regimes were authoritarian and nondemocratic. You can favor moving strongly in a socialist direction without favoring that kind of repression. Moreover, one can favor greatly increased collective control of the economy without advocating five-year plans and virtually complete state control of the economy. In the present context, the point is merely to rebut the conservative claim that the wonderful increases in human well-being over the last couple of centuries can all be credited to the rise of capitalism. You might not like statistics, but the data from the 20th-century state socialist countries paint a puzzling picture for

---

[18] "End of Communism Cheered but Now with More Reservations," Pew Research Center, November 2, 2009, http://www.pewglobal.org/2009/11/02/end-of-communism-cheered-but-now-with-more-reservations/.

[19] "Confidence in Democracy and Capitalism Wanes in Former Soviet Union," Pew Research Center, December 5, 2011, http://www.pewglobal.org/2011/12/05/confidence-in-democracy-and-capitalism-wanes-in-former-soviet-union/.

[20] Kristen Ghodsee, *Why Women Have Better Sex under Socialism and Other Arguments for Economic Independence* (New York: Hachette, 2018).

conservatives who insist that capitalism is the driving force behind all such progress.

Science and Technology as the Real Explanation

If capitalism cannot take credit for global increases in wealth, then whatever rough correlation there is between the rise of capitalism and increased wealth is merely that: a correlation between phenomena that are fundamentally unrelated. This was option (c), according to which the apparent correlation is coincidental and there must be some other explanation for the increase in wealth and increases in life expectancy.

What is that other explanation? The obvious answer: science and technology. The scientific revolution is usually dated back to the mid-1500s with the publication of Copernicus's model of the solar system. Subsequent thinkers like Galileo and Newton transformed the idea of how science should work, and science rather suddenly started making huge progress by the 18th century. This in turn led to the invention of things like the steam engine, inventions which propelled the industrial revolution and allowed for massive increases in agricultural production. With the work of people like Louis Pasteur in the 19th century and with the germ theory of disease, discovery of penicillin, medical advances increased longevity and health. One could go on and on about the story of scientific and technological advances making our lives better.

Conservatives might try to claim that only capitalism could properly take advantage of the scientific revolution, and that the socialist countries simply copied the science and technology that developed under capitalism. But such claims would clearly need empirical support. And the fact that it was the USSR that first put a satellite into space (Sputnik) and first put a man into space (Yuri Gagarin) will make it more difficult to maintain that they were just copying our technology. (I'll also mention that the Soviets put a *woman* into space, Valentina Tereshkova, fully 20 years before the United States did the same.)

Pinker does not disagree about the importance of science and technology to this story. After all, his book is called *Enlightenment Now*, and the subtitle is *The Case for Reason, Science, Humanism, and Progress*. Pinker allows that "science and technology" is the most important contributor to the great increase in wealth and decrease in poverty.[21] But his enthusiasm for capitalism

---

[21] Pinker, *Enlightenment Now,* 94.

130 SOCIALISM AND HUMAN WELL-BEING

(and distaste for socialism) apparently makes him overreach and claim causation when there is only a very rough and notably incomplete correlation between capitalism and the progress he rightly lauds. Perhaps he is also blinded by the fact that the state socialist countries were significantly poorer than the West at the end of the Cold War—ignoring the fact that these countries *started* much poorer than the West but then created wealth at a comparable rate.

Once again, one can make the points I have made in this chapter without advocating or defending the brand of state socialism practiced by the Soviet bloc countries, especially not their lack of democracy and restrictions on political rights. My point is limited to responding to a particular argument: Pinker and others claim that the great increase in human well-being—most notably wealth and life expectancy—must be attributed to capitalism and free markets. But the data from China and the Soviet bloc countries makes this hypothesis extremely problematic. At bare minimum, thinkers like Pinker and Friedman would need to explain, if it is capitalism that causes these good things, why similar or even greater increases in growth and life expectancy occurred in noncapitalist countries. They would also need to explain why the switch from communism to capitalism in the Soviet bloc was accompanied by an economic depression and by *lowered* life expectancies rather than the increases you would expect if capitalism explains the progress in human well-being.

Key Takeaways

- Conservatives like to point out that human well-being has increased tremendously in recent centuries, particularly in terms of life expectancy and wealth. Conservatives are right about this.
- Conservatives like to claim that these increases in well-being are *explained* by capitalism and free markets. This explanatory claim is rendered dubious by data from the 20th-century state socialist countries.
- The obvious explanation for gains in life expectancy and wealth is science and technology, not capitalism.
- No, I'm not advocating state socialism of the sort practiced in the Soviet bloc countries.
- *Socialism: A Logical Introduction* is a pretty lame book title compared with *Why Women Have Better Sex under Socialism*.

7

Redistribution: Inequality and Envy

The Pettiness of Envy

When I was a teenager, I was horribly envious of the boys on my baseball team who could hit the ball much further than me. One of them, Mike, hit the ball so hard that during batting practice we typically stationed at least one fielder *beyond* the home-run fence to track down all of his moon shots. I so wanted, just once, to be cheered as I rounded the bases in a home-run trot, like Mike got to do regularly. But the fact that I felt pangs of distress did not make it a bad thing when Mike hit a home run; my petty jealousy was not a reason worth considering at all. There would have been no justification for an attempt to equalize the cheers and pats on the back that every player received.

Socialism calls for more egalitarian distribution of resources, and socialists claim that this will make people happier in general: in other words, socialists support premise (1) of the *Master Argument for Socialism* by saying that redistribution will enhance human well-being. One conservative reaction is that such calls for redistribution merely stem from envy: the rest of us just envy the wealth of the 1% in the way that I envied Mike's hitting talent. "Complaining about inequality is basically a variation of envy or coveting," says Rand Paul.[1] Nearly 60 years earlier, F. A. Hayek quoted the early 20th-century Supreme Court justice Oliver Wendell Holmes saying, "I have no respect for the passion for equality, which seems to me merely idealizing envy."[2] That Mike was loudly cheered for hitting home runs did not really hurt me in any way, and when Bill Gates amassed a fortune worth over $100 billion, that likewise does not hurt me. I might envy him his wealth, but envy is a petty emotion; we should not make public policy decisions just to appease envious desires. Or so goes the conservative claim.

---

[1] Paul, *The Case against Socialism*, 51.
[2] Oliver Wendell Holmes and Harold J. Laski, *The Holmes-Laski Letters*, ed. Mark DeWolfe Howe, vol. 2 (Cambridge, MA: Harvard University Press, 1953), 942.

Socialism. Scott R. Sehon, Oxford University Press. © Oxford University Press 2024.
DOI: 10.1093/oso/9780197753330.003.0007

132 SOCIALISM AND HUMAN WELL-BEING

In fact, say the conservatives, envy can be a positively good thing—something to be encouraged rather than appeased. On my baseball team, we lesser players than Mike were, one might suppose, inspired to work on our hitting technique; even if we never hit home runs the way he did, our desire to be the hero, or at least avoid being the goat, made us concentrate and practice more. Mike's home-run hitting, and his disproportionate share of the cheers and accolades, ultimately benefited the whole team, not just Mike. Similarly with wealth creation: if I envy my neighbor's nice house and new car, that might spur me to work harder myself. And if we all work harder and produce more, then there is more wealth to be enjoyed.

The conservatives accuse the liberals and socialists of falsely thinking of societal resources as a pie of fixed size, such that if Bill Gates gets a bigger piece, then others must be getting smaller pieces. In terms of the baseball example, that would be as if there were one fixed supply of accolades for players on the team, and when Mike received a large share of them, there were simply less for the rest of us. The fans (mostly our parents and a few friends) could wildly cheer for Mike's home runs and still applaud for my (occasional) single up the middle. Inequality need not mean *less* in absolute terms for anyone. As Steven Pinker puts it:

> The confusion of inequality with poverty comes straight out of the lump fallacy—the mindset in which wealth is a finite resource, like an antelope carcass, which has to be divvied up in zero-sum fashion, so that if some people end up with more, others must have less. As we just saw, wealth is not like that: since the Industrial Revolution, it has expanded exponentially. That means that when the rich get richer, the poor can get richer, too.[3]

And Rand Paul argues similarly, adding some artificially concocted numbers to illustrate the point:

> In other words, would you rather make $10,000 where the rich earn ten times that or make $30,000 where the rich earn 20 times that? What really matters is your standard of living, not your neighbors'. In reality, the poor are getting richer all the time, and the rich are also.[4]

---

[3] Pinker, *Enlightenment Now*, 99.
[4] Paul, *The Case against Socialism*, 31.

REDISTRIBUTION: INEQUALITY AND ENVY   133

Let's lay out explicitly the two scenarios Senator Paul envisions:

Scenario A

Poor: $10K
Rich: $100K

Scenario B

Poor: $30K
Rich: $600K

In Scenario B, the gap between rich and poor is larger, both in absolute terms (a $570K gap vs. a $90K gap in A) and in percentage terms (the rich own about 95% of the wealth in B as opposed to 91% in A). But who would choose Scenario A? And if anyone would, why? That would appear to be a matter of just wanting the rich to be less well off because you envy them or don't like them. The rich person in Scenario B is not doing anything to harm the poor person; after all, the poor person is better off than the analogous poor person in Scenario A.

Diminishing Marginal Utility versus Incentives

Of course, we might ask why we are limited to a choice between Scenarios A and B. Why couldn't we tax the wealth of the rich person in Scenario B and give some of it to the poorer person? After all, money has what economists term "diminishing marginal utility." Nathan Robinson explains the basic point with a nice analogy:

> If you give me a piece of chocolate, I may enjoy it a lot. If you give me a second piece, I will enjoy it, but perhaps a little less than I enjoyed the first, since the difference between no chocolate and a piece of chocolate is greater than the difference between one piece of chocolate and two. Each additional piece of chocolate thereafter will be slightly less satisfying to the point where I will feel that I've had quite enough chocolate and will decline even if you offer me more.[5]

The point also applies to money. If you give $1,000 to someone struggling to support a family on a minimum wage job, it will make a considerable difference to their happiness. By contrast, if you add $1,000 to the net

---

[5] Nathan Robinson, *Why You Should Be a Socialist* (New York: St. Martin's Press, 2019), 88.

134 SOCIALISM AND HUMAN WELL-BEING

worth of millionaires, they will barely notice—it would amount to only 1/10th of 1% of their wealth; it is not as if they would now be able to buy something they wanted that they could not afford before the extra amount.

For those with billions of dollars, rather than a mere million, it gets even more extreme. To illustrate: Is it worth it to you to pick up a penny you see lying on the ground? Not because you think it will bring good luck, or because you think it looks pretty, but because you could use the money? Suppose you are middle class and your net worth is about $100K; then that penny is a quite small fraction of your wealth, namely 1/100,000th of 1%. In purely monetary terms it is probably not worth the tiny risk of throwing out your back to add that small percentage to your bank account; you might well just leave the penny there. Now suppose you are Bill Gates, with well over $100 billion in net worth. Suppose he is walking wherever Bill Gates walks in public and happens to see $10,000 lying on the ground. In terms of his net worth, this is somewhat less to him than would be the penny to you. Just as it probably wasn't worth it to you to pick up a penny, it would be not worth it to Bill Gates to pick up $10,000 from the ground. (Well, as a good deed, he should probably pick it up and report it to the police. What is $10,000 in cash doing lying on the ground? But the very fact that an amount of money that is utterly trivial to Gates—like less than a penny to you—is a police-worthy report shows us something about the extremes of wealth.)

There is a disanalogy between the chocolate case and the money examples: if you are considering being offered chocolate that you must eat right then, then at some point having yet more chocolate will be positively unpleasurable and even disgusting (it might take some of us longer to hit that point than others). By contrast, even if it is not worth the risk to his back to bend over and pick up $10,000, it doesn't hurt Bill Gates at all to have another $10,000 added to his bank account. It is not as if the very thought of another $1,000 will make him so disgusted that he vomits. (Thought experiment: would it be better for humanity if we *did* have this kind of reaction to truly excessive amounts of money in our possession?) But, in any event, it remains true that, in Scenario B, if we take $1K from the rich person's $600K and give it to the poor person, then it seems likely that rich person will miss it less than the poor person will benefit from it. Indeed, it seems that we could follow this line of reasoning and continue redistributing all the way until we reach this scenario:

Scenario C
Poor: $315K
Rich: $315K

Ah, the conservative replies, but it is not so simple. If you equalize income no matter what, then there will be no envy-based incentive to work harder. Instead of each party having $315K, each would just hope that the other would do all the work, and both incomes would plummet. Even granting the point about diminishing marginal utility, it would not make sense to split the pie evenly if by so doing we ensure that the pie starts to shrink and that everybody's piece becomes smaller. The point is, according to the conservative, that we cannot have Scenario C: if we let it be known that we will equalize incomes irrespective of productivity we would instead have a scenario in which both the rich and the poor person got much less than $315K.

Suppose we grant that much—that we cannot completely equalize income or wealth without thereby lowering the incentive to work so much that everyone would be worse off. It still seems that there must be *some* scenario that is better than the large inequality we see in Scenario B (which is far less than the inequality we actually see under capitalism). Suppose, for example, that we imposed a 60% top marginal tax rate on any income over $550K; thus, when the rich person earns $600K, $30K of that gets taxed and then redistributed in one way or another, yielding something like this:

Scenario D
Poor: $60K
Rich: $570K

Some conservatives will object that this sort of redistribution from rich to poor violates the *rights* of the rich person: that $30K belonged to her and you violate her rights if you take the money she earned and use it, without her explicit consent, to help others. However, that is a question I already dealt with in Chapter 4. At this point, the only issue is whether such redistribution will lead to greater human well-being.

If we are thinking on such broadly utilitarian grounds, will something like Scenario D make people happier than Scenario B? The diminishing marginal utility of money suggests that Scenario D will bring about more happiness overall than Scenario B, since the extra $30K will mean a lot more to the poorer person than it will to the one who starts the scenario with 20 times

136 SOCIALISM AND HUMAN WELL-BEING

as much. However, the conservative might object that even such moderate distribution will run afoul of the need for incentives. Taxing an extra $30K away from the rich and giving it to the poor will, the conservative maintains, diminish the motivation of each person. If the poor person is going to just be given $30K out of the rich person's earnings, then the poor person might decide, "I can get by on $30K; why should I work at all?" Moreover, the rich person might be annoyed as well, and think, "Well, if they are just going to tax my income at such high rates once I get above $550K, why should I keep working so hard to produce that much?" (I'm charitably assuming within the example that the rich person receives the $600K by *working* for it, rather than by, for example, inheriting it or receiving dividends from investments.)

It is worth noting that there is something insidious about the conservative's assumptions concerning this hypothetical. The conservative assumes that the poor person will be tempted simply not to work at all, once they are given a comfortable amount of money to live on; by contrast, the rich person will continue to work hard beyond their already high income, so long as you don't tax too much of it away. It's hard not to see in this combination of assumptions the view that poor people are inherently lazy as compared with those industrious rich types. (This was merely a hypothetical example and a hypothetical conservative objection, but one sees the same dynamic in contemporary debates. With any mention of strong social safety nets, let alone a universal basic income, conservatives are likely to talk about how poor people will just stop working and will not try to earn more, whereas they think that rich people will continue to work hard unless we make top marginal tax rates too high.)

In any event, if people do think like the conservative says they will, then Scenario D might be unstable; with the poor person deciding not to work, and the rich person saying she won't keep working so hard after hitting the top tax bracket, we would drift toward this instead:

Scenario E
Poor: $0K
Rich $550K

And nobody would choose Scenario E over Scenario D. So the poor person should be satisfied with what he has in Scenario B and stop whining about the gap between his income and that of the rich person. Or so goes the conservative argument.

On the most extreme version of the argument, *any* sort of redistributive taxation will backfire and make everyone less happy, for *any* handouts to the poor will diminish their incentive to work, and likewise any level of taxation on the rich will lessen their inclination to go out and work even harder and make more money. Even if we reject the extreme version of the argument, it is perhaps reasonable to assume that there is a tipping point somewhere, some point beyond which the redistribution destroys incentives and lowers the overall amount of wealth available.

There are complicated issues intertwined here: first, whether and to what degree inequality is good (because it provides incentives to productivity or innovation) or bad (beyond causing pangs of envy); and, second, at what point redistributive taxation diminishes incentives enough to make everyone worse, rather than better, off. These are empirical questions. We cannot simply *assume* that taxation will have little effect on incentives (as some liberals might be wont to do), but neither can we simply assume (as might some conservatives) that we should always err on the side of much lower taxation, lest we create a situation in which nobody wants to work.

The Empirical Evidence: Optimal Rates of Taxation

The question of whether high taxation rates will lead the rich to produce less is related to the economic question of the *optimal* rate of taxation. "Optimal rate" is here being used as a technical term, meaning the rate of taxation that produces the most revenue for the government. Your first thought might be that the higher the taxation, the more revenue. But that is clearly wrong: if we tax all income at 100%, people will have no incentive to make any money at all, will stop working, and there will be no revenue. The question is where the tipping point is: at what level of taxation rates become so high that government revenue starts to fall?

Economist Arthur Laffer famously convinced Ronald Reagan in the early 1980s that US tax rates were well past that point. He claimed that if we cut taxes on the wealthy, this would spur more productivity and that there would actually be *more* (or at least not less) government revenue from taxation. Reagan then instituted a large tax cut on the promise that the tax cuts would pay for themselves. George W. Bush cut taxes in 2001 and 2003 on the same theory. More recently, Donald Trump and the Republicans in Congress cut taxes in 2017, and Trump's Treasury secretary, Steven Mnuchin promised,

"Not only will this tax plan pay for itself, but it will pay down debt."[6] When Reagan cut the top tax rate, it was 70%; he ultimately brought that rate down to 28%. It went back up slightly under the first President Bush, and then up to 39.6% under Clinton. The Trump tax cut took the top marginal rate down from 39.6% to 37%.

In none of these cases did it actually work as promised: government revenues went down and the deficit increased.[7] This by itself would indicate that the optimal tax rate is well above 37%, and perhaps even above 70%, since even the original Reagan tax cut likewise decreased revenue. (There are, of course, many complications here: given deductions and various ways of avoiding taxes, it is not as if everyone actually pays the marginal rates that are specified in the tax code.)

Where is the optimal rate? Economists Peter Diamond and Emmanuel Saez put the optimal overall top rate, including state and local taxes, at 73%.[8] Andrew Fieldhouse calculates that this means that the highest marginal federal income tax rate could go to 66% before reaching the point at which revenue is maximized.[9] Other economists argue that the top tax rate could go even higher, perhaps as high as 83%.[10]

I'm not qualified to take a position on the details here, but the general picture seems clear: especially in the United States, where the current top marginal federal rate is 37%, we could make that much higher without worrying about going past the tipping point. That is to say, we could do much

---

[6] John Harwood, "The Number Are in, and Trump's Tax Cut Didn't Reduce the Deficit—Despite His Many Promises," CNBC, October, 16, 2018, https://www.cnbc.com/2018/10/16/trumps-tax-cut-didnt-reduce-the-deficit--despite-his-many-promises.html.

[7] That the Trump tax cut did not pay for itself: see William Gale, "Did the 2017 Tax Cut—the Tax Cuts and Jobs Act—Pay for Itself?," Brookings, February 14, 2020, https://www.brookings.edu/policy2020/votervital/did-the-2017-tax-cut-the-tax-cuts-and-jobs-act-pay-for-itself/. That tax cuts for the rich have in general, across 18 OECD countries, not increased economic productivity, as they would have to do in order to increase (or even maintain) the same amount of government revenue: David Hope and Julian Limberg, "The Economic Consequences of Major Tax Cuts for the Rich," London School of Economics, Working Paper no. 55, December 2020. Available at http://eprints.lse.ac.uk/107919/1/Hope_economic_consequences_of_major_tax_cuts_published.pdf.

[8] Peter Diamond and Emmanuel Saez, "The Case for a Progressive Tax: From Basic Research to Policy Recommendations," *Journal of Economic Perspectives*, vol. 25, no. 4 (Fall 2011): 165–190.

[9] Andrew Fieldhouse, "How High Should Top Income Tax Rates Be? (Hint: Much Higher)," *Fiscal Times*, April 10, 2013, https://www.thefiscaltimes.com/Columns/2013/04/10/How-High-Should-Top-Income-Tax-Rates-Be.

[10] Thomas Piketty, Emmanuel Saez, and Stefanie Stantcheva, "Taxing the 1%: Why the Top Tax Rate Could Be over 80%," *VoxEU*, December 8, 2011, https://voxeu.org/article/taxing-1-why-top-tax-rate-could-be-over-80#:~:text=It%20says%20the%20optimal%20top,and%20Piketty%20and%20Saez%202003.

more redistribution than we do now, increasing happiness because of the diminishing marginal utility of extra dollars, while not encountering any overall drop in productivity from the rich that might lower overall utility. Given this, and the diminishing marginal utility of extra dollars, it certainly seems we should go strongly in that direction.

"Hold on!" says the conservative; "the only reason that inequality per se causes any unhappiness is that some people feel pangs of envy about not having as much as others, and that's just a petty emotion that we should not aim to appease." One might respond that suffering from pangs of envy is still *suffering*, so it doesn't matter if the concerns about inequality stem from this particular emotion. But something does seem awry about counting mere envy-inspired unhappiness. More generally, when we say that we should prefer styles of governance that lead to greater happiness (so long as they don't violate rights), we don't count *all* pleasures and displeasures as part of being happy in the relevant sense. This is a general issue for utilitarian theories, according to which the right action is the one that leads to the greatest happiness for the greatest number: some forms of pleasure or happiness shouldn't count. For example, if someone tortures an innocent child, then it doesn't make the action any better if the torturer really enjoyed himself in the process; indeed it seems to make the action even worse. Accordingly, to the extent that the unhappiness resulting from economic inequality is *just* a matter of envy, perhaps we can disregard it.

Philosopher Robert Nozick would go further. He suggests that redistribution will not even make the feelings of envy go away, for envy is, he asserts, connected with self-esteem. To illustrate, let's go back to my baseball-playing days, when I envied Mike's home-run power, given that I was lucky to hit the ball out of the infield. The real source of my envy in that case was my diminished self-esteem: Mike was just a much better hitter than I was, and that's what stung. My feelings would not have been buoyed by having everyone cheer when I grounded out to the pitcher; it wasn't that I really envied hearing the cheers, but that I envied the ability that Mike had. It wasn't that I thought I too deserved as many cheers as he received, and that it was unfair that I didn't receive them. Rather, it was precisely because I thought the cheers for Mike, and my lack thereof, were completely deserved. Applied to wealth and inequality, Nozick suggests that the situation might be similar: "This would be one possible explanation of why certain inequalities in income, or position of authority within

140 SOCIALISM AND HUMAN WELL-BEING

an industry, or of an entrepreneur as compared to his employees, rankle so; not due to the feeling that this superior position is undeserved, but to the feeling that it is deserved and earned."[11]

If this is right, then not only should we not really dignify alleged suffering that merely amounts to envying the wealth of others; if the real source of our feelings of envy is that those people actually deserve that wealth in a way that I don't, then redistributing the money won't even make the feelings of envy go away—I will still know, at least deep down, that the successful entrepreneur is really a more diligent, talented, and productive person than I am, and this will trigger the same feelings in the end. Or so Nozick suggests.

However, Nozick's suggestion seems wrong. There are two key differences to keep in mind between the baseball case, where I did envy Mike's talent, and the case of economic inequality. First, the cheers that Mike received undoubtedly made him feel good, but he couldn't use them to go off and buy the latest album by Led Zeppelin (this was the 1970s!). The cheers were *merely* a recognition of his talent and role in winning baseball games, but had no other tradeable, intrinsic value. By contrast, if an entrepreneur is rewarded by having Microsoft buy his start-up business for $100 million, then the entrepreneur *can* use that money for rent, food, yachts, or even Led Zeppelin albums. And if some of that money is instead given to a poor person, then while they may not have the pleasure of knowing that they received the money because of their diligence and good ideas, they can still use it for rent and food. Second, while we laud entrepreneurs and hold them up as the poster children for capitalism, I think it is fair to say that most wealth in this country is *not* a matter of pure diligence and talent. Much wealth (approximately 60%)[12] is simply inherited, and even the successful entrepreneurs often were the beneficiaries of the lucky moment of being in the right place at the right time. While I might envy Mark Zuckerberg's programming ability a little bit, seeing the billionaire children and grandchildren of Sam Walton (the founder of Walmart) does not make me envy their talent; the only talent they needed for unimaginable wealth was to be born to the right parents. While I might feel bad about my lack of hitting ability, it would be rather crazy for me to chastise myself for having chosen less than rich parents.

---

[11] Nozick, *Anarchy, State, and Utopia*, 21.
[12] Alvaredo, Garbinti, and Piketty, "Share of Inheritance."

Inequality Is Toxic

In any event, we need not speculate on whether inequality merely leads to pangs of envious desire to have the wealth of Mark Zuckerberg or your now rich college roommate; we could, instead, look to empirical data on what happens in different countries that have different degrees of inequality. Luckily, we don't have to look very far for data, for there have been a raft of such studies, and they were ably discussed and summarized by Richard Wilkinson and Kate Pickett in two books, *The Spirit Level* (2009) and *The Inner Level* (2018).[13] Wilkinson and Pickett start by taking on the idea that concerns about inequality merely stem from envy:

> Inequality is often seen as a relatively trivial issue, dismissed as "the politics of envy," and it is treated as if it only matters when it creates extreme poverty or is seen as very unfair. But this is a naïve view. There is a deep psychology of inequality that we need to understand if humanity is to flourish. We have evolved to be extremely sensitive to social status.[14]

Their claim about evolution is a good starting point. The picture presented by neoliberal economists like Hayek and Friedman is that human beings are by nature selfish and greedy, and that a capitalistic economic system is thus quite natural. In fact, however, it was less than 10,000 years ago that human beings moved away from a purely hunter-gatherer model to having state-like entities and differentiation into classes.[15] As Wilkinson and Pickett note: "it is clear that throughout most of our specifically human prehistory, we lived in extraordinarily egalitarian hunting and gathering societies, in which food was shared and goods were passed between people, not through barter but through systems of reciprocal gift exchange."[16] During the long hunter-gatherer period, "equality was the norm in human societies."[17] In evolutionary terms, the last 10,000 years are the blink of an eye—less than 5% of the time since anatomically modern humans evolved. Conservatives like to

---

[13] Richard Wilkinson and Kate Pickett, *The Spirit Level: Why Greater Equality Makes Societies Stronger* (New York: Bloomsbury Press, 2009) and *The Inner Level: How More Equal Societies Reduce Stress, Restore Sanity and Improve Everyone's Well-Being* (New York: Penguin Random House, 2018).

[14] Wilkinson and Pickett, *The Inner Level*, x.

[15] James C. Scott, *Against the Grain: A Deep History of the Earliest States* (New Haven: Yale University Press, 2017), 5.

[16] Wilkinson and Pickett, *The Inner Level*, 129.

[17] Wilkinson and Pickett, *The Inner Level*, 27.

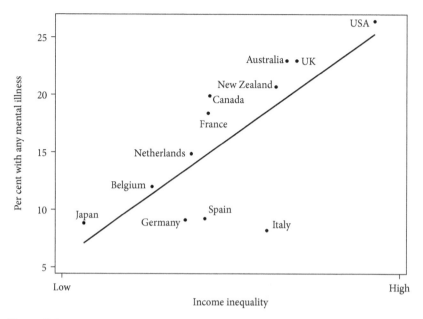

Figure 7.1

claim that they are just being realistic about human nature, but this seems to be an extremely narrow view, taking the last blip of our history as definitive of how human beings just *are*.

Though we humans spent the vast majority of our history in highly egalitarian settings, things are rather different now, to say the least. It is also clear that, in many ways, the inequality is not good for us. Wilkinson and Pickett looked at research across a number of countries with differing levels of inequality, as measured by the Gini coefficient. For starters, people in more equal societies exhibit greater feelings of solidarity and willingness to help others: "Where there is greater inequality, community life is weaker and levels of interpersonal trust decline—almost certainly because the stress of status insecurity makes people withdraw from social engagement."[18] If people are experiencing more stress because of status insecurity in countries with greater inequality, one might expect mental illness to be on the rise in those countries as well, and indeed Wilkinson and Pickett found a strong correlation in that regard (Figure 7.1).[19]

---

[18] Wilkinson and Pickett, *The Inner Level*, 243.
[19] Wilkinson and Pickett, *The Spirit Level*, 44.

REDISTRIBUTION: INEQUALITY AND ENVY   143

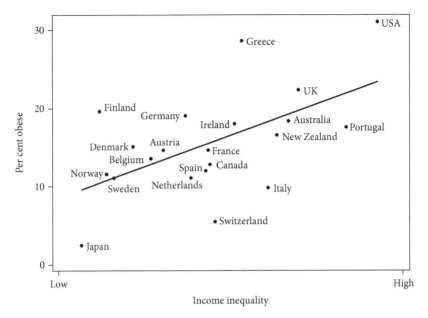

Figure 7.2

In general, they found that across studies "that used objective measures like death rates, or life expectancy" they could confirm that "health is worse in more unequal societies."[20] It may or may not come as a surprise to find out that the United States, which has the highest nominal GDP in the world, nonetheless ranks 30th in life expectancy out of the 38 countries in the OECD (Organization for Economic Co-operation and Development): life expectancy in the United States is 77.0 years, whereas it is 83.2 for Norway, 83.2 for Sweden, and in general is above 82 for 14 of the member states.[21] One might think that that one reason for poor life expectancy in the United States is our obesity problem, and it is true that the percentage of overweight or obese people is higher in the United States than in almost any of the OECD countries.[22] However, obesity is itself likewise correlated with inequality: the more unequal the countries, the more obesity (Figure 7.2).[23]

---

[20] Wilkinson and Pickett, *The Spirit Level*, 69.
[21] "Life Expectancy at Birth," OECD, 2021, https://data.oecd.org/healthstat/life-expectancy-at-birth.htm.
[22] "Overweight or Obese Population," OECD, 2021, https://data.oecd.org/healthrisk/overweight-or-obese-population.htm.
[23] Wilkinson and Pickett, *The Spirit Level*, 128.

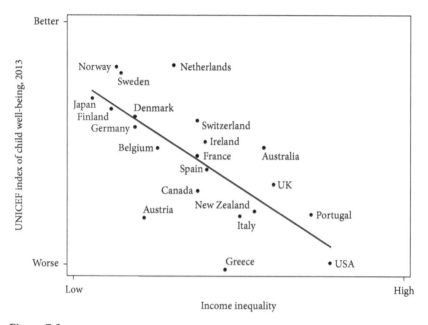

Figure 7.3

In some ways the most disturbing chart in the Wilkinson and Pickett books is one that plots the UNICEF index of child well-being on the vertical axis against increasing degrees of inequality on the right (Figure 7.3).[24] It is especially important that this chart concerns children. With adults, one can at least raise the question of whether the poorer people in very unequal countries might be, at least partially, to blame for their situation, and that they should pull themselves up by their bootstraps. (It is always interesting to me that anyone was ever attracted to the bootstraps metaphor as an exhortation to make something of yourself, since it is an obvious physical impossibility.) However, when we are talking about the well-being of children, there is even less plausibility to the claim that the children are in any way to blame for their poverty.

You might hope that children in the United States can be saved by the American Dream: that the United States is the land of opportunity where even if you are born poor, you can outdo your parents and rise through the ranks of society through your own hard work and skill. However, while there are indeed some great success stories, the data show the American Dream to

---

[24] Wilkinson and Pickett, *The Inner Level*, 115.

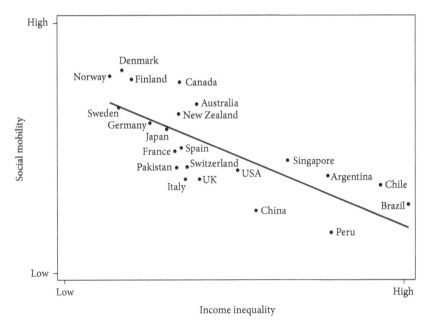

Figure 7.4

be more of a fantasy than a realistic possibility. If you measure the income of a child's parents when the child is born, and then compare the income of the child when he or she reaches age thirty, you get a measure of how correlated the incomes are—the extent to which rich parents have rich kids and poor parents have poor kids. However, based on this measure, the United States does not do well. Moreover, there is a general trend: countries with greater inequality *also* have less social mobility (Figure 7.4).[25]

As Wilkinson and Pickett report: in countries with large differences in income, "people are more likely to remain in the classes they were born into because larger income differences increase class barriers, make the social hierarchy more rigid and opportunities for children even more unequal."[26] Part of the reason for the lack of social mobility in unequal countries is that income inequality generally translates into educational inequality—children with the poorer parents have poorer educational performance.[27]

---

[25] Wilkinson and Pickett, *The Inner Level*, 186.
[26] Wilkinson and Pickett, *The Inner Level*, 243.
[27] Wilkinson and Pickett, *The Inner Level*, 141.

146 SOCIALISM AND HUMAN WELL-BEING

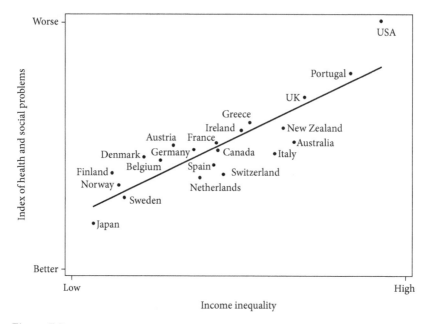

Figure 7.5

Wilkinson and Pickett put together their findings in an overall chart that is impressive. And depressing. On the y axis they have an index of health and social problems, which measures "life expectancy, trust, mental illness (including drug and alcohol addiction), obesity, infant mortality, children's maths and literacy scores, imprisonment rates, homicide rates, teenage births and social mobility."[28] On the x axis we have degrees of income inequality in each country. The correlation is obvious and strong: increasing income inequality means greater health and social problems (Figure 7.5).[29]

For those doing reasonably well under US-style capitalism with its rampant economic inequality, one might take some selfish solace in the thought that these negative consequences of inequality mostly affect poor people. However, Wilkinson and Pickett report that even this is not true: "One of our more surprising findings was that inequality affects the vast majority of the population, not only a poor minority. Although its severest effects are on those nearer the bottom of the social ladder, the vast majority are also affected to a lesser extent."[30]

---

[28] Wilkinson and Pickett, *The Inner Level*, 3.
[29] Wilkinson and Pickett, *The Inner Level*, 3.
[30] Wilkinson and Pickett, *The Inner Level*, 5.

REDISTRIBUTION: INEQUALITY AND ENVY   147

In the previous chapter, I considered the conservative argument in favor of capitalism which started with the apparent correlation of the rise of capitalism with great increases in human well-being, and I cautioned that one must take great care not to hastily infer a genuinely explanatory relation from mere correlation. One can, of course, have a similar worry here: the data provided by Wilkinson and Pickett comprise correlations between levels of inequality and various outcomes indicative of lower overall well-being. How can we know that the inequality *explains* the lower levels of well-being, rather than being, say, a spurious or merely coincidental correlation (like that between Putin's hold on power in Russia and major league baseball salaries)? Wilkinson and Pickett are certainly aware of this possibility, and they have this to say about it:

> The step from evidence of correlation to evidence of causality is obviously a crucial one. Why do we think it can be made confidently? Epidemiology has been centrally concerned with statistical evidence identifying the causes of disease and has therefore developed a set of criteria for judging whether relationships are likely to be causal. As well as the obvious point that causes must precede their effects, they also include the strength of the relationship, whether there is a "dose-response" relationship—i.e., higher levels of inequality lead to successively worse outcomes—whether the relationship is biologically plausible, whether or not there are other likely explanations, and whether research results present a consistent picture. Judged on this basis, the evidence from several hundred research studies suggests that the relationship between larger income differences and a worsening of a wide range of health and social problems is indeed causal.[31]

One can complain, as conservatives from Hayek on down have done, that there is no reason to worry about issues of income inequality. People who get rich are not doing any harm to the rest of us; if I envy their wealth, that's merely my problem, just as it was my problem that I envied Mike's hitting ability. But the data that Wilkinson and Pickett have collected and analyzed paints a very different picture: vast economic inequality has truly corrosive effects throughout society. Moving in the direction of socialism, with its much more extensive welfare state and redistribution, will lead to greater overall happiness.

---

[31] Wilkinson and Pickett, *The Inner Level*, 3–4.

148 SOCIALISM AND HUMAN WELL-BEING

How far should we go in that direction? How much should we redistribute? That is, essentially, an empirical question: insofar as redistribution does not violate rights (see Chapter 4), we should engage in that level of redistribution that best maximizes human well-being. (And we need to keep in mind the complications concerning that questions canvassed in Chapter 3: we are not necessarily looking to maximizes total or average well-being, for we might conclude that justice requires that well-being itself in a fair way, where this might differ from the distribution simply maximizes total or average well-being.) Perhaps the conservative is right that there is a tipping point at which too much equality diminishes incentives to the point that we are all less well off. But, as noted above, the economists tell us that we can certainly raise taxes on the wealthy far higher than they are now without diminishing government revenue, indicating that top marginal tax rates above 70% would still not lower productivity or overall happiness. The data analyzed by Wilkinson and Pickett likewise suggest that we can go way further than we have in the United States:

> We cannot say exactly by how much income differences must be reduced to maximize well-being. What we do know is that, rather than levelling off among the more equal countries, both our own Index of Health and Social Problems and the UNICEF Index of Child Well-being show a continuous rate of improvement from the most unequal to the most equal developed countries. This suggests that the benefits of greater equality persist at the very least up to the levels of equality found in the Scandinavian countries, which are among the most equal developed countries. Beyond that we have no data and so cannot say what happens. However, by the time the most unequal countries have reduced income differences to those levels there will, perhaps, be examples of countries that will show if it is worth going further.[32]

Since we are talking about happy people and the Scandinavian countries, it is worth bringing up another well-known piece of data. Every year, the United Nations puts out a *World Happiness Report*, in which countries are ranked on their overall levels of happiness. The 2020 edition of this report adds a special chapter entitled "The Nordic Exceptionalism: What Explains Why the

---

[32] Wilkinson and Pickett, *The Inner Level*, 245.

Nordic Countries Are Constantly among the Happiest in the World."[33] As the report notes: "From 2013 until today, every time the *World Happiness Report* . . . has published its annual ranking of countries, the five Nordic countries—Finland, Denmark, Norway, Sweden, and Iceland—have all been in the top ten, with Nordic countries occupying the top three spots in 2017, 2018, and 2019."[34]

The authors of the report debunk some alleged explanations for this phenomenon. For example, they reject a hypothesis that the level of happiness in these countries is to be explained by the fact that they are "small and homogenous." As they note, some of the Nordic countries "are actually quite heterogeneous, with some 19% of the population of Sweden being born outside the country."[35] They suggest instead that a key part of the explanation is redistribution and heavy regulation of the labor market: "These and other studies suggest that one secret to Nordic happiness is the institutional framework of the Nordic welfare state. People tend to be happier in countries where there is easy access to relatively generous welfare benefits, and where the labor market is regulated to avoid employee exploitation."[36]

Both Wilkinson and Pickett and the *World Happiness Report* tend to avoid the word "socialism," but I won't: the data show that the way to happier people is to have more socialism.

Key Takeaways

- Conservatives often claim that any concerns about inequality stem merely from the petty emotion of envy.
- Socialists point out that it goes beyond envy: since money has diminishing marginal utility we would, all things being equal, expect well-being to increase if wealth is distributed in a more egalitarian fashion.
- Conservatives reply that all things are not equal, and that redistribution leads to decreased incentives and less wealth overall.

---

[33] Frank Martela, Brent Greve, and Juho Saari, "The Nordic Exceptionalism: What Explains Why the Nordic Countries Are Constantly among the Happiest in the World," Chapter 7 in *World Happiness Report*, ed. John Helliwell (New York: Sustainable Development Solutions Network, 2020).

[34] Martela, Greve, and Saari, "The Nordic Exceptionalism," 131.

[35] Martela, Greve, and Saari, "The Nordic Exceptionalism," 132.

[36] Martela, Greve, and Saari, "The Nordic Exceptionalism," 133.

150 SOCIALISM AND HUMAN WELL-BEING

- Empirical evidence from economists indicates that we could make the tax system significantly more progressive, and thereby make for more egalitarian distribution, without leading to less wealth overall.
- Empirical evidence also indicates that inequality is toxic, and that greater inequality in a society leads to lower well-being.
- Thus, there is good reason to believe premise (1) of the *Master Argument for Socialism*, that socialism, with its more egalitarian distribution of resources, leads to greater well-being.
- I still wish I had managed to hit a home run during my baseball-playing days.

8

Collective Control:
The Democracy Argument

The first premise of the *Master Argument for Socialism* is that socialism leads to greater happiness than extant alternative styles of governance. I defined socialism as coming in degrees along two axes: collective ownership and control of the means of production, and egalitarian distribution of resources. In the previous chapter, I argued that moving in the socialist direction on the second axis—making things more egalitarian—leads to greater well-being. In this chapter I want to look at the first axis: does more collective ownership and control lead to greater well-being?

Empirical Correlations: Scandinavia Again

When I made the case for more egalitarian distribution producing greater happiness, I was able to draw on two different sorts of considerations or evidence. First, there was the brute empirical data: there were strong correlations between societies with greater degrees of equality and societies with greater happiness and well-being among its population. But, second, even without looking at that detailed data, we had general reasons for expecting this might be the case, for we know that money has diminishing marginal utility, meaning that an extra $1,000 for Elon Musk means a lot less than it would to a poor person scraping by.

We can make the same sort of distinction between two types of evidence when investigating whether collective ownership and control will lead to greater happiness. We could first look at brute empirical data and see what correlation there is between a society's degree of collective ownership and control on the one hand and the happiness and well-being of its people on the other. Beyond that, we could also look at more general reasons for *expecting* that collective ownership and control will lead to either greater or less happiness.

Socialism. Scott R. Sehon, Oxford University Press. © Oxford University Press 2024.
DOI: 10.1093/oso/9780197753330.003.0008

152 SOCIALISM AND HUMAN WELL-BEING

When we were considering the correlation between egalitarian distribution and happiness, we had a lot of solid data to work with: there are substantial data on income inequality around the world, as well as patchier data on wealth inequality. We could then simply correlate those measures of inequality with various measures of well-being. The situation is more difficult when attempting the same brute correlation approach concerning the issue of collective ownership and control. Unlike the case of income or wealth inequality, there is no simple way of measuring the degree of collective ownership of the means of production or collective control of the economy. We have various crude measures: size of government in relationship to GDP, or percentage of the workforce that is in the public sector, but these are far from perfect measures of the degree of collective ownership and control—or, to look at it from the other direction, the degree to which the market is completely free.

There are organizations which purport to rate countries on the basis of the freeness of their market and economies: the Heritage Foundation's so-called "Index of Economic Freedom" being the main one.[1] However, their index includes factors that are, at best, somewhat orthogonal to the degree of government control of the economy. Some of what the index measures are things like the degree to which the judiciary is independent and the absence of bribing government officials; worthy ideals to be sure, but not the same as a measure of degree of government involvement in the economy. The Heritage Foundation also takes points off for governments that run large budget deficits, which, again, would seem to be neither here nor there with respect to the degree of government control. On the other hand, they give positive points for strong government protection of intellectual property claims, even though this is, on its face, a matter of *more* government involvement rather than less.

All that said, it is worth noting, as I did in Chapter 2, that the Nordic countries do seem to have more collective ownership and control than most other Western countries, and more than the United States in particular. We saw this both in terms of the size of the governments there, the percentage of wealth that is privately owned, and the percentage of the workforce that is in the public sector. I don't think that any of these are precise enough to allow us to make graphs like those presented in Chapter 7, where we have degree of collective ownership and control on one axis and a measure of well-being

---

[1] "2023 Index of Economic Freedom," Heritage Foundation, https://www.heritage.org/index.

COLLECTIVE CONTROL: THE DEMOCRACY ARGUMENT   153

on the other. But there was nonetheless a generally clear picture: the Nordic countries have *more* collective ownership and control.

This is important, because as we saw with so much of the data presented in the last chapter, the Nordic countries also do quite well by various measures of well-being, whether objective health-related measures or self-reported happiness levels. Thus there is at least some empirical correlation between more happiness and greater collective ownership and control. If nothing else, the conservative who wants to claim that capitalism and freer markets are the way to happiness has some explaining to do: Why does the claim seem not to hold up when we look at the Nordic countries?

Community versus Competitiveness

In the absence of further detailed and specific correlational data, I now turn to more general reasons and evidence concerning the relationship between increased collective control of the economy and happiness. One such general reason is this: people are happier when they work together communally rather than competitively, and there is more community under socialism and more competitiveness under capitalism. This sort of point was suggested by a noted socialist thinker, Albert Einstein. (He was also noted for a few other things.) In a 1949 article titled "Why Socialism?" Einstein says that the "worst evil of capitalism" is the "crippling of individuals" resulting from the "exaggerated competitive attitude" that is inculcated into us, whereby we are "trained to worship acquisitive success."[2] We could put this together as a simple argument:

Community Makes People Happier

(1) All things being equal, people are happier to the extent that they operate communally rather than competitively. [P]
(2) Under socialism rather than capitalism, people operate more communally rather than competitively. [P]
(3) All things being equal, people will be happier under socialism rather than capitalism. [1,2]

---

[2] Albert Einstein, "Why Socialism?," in *Ideas and Opinions* (New York: Crown Publishers, 1954), 158.

154 SOCIALISM AND HUMAN WELL-BEING

G. A. Cohen illustrates the first principle with an example of a camping trip.[3] He notes that on typical camping trips, people work together in a largely communal fashion. There is, of course, work to be done: setting up tents, starting a fire, cooking, gathering water, etc. On a normal camping trip, a group of people walking and camping together will just pitch in and work together. The work might be divided, perhaps in accord with people's preferences and skills; I might start the fire and start cooking, while you set up the tents, and someone else heads down to the stream to get water for the evening. Naturally, if there is one person who persistently lies about while the rest of us are doing such tasks, we might get annoyed and prod them into doing more of their share, but that is generally not necessary, and we don't bother to keep track of exactly how much work each person is doing.

Cohen notes that a camping trip could work differently.

> You could imagine a camping trip where everybody asserts her rights over the pieces of equipment, and the talents, that she brings, and where bargaining proceeds with respect to who is going to pay what to whom to be allowed, for example, to use a knife to peel the potatoes, and how much he is going to charge others for those now-peeled potatoes that he bought in an unpeeled condition from another camper, and so on. You could base a camping trip on the principles of market exchange and strictly private ownership of the required facilities.[4]

I think it is safe to say that most of us would prefer to be on the first sort of camping trip. (Some, including Cohen himself,[5] would prefer to stay home or at a hotel and not go camping in the first place, but that's different.) Why? There is something *nice* about helping in a communal fashion toward the common goal of everyone's enjoyment, and there is something nice about knowing that others are doing the same. If I run into problems setting up my tent, you will likely just help me, rather than negotiate a price first and then offer your labor. If you treated the camping trip as a market, where work and supplies were bought and sold as commodities, there would be two obvious disadvantages. First, it would take time and effort to negotiate all of those transactions; you might well prefer to spend that time enjoying nature and

---

[3] G. A. Cohen, *Why Not Socialism?* (Princeton, NJ: Princeton University Press, 2009).
[4] Cohen, *Why Not Socialism?*, 5.
[5] Cohen, *Why Not Socialism?*, 9.

COLLECTIVE CONTROL: THE DEMOCRACY ARGUMENT   155

the company of others. But, second, the *mindset* that would go with perpetual bargaining and checking would, for most of us, be corrosive. It would tend to change our attitude to one another, from being comrades on an enjoyable enterprise to being competitors constantly looking over our shoulders.

An experiment by psychologist Dan Ariely serves as an illustration.[6] The experimenters parked a truck with a heavy couch near a busy sidewalk. They would then ask some passersby if they would spend a few minutes helping to move the couch. Other pedestrians were asked a slightly different question: would they spend a few minutes helping to move the couch for $20? People were more likely to help, and felt better about doing so, if they were *not* paid for it. Most people were willing to help and felt good about doing so; but if it became an economic transaction, that, apparently, changed the whole character of the experience.

This is not to deny that many of us also like some friendly (or even not so friendly) competition now and then. Sporting events are a prime example. One of my fondest memories from college was an informal softball game arranged by the Department of Philosophy at Harvard. John Rawls and Robert Nozick became the opposing captains, with various graduate students and a few of us lucky undergraduates taking our positions under one or another of these philosophical giants. At one point in the game, Rawls, then about 64 years old, went from first to third on a single to right field and *slid* into third base—meaning that he dropped his body to the ground and slid across the last few feet of grass before the base in order to lessen his chances of being thrown out. Rawls thereby demonstrated that even a left-leaning political philosopher can still have quite the competitive instinct under the right circumstances. However, it's one thing to compete, and even compete fiercely, in a game-like context, after which everyone enjoys a friendly beer. The suggestion by Einstein and Cohen is that typical enjoyment of competition has its limits. On a camping trip, or in life in general, if everything is marketized, if the provision of basic goods is essentially a competitive matter, then this would be a bit like being caught in a perpetual softball game that you can't get out of, where whether you have food to eat or shelter at night depends on how well you play the game and whether you beat the others.

Philosopher Jason Brennan disputes Cohen's analogy and offers a story of his own, based on the Mickey Mouse Clubhouse Village, run on capitalist

---

[6] Dan Ariely, *Predictably Irrational: The Hidden Forces That Shape Our Decisions* (New York: Harper Collins, 2008).

156 SOCIALISM AND HUMAN WELL-BEING

principles. But Brennan notes that "Village life is not all about work! The villagers spend much of their time having fun."[7] He asserts that within the village, various principles of justice apply, including "the principle of voluntary community, the principle of mutual respect, the principle of reciprocity, the principle of social justice, and the principle of beneficence."[8] The basic idea is that if reasonable and nice capitalists were on a camping trip, they wouldn't be acting at all like the way Cohen imagines. Cohen makes the mistake, according to Brennan, of assuming nicely motivated socialists on a camping trip, while assuming that those on the capitalist camping trip are jerks.

But one might argue, as Sam Arnold does in reply to Brennan, that "capitalism—even among morally perfect agents—inevitably runs roughshod over community."[9] The reason is that when it comes to the economy—providing goods, services, and thereby gaining the resources one needs to survive—the logic of the market forces business owners to maximize profits and grow. If they do not, they will be run out of business: "As any introductory economics textbook explains, market competition forces firms to maximize profits."[10] We could also turn to an ardent defender of capitalism, the economist Milton Friedman, to make a similar point. According to title of one of Friedman's articles, "The Social Responsibility of Business Is to Increase Its Profits." Friedman argues that if managers or others within a business do anything *other* than aim to make as much money as possible, for example if they try to get a company to do something for " 'social' causes favored by the activists," they are effectively imposing taxes on the owners and are violating their moral obligations.[11] According to Friedman, "there is one and only one social responsibility of business—to use its resources and engage in activities designed to increase its profits so long as it stays within the rules of the game."[12] It is the *obligation* of managers and workers within a company to make as much profit as possible.

None of this is to say that capitalists (whether of the Mickey Mouse or Milton Friedman variety) cannot take camping trips and act like perfectly reasonable human beings (or reasonable cartoon characters, as the case

[7] Jason Brennan, *Why Not Capitalism?* (New York: Routledge, 2014), 25.
[8] Brennan, *Why Not Capitalism?*, 29–30.
[9] Sam Arnold, "No Community without Socialism: Why Liberal Egalitarianism Is Not Enough", *Philosophical Topics*, Vol. 48, No. 2, (2020): 3.
[10] Arnold, "No Community without Socialism," 16.
[11] Milton Friedman, "A Friedman Doctrine—The Social Responsibility of Business Is to Increase Its Profits," *New York Times*, September 13, 1970, https://www.nytimes.com/1970/09/13/archives/a-friedman-doctrine-the-social-responsibility-of-business-is-to.html.
[12] Milton Friedman, *Capitalism and Freedom* (Chicago: University of Chicago Press, 1962)

COLLECTIVE CONTROL: THE DEMOCRACY ARGUMENT   157

might be). It was never the point of Cohen's analogy to claim that capitalists are always jerks. But within the economic realm, the imperative under capitalism is to compete and make profits. For laborers who have none of the means of production, this means that, as far as their economic life is concerned, they engage in work with salaries paid by owners whose motivation is and must be simply to make as much money off the laborers' work as possible. Naturally, this does not rule out the possibility of treating one's employees well; under the right circumstances that might be the best way to maximize profits in the long run. But the underlying motivation remains that of profit. As Arnold argues, "profit-maximizing owners and managers must *handle* their employees, customers, and competitors, must treat them as tools to be exploited (employees), or sources of enrichment to be fleeced (customers), or as rival predators to be vanquished (competing firms)."[13] That is to say, under capitalism, people are indeed forced to operate competitively, as indicated by premise (2) of *Community Makes People Happier*; and, as the analogy to the camping trip illustrates (and as claimed in premise (1) of the argument), most people would, all things being equal, prefer a situation in which people are genuinely acting communally—where respecting laborers and customers is not essentially a *strategy* for making more money but is itself part of the ultimate aim.

However, all of this is a far cry from showing that *Community Makes People Happier* serves as a sound argument for favoring socialism rather than capitalism. For starters, the capitalist might just agree with the conclusion:

(3) All things being equal, people will be happier under socialism rather than capitalism.

That conclusion contained the important caveat, "all things being equal." It is possible that there are circumstances in which competition yields more happiness, and such circumstances might go beyond the confines of a limited sporting event. The capitalist will claim that competition gives us incentives, and incentives increase productivity, and increased productivity gives greater wealth across the board. Wealth, in turn, allows one to live in more comfort, with plenty of food, adequate housing, and various goods that make our lives better (books, music, entertainment opportunities, hot baths, etc.). If you take away the competitive aspect of capitalism, you will lose all of that.

---

[13] Arnold, "No Community without Socialism," 17.

158 SOCIALISM AND HUMAN WELL-BEING

Or so the capitalist claims. Thus the capitalist might agree that *if* we could create a fully communal economic system that would produce a comparable amount of wealth as capitalism, then, sure, it might be the thing to do. But the capitalist will insist that it can't work—that human nature is such that we need competition to spur us to greater productivity and more comfort. Cohen himself admits that we don't know whether socialism can be made to work on a broad scale such that we can attain the advantages of community without losing productivity that also makes our lives better.[14]

Were the capitalist to rest content with this response to the argument, it might seem to be quite an admission: "Yes, socialism, if it could be made to work, would be better than cutthroat competition and capitalism; alas, it can't be made to work." If one admits that socialism would be nice if it worked, then surely one shouldn't be *too quick* to conclude that it can't work. However, there is another lingering issue with the argument, for the second premise of the argument is not to be taken for granted:

(2) Under socialism rather than capitalism, people operate more communally rather than competitively. [P]

What the camping trip scenario seems to illustrate is that we would, all things being equal, prefer an economic system based on the feeling of working together for a common goal (especially if that goal is our mutual happiness and well-being) rather than a competitive system. But I have also defined "socialism" as coming in degrees—the extent to which the economy is collectively owned and controlled can vary greatly. We have been concerned to see whether the arguments support us moving in the socialist direction. But one might think that any advantages of the feeling of community will only accrue if we fundamentally eliminate the competitive aspect of markets, and this, in turn, would require that we entirely (or at least almost entirely) eliminate private ownership of the means of production. As noted in earlier chapters, even in countries that are on the more socialist end of the spectrum, markets and private ownership of productive property have by no means been eliminated. Even if we adopt one of the various forms of market socialism where workers effectively own the enterprises in which they work, market forces and the need for profit maximization would still be at work, and one might think that

---

[14] Cohen, *Why Not Socialism?*, 57.

COLLECTIVE CONTROL: THE DEMOCRACY ARGUMENT   159

few, if any, of the advantages of additional communal feeling would be possible under those circumstances.

On the other hand, it could be that the feeling of community comes in degrees, and that we can get some of these advantages by moving in the socialist direction even without going all the way to complete collective ownership of the means of production. For example, if we move toward worker-owned cooperatives, then we might lament the fact that market logic still forces a general attitude of competitiveness: your customers are sources of profit, and your competitors are rivals. But at least you would be on the same team as your fellow workers, rather than just being a tool in the process of gaining profit for the owner of your business.

More generally, there could be a society-wide effect of more being done out of communal purpose. Even in the most capitalist societies, some proportion of employment is in the nonprofit sector and in government. Even if you happen to work for a for-profit corporation, you might benefit from a general sense of greater community in a society where there is a greater proportion of work not dictated by market logic. This might in turn be tied with the degree of redistribution. The economic *stakes* of competition will be lower in a society where degrees of inequality are less.

There is indeed some evidence that a sense of community can be greater in countries that move toward the socialist end of the spectrum. The World Values Survey asks people around the world the following question: "Generally speaking, would you say that most people can be trusted or that you need to be very careful in dealing with people?" You might take answers to this question to be a reasonable proxy for a general sense of community; if you generally trust the people around you, that yields a positive sense of community, and, conversely, if you distrust people and feel you need to watch your back, this is the opposite of community. Here are the results that they found for the Nordic countries as opposed to the United States:[15]

---

[15] "World Values Survey," data from 2017–2022, https://www.worldvaluessurvey.org/WVSOnline.jsp.

	Denmark	Finland	Norway	Sweden	United States
Most people can be trusted	73.9%	68.4%	72.1%	62.8%	37%
Need to be very careful	25.8%	29.6%	26.9%	35.7%	62.5%
Don't know	0.1%	2%	0.9%	1.2%	0%
No answer	0.2%	0%	0.1%	0.4%	0.4%

The results are quite striking, with over 60% of people in the United States feeling that they need to be very careful with people, while only about 30% of people in the Nordic countries feeling that way. Of course, one cannot infer too much from such data; there can be many other cultural factors at work here, and one might suggest that how you answer a survey question of this sort may or may not accurately indicate much about your positive feelings of community. But the data are at least suggestive, and they point to something being right about the *Community Makes People Happier* argument.

Why Is Democracy Good? The *All Affected Principle*

Another general reason for expecting greater well-being from collective control of the economy has to do with democracy. We can start with a banal observation: most people think democracy is a good thing; relatively few people advocate getting rid of democracy and replacing it with something else. Though most people do at least pay lip service to the ideals of democracy, it is not as easy to answer the question of exactly *why* it is a good thing. Clearly, democracy does not always lead to good results. According to many, the Brexit vote in the UK and the election of Donald Trump as president in 2016 serve as examples of terrible outcomes; for others, the fact that Donald Trump was *not* reelected in 2020 is as an example of a bad outcome. Nearly everyone would agree that the November 1932 election in Germany was horrible: the Nazi Party received more votes than any other party, ultimately making it possible for Hitler to take power.

One might despair of democracy. Winston Churchill is often alleged to have said, "The best argument against Democracy is a five-minute

COLLECTIVE CONTROL: THE DEMOCRACY ARGUMENT   161

conversation with the average voter." Even though that attribution is apparently false,[16] we do have data indicating that voters are not nearly so well informed as we might like. As philosopher Jason Brennan reports:

> For as long as we've been measuring, the mean, model, and median voters have been misinformed or ignorant about basic political information; they have known even less about more advanced social scientific knowledge. Their ignorance and misinformation causes them to support policies and candidates they would not support if they were better informed. As a result, we get suboptimal and sometimes quite bad political outcomes.[17]

Despite our well-deserved pessimism about the knowledge possessed by the average voter, many of us are still inclined to give grudging approval to democracy, which is embodied in something Churchill actually did say: "democracy is the worst form of Government except for all those other forms that have been tried from time to time."[18] Another grudging approval of democracy comes from W. E. B. DuBois: "The theory of democratic government is not that the will of the people is always right, but rather that normal human beings of average intelligence will, if given a chance, learn the right and best course by bitter experience."[19]

Even Brennan reports, "I'm a critic of democracy, but I'm also a fan.... I argue that as a matter of fact, democracy is positively correlated with a number of important outcomes, and this appears not to be mere correlation, but causation."[20]

Even if your approval of democracy is only grudgingly given, we can still ask *why* we approve of it, why it is better than the other forms of government that have been tried. When political theorists talk about democracy, they sometimes bring up a principle like the following:[21]

---

[16] Michael Richards, "History Detectives: A Concise List of Attributed Churchill Quotes Which Winston Never Uttered," International Churchill Society, June 9, 2013, https://winstonchurchill.org/publications/finest-hour/finest-hour-141/red-herrings-famous-quotes-churchill-never-said/.

[17] Jason Brennan, *Against Democracy* (Princeton, NJ: Princeton University Press, 2017), x.

[18] Richard Langworth, "Churchill's 'Democracy Is the Worst Form of Government . . . ,'" June 20, 2022, https://richardlangworth.com/worst-form-of-government.

[19] W. E. B. Du Bois, *The Negro* (New York: Henry Holt, 1915), 216.

[20] Brennan, *Against Democracy*, ix.

[21] See, e.g., Robert Dahl, *After the Revolution? Authority in a Good Society*, rev. ed. (New Haven: Yale University Press, 1990); Robert Goodin, "Exploiting a Person and Exploiting a Situation," in *Modern Theories of Exploitation*, ed. Andrew Reeve (Beverly Hills, CA: Sage Publishing, 1987); Erik Lagerspetz, "Democracy and the All-Affected Principle," *Res Cogitans*, vol. 10, no. 1 (2015): 6–23. These authors do not discuss the principle in connection with socialism and collective control of the economy. Arnold, "Socialism," explicitly makes that connection.

> *All Affected Principle*: People significantly affected by a decision should have a say over that decision.

There are, of course, exceptions to this principle. If a decision of mine affects me greatly but affects you in only an extremely minor way, then we would probably not say that you should have *equal* say in the decision. Or if a decision by one citizen involves exercising a genuine *moral right*, then we presumably do not want the decision to be put to any sort of democratic vote. But, granting such exceptions, the principle has a certain plausibility. Why? Why should people be allowed a say over decisions that significantly affect them? We might say that the *All Affected Principle* is just a brute moral fact, perhaps claiming that people have a *right* to have a voice in decisions that affect them. There might be something to that, and it might be used as the basis of rights-based argument for greatly increased democratic control over the economy. I raise that possibility only to set it aside, for I considered rights-based arguments for and against socialism in Part II of the book. Here we are considering arguments concerning increased overall well-being.

Instead of (or in addition to) any claim of a right to a democratic voice, I suggest that the *All Affected Principle* is plausible because we think that, by allowing everyone affected by a decision to have a say of some sort in the decision, we can maximize human well-being. Usually. On average. There will certainly be exceptions, as I will go on to discuss later. But the principle is plausible for two reasons. First, by letting everyone have a say, the ultimate decision draws on the experiences of a greater number of interested people. In general, one might at least hope that this extra information and broader set of perspectives will lead to better decisions. Second, if everyone had a say in a decision, then people might feel a greater degree of buy-in, and that by itself might lead to happier people after the decision is made.

The alternative to letting all those significantly affected have a say would be to cede control to some subset of the people. And there are times when some of us might despair enough about the "average voter" to contemplate granting such power. If, for example, we could have a dictator, but stipulate that she is truly benevolent and wise, then this would presumably produce more happiness for the people than we would get from majority rule. Obviously, in practice we cannot simply stipulate that our dictator have those properties; even if we did find one, we know better than to think that a

COLLECTIVE CONTROL: THE DEMOCRACY ARGUMENT   163

currently benevolent and wise despot will inevitably be followed by another equally benevolent and wise despot. If you believe in God and think that God has designated rulers that he deems to best represent him (whether through a hereditary monarchy or a theocracy in which church leaders rule), and if you believe that God carefully chooses and communicates with the leaders governing in his name, then this would be a good system; but, to say the least, those are some big *ifs*.

Rather than any of the obvious alternatives, it seems better, in the long run, to trust the people to make the ultimate decisions. Of course, this trust will pan out better if we also try to make sure that the people are well educated, have access to good information, and have good critical skills. We might even go so far as to limit access to power who exhibit some appropriate degree of knowledge about the relevant situations, though we would then be faced by questions of how we test for that and who devises the tests.[22] Even this approach grants basic plausibility to the *All Affected Principle*, reluctantly taking some of that say away from people who are demonstrably too ignorant to use it properly.

Democracy and Traditional Governmental Functions

Accordingly, we could translate this into an argument justifying our belief in democracy. The motivating thought would be in accord with the *All Affected Principle*, namely that we think that, in most cases, decisions will be better for everyone if everyone who is affected has a say in them; this in turn leads to the idea that these decisions should be made democratically. We could, in the first instance, make the argument about what we might call *traditional governmental functions*, where these would include police, courts, national defense, public services (e.g., public schools and roads), and redistributive programs. As suggested by the *All Affected Principle*, we could simply assert that democratic governance (letting everyone have a say) will have the best overall results for human well-being; in that case, the argument would look like this:

---

[22] Jason Brennan proposes *epistocracy*, according to which "more competent or knowledgeable citizens have slightly more political power than less competent or knowledgeable citizens." *Against Democracy*, x.

164 SOCIALISM AND HUMAN WELL-BEING

> *Democracy Argument for Traditional Governmental Functions 1.0*
>
> (1) Human well-being is maximized by allowing those affected by a decision to have democratic control over the decision.
> (2) Human well-being is maximized by allowing those affected by decisions concerning traditional governmental functions to have democratic control over them. [1]

However, it seems clear that premise (1) is not universally true about *all* decisions. When it comes time to assign grades in my courses, I do not submit them to a democratic vote. Robert Nozick gives a different example:

> If four men propose marriage to a woman, her decision about whom, if any of them, to marry importantly affects each of the lives of those four persons, her own life, and the lives of any other persons wishing to marry one of these four men, and so on. Would anyone propose, even limiting the group to include only the primary parties, that all five persons vote to decide whom she shall marry?[23]

We might suggest that a democratic vote in a case like this would violate the *rights* of the woman, that a woman has a right not to be forced into a marriage against her will. But even apart from the woman's rights, we might say that marriage decisions are not a case where we maximize happiness by giving an equal vote to everyone who might be affected by the decision (which would include many more people than the potential couple and other suitors); we might well surmise that we will maximize happiness when both parties to a proposed marriage want it, largely irrespective of the preferences of other people.

Nonetheless, I think premise (1) is in the right direction; it captures something of our thinking about why we prefer democracy. Rather than bluntly stating that it is true in all cases that democratically made decisions work out for the best, we could say that it is our default assumption—that unless we have specific reason to think it false in a particular realm of cases, we will assume that democratic decision-making is the best way to make decisions. More carefully phrased, then, the argument goes like this:

---

[23] Nozick, *Anarchy, State, and Utopia*, 269.

COLLECTIVE CONTROL: THE DEMOCRACY ARGUMENT   165

Democracy Argument for Traditional Governmental
Functions 2.0

(1) Human well-being is maximized by allowing those affected by a decision to have democratic control over the decision, unless there is special reason to think that there is a nondemocratic way of making this type of decision that is better for overall human well-being. [P]
(2) There is no special reason to think that there is a nondemocratic way of making decisions about traditional governmental programs that is better for overall human well-being. [P]
(3) Human well-being is maximized by allowing those affected by decisions about traditional governmental functions to have democratic control over them. [1,2]

Note that the argument now needs an extra premise: we assume in (2) that, in the case of decisions about traditional governmental programs, we have no special reason to think that there is some nondemocratic way of making these decisions that would be better.

The *Democracy Argument* conspicuously leaves open exactly what we mean by "democratic control" over a decision. We would not want this to mean that everyone votes on every single issue that arises. If nothing else, that would be highly impractical. Instead, I might get my say over a given set of issues by having been allowed to play my part in choosing a representative, who then gets involved matters of more detail. In some areas, especially those involving technical matters or specialized knowledge, we appoint experts and defer to their judgment. Courts are one example of that: instead of just having votes among the parties to a conflict, we have a process by means of which we appoint disinterested judges, who are experts on the relevant portions of the law involved. But appointing experts is not incompatible with the general idea of giving everyone a say, for we the people could *say* that we defer to experts appointed in such-and-such way on this issue. The deference itself would ultimately come back to a decision in which everyone has a say.

There is a much bigger question that gets left open by the *Democracy Argument* in its current form: Who gets counted in among those who are affected, and thus who should we allow to have democratic control if we want to maximize well-being? In practice, there are many people affected by decisions about governmental functions who are not given a say in those

166   SOCIALISM AND HUMAN WELL-BEING

decisions. For starters, future generations are affected by many decisions we make, but there is no way to let not-yet-existing people register and vote. But there is another group who are clearly affected by many such decisions but are not given a say: children under the age of 18. One can raise good questions about what the voting age should be, but nobody proposes that toddlers should be able to cast ballots. Perhaps we could amend the argument to say that human well-being is maximized by allowing all those *fully rational beings* affected by a decision.

Even among fully rational adults, we have never truly let *all* people have a say. For many years in many countries, it was just white men, or white men who owned property. The United States did not grant black men the right to vote until 1870. American women only won the right to vote in 1920. The UK extended women the franchise in 1928. Switzerland did not grant women the right to vote in federal elections until 1971. Prisoners cannot vote in many countries. In many states in the United States, those who have been convicted of serious crimes, even if they have served their time, cannot vote. We don't allow noncitizens to vote, even when these people live (legally or otherwise) within the country. Moreover, many governmental decisions profoundly impact people outside the territorial boundaries of the country in question. For example, when Britain's government declared war on Germany on September 3, 1939, this declaration and subsequent governmental actions had substantial effects on many non-British citizens. Similarly, if a government does something less dramatic, like impose tariffs on whiskey, this will have effects on citizens outside the country.

Such examples do not show that the argument is unsound. The argument might still be sound, and it might be true that we *would* maximize well-being by truly allowing those affected by governmental decisions to have democratic control over them, even if no government has truly followed such a policy. *Of course* the vote should never have been restricted to white men, and it is scandalous and maddening that countries took so long to grant suffrage to women. It is at least arguable that prisoners (and especially ex-cons who are fully living within the society again) *should* be allowed to vote, and the *All Affected Principle* might well be taken to mean that we should extend democracy further than national boundaries, at least insofar as governmental decisions involving international relations are concerned—or that such decisions should at least be regulated by a democratically elected international body.[24] Such ideas are interesting, but lie well beyond the scope of a book like this.

---

[24] See Goodin, "Enfranchising All Affected Interests," for discussion and advocacy of this position insofar as it would be practically possible.

Democracy and Economic Decisions

The socialist now asks: If democracy is a good thing for this reason (that it is best if people should have a say over decisions that affect them), then why stop at what I have denoted as "traditional governmental programs"? David Schweickart notes: "It is a striking anomaly of modern capitalist societies that ordinary people are deemed competent enough to select their political leaders—but not their bosses."[25] Why not bring democracy further into economic decisions? As Sam Arnold puts it:

> [M]any economic issues affect the public. When a local business fires 20% of its workers, this affects the public. When financiers withdraw support for a new shopping center, this affects the public. When society's productive assets are deployed to make yachts for millionaires rather than affordable housing, this affects the public. When corporations pull up roots and relocate production to greener pastures, this affects the public.[26]

Admittedly, not all economic transactions are so grand in scope as Arnold's examples. If I go to the local beverage store and buy a six-pack of Rothaus Pils (my favorite German pilsener that I've found outside of Germany), this economic decision has minor effects on my bank account and on the owner and employees of the store. The financial effects on anyone else are negligible. But major actions by large corporations are quite different. As one example, in the financial crisis of 2008, actions by investors and banks had significant ripple effects throughout the economy, affecting the lives of all of us. Accordingly, we could now suggest the following argument:

Democracy Argument for Socialism

(1) Human well-being is maximized by allowing those fully rational beings affected by a decision to have democratic control over the decision, unless there is special reason to think that there is a nondemocratic way of making this type of decision that is better for overall human well-being. [P]

---

[25] David Schweickart, *After Capitalism* (Lanham, MD: Rowman and Littlefield, 2002), 46.
[26] Arnold, "Socialism."

(2) There is no special reason to think that there is a nondemocratic way of making major economic decisions that is better for overall human well-being. [P]

(3) Human well-being is maximized by allowing those fully rational beings affected by major economic decisions to have democratic control over them. [1,2]

Often when people speak of government control of the economy, they tend to speak of the government as an alien force that uses its coercive authority, rather than just leaving people with freedom and liberty. There is a temptation to leave out two aspects of the situation. First, insofar as the government is democratically elected, then the government is, in a real sense, *us* and not some alien force. Second, just because the *government* does not involve itself in economic decisions affecting everyone does not mean that we all have more liberty and freedom. When Jeff Bezos sets things up such that many of his half million employees cannot easily take bathroom breaks, I think the affected employees might not see this as a matter of *their* liberty. With a private corporation free from government regulation, the owner has something like dictatorial power over the conditions under which the employees work, as well as a great deal of power over others who interact with the company. Of course, Amazon workers are free to quit their jobs, and that distinguishes the power that corporate owners have from the power the government has. But if someone desperately needs a job, then they are unlikely to quit the only one they have been able to find. In practice, the alternative to democratic control of large-scale economic decisions is not more freedom for all. Instead, the alternative to democracy is to cede a large amount of control to, for example, Jeff Bezos, concerning economic decisions involving Amazon, even though such decisions directly affect the half million employees of the company and somewhat less directly affect the rest of us. However, in accord with the *Democracy Argument for Socialism*, we might say that there is no good reason to assume that this nondemocratic way of making major economic decisions is better for overall human well-being.

One possible libertarian or conservative response to the *Democracy Argument for Socialism* would be simply to grant its conclusion, at least for the sake of argument, but to dispute its relevance. If you think that Jeff Bezos (or other owners of large chunks of productive property) have the *right* to do as they choose with their property and have the right to contract with workers in ways they see fit, then you might even grant that well-being might be maximized by more democratic control over these economic matters while insisting that this is irrelevant. If democratic control over such economic matters would violate Bezos's economic rights, then we should not allow such democratic control irrespective of concerns about human well-being. However, I already argued in Chapter 4 that there are no such strong economic rights—while we should regard economic liberties as important when doing utilitarian calculations, I saw no grounds for the claim that there are economic rights in the trump-card sense, which is precisely the sense that would be necessary if one were to claim that the conclusion of the *Democracy Argument for Socialism* is simply irrelevant.

Market Socialism

Notice what having more democratic control over major economic decisions would mean: greater collective ownership and collective control of the economy. This comes in degrees, and steps in this direction could take any number of forms. One key question is whether and how to incorporate markets. One model of collective control would be to have a centrally planned economy, with little or no role for the profit motive. However, some socialists advocate *market socialism*, where markets are still allowed to function but with more collective control and regulation and less (potentially *far* less) private ownership of the means of production.

David Schweickart gives one example of how market socialism might work. On his proposed system, which he calls "Economic Democracy," we would still use markets as a way of making production of goods responsive both to consumer demand and external circumstances, for he acknowledges that "Without a price mechanism sensitive to supply and demand, it is extremely difficult for a producer or planner to know what and how much to produce and which production and marketing methods are the most efficient."[27] Schweickart's Economic Democracy would still include businesses or enterprises that aim to make a profit in a relatively unencumbered market. However, each of these enterprises would be "controlled democratically by

---

[27] Schweickart, *After Capitalism*, 51.

170 SOCIALISM AND HUMAN WELL-BEING

its workers": the workers themselves would collectively control the operation, including the "organization of the workplace, enterprise discipline, techniques of production, what and how much to produce, what to charge for what is produced, and how the net proceeds are to be distributed."[28] Under Schweickart's system, workers would not be paid a normal wage; instead, the profits of the enterprise would be divided among the workers, in accord with whatever arrangement the workers collectively decided. This need not mean that each worker receives an equal share; the workers might decide to provide incentives or give higher percentages to those in certain positions.

Schweickart's Economic Democracy might still seem to amount to private ownership of the means of production where the private owners happen to consist of the workers of each of the enterprises. But Schweickart introduces some key features that mean that *worker control* and profit-sharing would still not really amount to private ownership. First and foremost, the workers "are not free to sell off their capital assets and use the proceeds as income."[29] If an enterprise declares bankruptcy, the capital assets revert to state control. In addition, each enterprise must pay a tax on the capital assets, essentially a property tax; Schweickart says that this means that "In effect, workers lease their capital assets from society."[30]

A final central aspect of Schweickart's system is that all investment would be done publicly, through democratically controlled banks:

> Unlike banks under capitalism, these banks are not themselves private, profit-maximizing institutions. They are public institutions charged with effectively allocating the funds entrusted to them in accordance with at least two criteria: profitability and employment creation. A region or community may impose additional criteria to better control its pattern of development. It may, for example, offer loans at lower rates to businesses creating green jobs, or retooling to use more ecologically sound technologies.[31]

With investment controlled democratically, we would no longer need to worry about "capital flight," whereby private owners of the means of production take their assets to wherever they can, for the moment, get the cheapest labor costs or the most favorable tax and regulatory situation from local governments.

---

[28] Schweickart, *After Capitalism*, 47.
[29] Schweickart, *After Capitalism*, 48.
[30] Schweickart, *After Capitalism*, 48.
[31] Schweickart, *After Capitalism*, 54.

COLLECTIVE CONTROL: THE DEMOCRACY ARGUMENT   171

Erik Olin Wright proposes a somewhat different model that he also terms "market socialism."[32] As with Schweickart, Wright proposes that markets would still play a significant role, but he would aim for a more "cooperative market economy."[33] There would be various forms of cooperative organizations, including consumer cooperatives, credit unions, and, especially, worker cooperatives. Worker cooperatives would be, as under Schweickart's model, enterprises that are governed democratically by the workers themselves.[34] However, the worker cooperatives under Wright's system would still genuinely own the enterprise in question. Moreover, Wright does not rule out the continued existence of businesses that are owned by individuals or investors other than the workers. He says instead, "In a democratic socialist economy, worker cooperatives would potentially constitute a substantial sector, perhaps even the dominant form of organization engaged in market production for many goods and services."[35] Those who insist that virtually complete collective ownership of the means of production is the definitive feature of socialism might doubt that Wright's version of Economic Democracy truly counts as socialist. Wright, however, shares the approach I have taken to the definitional question, saying that we should not regard the distinction between capitalism and socialism as "a simple dichotomy" and that, instead, "we can talk about the degree to which an economic system is capitalist or socialist."[36]

Markets and the Capitalist Reply to the *Democracy Argument for Socialism*

Of course, there are other models for how we might increase collective ownership and control of the economy,[37] and I will not attempt to evaluate the details of the different proposals. The *Democracy Argument for Socialism*, even if sound, does not specify exactly *how* we should allow those affected

---

[32] Erik Olin Wright, *How to Be an Anti-capitalist in the 21st Century* (New York: Verso, 2019), p. xiv.

[33] Wright, *Anti-capitalist*, 75.

[34] Wright, *Anti-capitalist*, 76.

[35] Wright, *Anti-capitalist*, 77.

[36] Wright, *Anti-capitalist*, 71.

[37] See, for example, John Roemer, *A Future for Socialism* (Cambridge, MA: Harvard University Press, 1994); Richard Wolff, *Democracy at Work: A Cure for Capitalism* (Chicago: Haymarket Books, 2012); Joseph Carens, *Equality, Incentives, and the Market: An Essay in Utopian Politico-Economic Theory* (Chicago: University of Chicago Press, 1981); and Giacomo Corneo, *Is Capitalism Obsolete? A Journey through Alternative Economic Systems* (Cambridge, MA: Harvard University Press, 2017).

172 SOCIALISM AND HUMAN WELL-BEING

by major economic decisions to have control over them. The argument does show, however, that the word "democratic" in "democratic socialism" is more than just an ornament meant to assuage fears that socialists are aiming for something like the authoritarian communist states of the 20th century. Rather, proponents call it "democratic socialism" precisely because the proposal is to *expand* democracy by extending it to parts of the economic realm that, under capitalism, are individual, profit-oriented decisions.

Nobody thinks that *everything* should be subject to democratic control; nobody thinks that your decision about whom to date or marry (or whether to date or marry at all) should be decided by the legislature. (However, legislatures do typically place limits on your choice by prohibiting marriages between close biological relatives. Moreover, those conservatives who are still opposed to same-sex marriage would like to greatly restrict your choice of whom to marry, but even they don't propose that the legislature will tell you which specific person of the opposite sex you are allowed to marry.) And, of course, free-market-loving capitalists will be aghast at the thought of more collective control of the means of production, despite that being an expansion of democracy. Capitalists will think that it is indeed better, for example, to let Jeff Bezos run Amazon as he sees fit, hoping that his drive to increase his own profits will ultimately benefit us all. The defender of capitalism will claim that it is better for all of us if the economy is left to the control of the "invisible hand" that is brought about by decisions by individuals each acting in accord with their own economic self-interest, rather than being determined by anything like a democratic process.

What these doubts mean in terms of the *Democracy Argument for Socialism*: capitalists will deny premise (2). They will claim that we *do* have special reason to doubt the efficacy of democracy when it comes to economic decisions, and that leaving such decisions to the free market will be the best way to maximize overall human well-being. The capitalist thus thinks that democracy should not extend very far into the economy: we should leave economic decisions to the dictatorial control of the principal actors, even when those decisions have substantial effects on the rest of us. Capitalists do not say this because they are heartless and don't care about the rest of us. Instead, most charitably interpreted, the capitalists think that by letting the legal owners of capital make the economic decisions involving that capital, we will achieve outcomes that are ultimately better for everyone.

In the next chapter, I will explore this thought by looking at two famous arguments for why we should rely on markets rather than democratic control. I will then spend several chapters looking at circumstances where these arguments fail, circumstances in which we can presume that leaving things to the market will not maximize overall human well-being.

Before proceeding into that, let me reiterate that we are not talking about rights here. *Some* conservatives think that economic decisions should be privately made by individuals not because they think that will be better for all of us, but because they think that it would violate *rights* of individuals if government were to control the economy or own the means of production. However, that approach was already discussed in Chapter 4; the concern now is the question of which approach is better for increasing human well-being in the best way.

Key Takeaways

- The Scandinavian countries provide some evidence that greater collective control of the economy leads to greater human well-being.
- It is plausible that moving in a more socialist direction increases a sense of community and thereby increases overall well-being.
- Democracy is good, and its goodness presumably lies in our expectation that human well-being is maximized when we let those affected by decisions have some sort of say in making those decisions, unless there is some special reason to think that certain decisions should be made another way.
- But if democracy is good for that reason, then it seems that we would have reason to expand democracy further into the realm of major economic decisions, meaning that we would have reason to move in the socialist direction of increased collective control over the economy.
- Capitalists will reply that there *is* good reason to make economic decisions another way, namely that a free market will be best for everyone. See Part IV.
- Rothaus Pils ("Red house pilsner") is the best German pilsener you can buy outside of Germany.

PART IV
CAPITALISM AND HUMAN WELL-BEING

9

The Case for Markets

In the previous chapter, I presented an argument for more collective control of markets and the economy, an argument based on the simple idea that this would be more democratic. This is not to say that I am advocating collective control over the entire economy, let alone advocating having government control over *everything* in our lives. If nothing else, I know myself better than the government does, so I will generally know better than elected representatives which choices of mine will make me happier; so long as these are choices that have quite minimal impact on others, then it seems best for maximizing overall human well-being to leave those decisions to me.

But major economic decisions involving large amounts of capital or jobs are not like this: by their very nature, such decisions will have large effects on many other people. So, on the face of things, it seems that we would still be right to affirm both premises of this argument from the last chapter:

Democracy Argument for Socialism

(1) Human well-being is maximized by allowing those fully rational beings affected by a decision to have democratic control over the decision, unless there is special reason to think that there is a nondemocratic way of making this type of decision that is better for overall human well-being. [P]

(2) There is no special reason to think that there is a nondemocratic way of making major economic decisions that is better for overall human well-being. [P]

(3) Human well-being is maximized by allowing those fully rational beings affected by major economic decisions to have democratic control over them. [1,2]

Capitalists, especially since the Reagan-Thatcher era beginning in the 1980s, tend to be highly suspicious of government involvement, particularly in the economy. In his first inaugural address, speaking of the economic ills facing

Socialism. Scott R. Sehon, Oxford University Press. © Oxford University Press 2024.
DOI: 10.1093/oso/9780197753330.003.0009

the nation, Reagan famously said, "Government is not the solution to our problem; government *is* the problem."[1] Why think this? Why think that we will do best to have democratically elected government when it comes to things like courts, police, defense, and primary and secondary education (none of which was questioned by Reagan), but not when it comes to major economic decisions? Why think that premise (2) of the *Democracy Argument for Socialism* is false?

For help in understanding the conservative case against democratic control over markets and major economic decisions, I'll turn to two heroes of the conservative movement, both of whom had substantial influence over the Reagan-Thatcher era. First is an argument from Austrian-born economist F. A. Hayek (1899–1992). Margaret Thatcher was very taken with his works, and Reagan's vice president, George H. W. Bush, awarded Hayek the Presidential Medal of Freedom after succeeding Reagan as president. The second argument is from American economist Milton Friedman (1912–2006) who was an adviser to both Thatcher and Reagan.

Hayek: The Better Information Argument

Hayek was a noted critic of socialism. Actually, to say he was a *critic* of socialism rather understates the point, since he literally feared for the survival of humanity if we allow socialism to displace capitalism: "The dispute between the market order and socialism is no less than a matter of survival. To follow socialist morality would destroy much of present humankind and impoverish much of the rest."[2] How could socialism possibly lead to such dire results? Basically put, Hayek's idea is that the "fatal conceit" of socialism is the thought that "man is able to shape the world around him according to his wishes."[3] According to this economist, the attempt to shape things in some sort of centrally planned way, even through a democratically elected government, is doomed to fail.

We can begin to understand why Hayek thinks this by looking at a comparison he makes with evolutionary biology. The mistake many thinkers

---

[1] Ronald Reagan, "Inaugural Address," Reagan Foundation, January 20, 1981, https://www.reaganfoundation.org/ronald-reagan/reagan-quotes-speeches/inaugural-address-2/.

[2] F. A. Hayek, *The Fatal Conceit: The Errors of Socialism*, ed. W. W. Bartley III (Chicago: University of Chicago Press, 1988): 7.

[3] Hayek, *The Fatal Conceit*, 27.

made prior to Darwin was to assume that the appearance of *order* in biology implied the existence of a rational mind designing that order, whereas in fact this was the result of a natural process of evolution: some random mutations led some organisms, in their particular ecological niche, to thrive—in the specific sense of having more offspring. Those mutations that had this effect came to dominate the population of that species in that area. All of this can take place without a central planner thinking to herself, "Those finches in the Galapagos islands could use slightly larger beaks right now, and I think somewhat longer necks would do well for giraffes in Africa; oh, and I may have gone too far with those hagfish eyes—since they no longer need to see, I'll make the eyes nonfunctional." For any human designer, there would be too much information to keep track of, too many environmental changes to adjust to. But the process of evolution manages to respond to all of that quite well without central planning.

Hayek makes an analogous claim about economic practices, asserting that the *market* enables each person "to use his own individual knowledge for his own individual purposes while being ignorant of most of the order into which he had to fit his actions."[4] As with biological evolution, this process is highly decentralized and responds to forces and circumstances in real time all over the globe. Under the theory of biological evolution and natural selection, the mutations are random and there is no design or intelligence involved at any stage. Obviously, that is different in the economic case: individual producers, traders, and consumers make all kinds of intelligent decisions along the way. (Or sometimes stupid decisions—I really did not need to join the Columbia Record Club as a teenager, but the lure of 12 records for a penny was too much.) But just as a human central planner would not be able to outdo biological evolution in producing well-adapted organisms, Hayek asserts that central planning of the economy can never outdo the market: "Modern economics explains how such an extended order can come into being, and how it itself constitutes an information-gathering process, able to call up, and to put to use, widely dispersed information that no central planning agency, let alone any individual, could know as a whole, possess or control."[5]

The basic idea seems to be this: if economic decisions are made under free markets, then the market process, being decentralized, will lead "to the generation and use of more information than is possible under central

---

[4] Hayek, *The Fatal Conceit*, 47.
[5] Hayek, *The Fatal Conceit*, 14.

180 CAPITALISM AND HUMAN WELL-BEING

direction."[6] Economic decisions will thus be better, for if there is more information there will be better decisions. Laying out Hayek's argument explicitly, we would have something like this:

Better Information 1.0

(1) To the extent that economic decisions are made under free markets rather than under democratic control, more information is available and used in making those decisions. [P]
(2) To the extent that more information is available and used in making decisions, the better the decisions will be. [P]
(3) To the extent that economic decisions are made under free markets rather than under democratic control, the better the decisions will be. [1,2]

If *Better Information* is sound, then premise (2) of the *Democracy Argument for Socialism* would appear to be false: we would know that economic decisions made through individual free market decisions will be better than those made democratically.

However, before getting to other issues one might have with this argument, let me start with an oddity about the word "better" as used in steps (2) and (3). Suppose that someone is making plans to rob your house. They will have a greater chance of success (of taking your valuables and not being caught) to the extent that they have more information—e.g., information about when you are home, whether you have an alarm system, where your valuables are, where you keep a hidden key, etc. So it will be better *for them* if they have more information. But that does not make it better *in general*; you would probably prefer the outcome if they do not have good information.

Applied to the argument, the point is that premise (2) of *Better Information* is plausible to the extent that Hayek means that the decisions made will be better *for the person making the decision*. But as the house burglar example makes clear, that a particular decision is better for the person making it does not mean it is *better for people in general*. We would only really care about the conclusion of *Better Information* if the claim in the conclusion is that decisions made under free market capitalism will be better for people in general. After all, the whole point of the capitalist critique of *Democracy*

---

[6] Hayek, *The Fatal Conceit*, 86.

THE CASE FOR MARKETS   181

Is Good is to show that we *do* have special reason to think that there is a nondemocratic way of making major economic decisions that is better for overall human well-being. So it seems that *Better Information* equivocates on the word "better": to make the second premise seem plausible, Hayek uses one sense of the word "better," but to make the conclusion in (3) relevant to socialism, he uses a different sense. That would make *Better Information 1.0* simply invalid.

The obvious reply for Hayek is to add an additional assumption: if each person is left free to make her own economic decisions in a free market, then each person will succeed in doing what is in her own best interest, and if we just add all of that up, that means it will be better for everyone. In other words, Hayek would acknowledge that *Better Information 1.0* is invalid, but say that we need merely add a new premise to make the argument work:

Better Information 2.0

(1) To the extent that economic decisions are made under free markets rather than under democratic control, more information is available and used in making those decisions. [P]
(2) To the extent that more information is available and used in making decisions, the better the decisions will be for the person making the decision. [P]
(3) To the extent that each person makes economic decisions that are *better for them*, the decisions will cumulatively be *better for all*. [P]
(4) To the extent that economic decisions are made under free markets rather than under democratic control, the *better for all* the decisions will be. [1,2,3]

Now the argument looks valid, and premise (2) looks reasonably plausible: all things being equal, if you have more information when you are making a decision, you will make a better decision for you, just as the person planning to burgle your house will have greater success with more information. I will raise substantial questions, however, about premise (3) after considering an analogous argument from Milton Friedman.

Before getting to those concerns, let me note that there are other ways (in addition to denying premise (3)) that socialists could respond to *Better Information*. When Hayek speaks of "central planning" or socialism in this book (written in the mid-1980s), he has the Soviet model in mind, where

182 CAPITALISM AND HUMAN WELL-BEING

the state owned the vast majority of the means of production and attempted to centrally plan the economy as a whole, and Hayek's point about loss of information almost certainly applied then. However, as we saw in the previous chapter, D-socialist models do not (and certainly *need* not) involve Soviet-style planning. There are varieties of socialism, like David Schweickart's Economic Democracy, that do incorporate markets even while abolishing truly private ownership of the means of production. Moreover, other market socialist models, like that of Erik Olin Wright, still have markets and allow for some private ownership of the means of production. In any such model of socialism, it is not at all clear why there would be any loss of information as compared to market-based capitalism, since socialism would still be using markets to get information.

In terms of the specifics of *Better Information 2.0*, the point is that Hayek seems to presuppose a sharp distinction between making economic decisions through a market versus making those decisions in a way that is under democratic control: he seems to assume that, to the extent that the economy is under democratic control the economy does *not* utilize markets. This is a version of a false dichotomy, an argument that presupposes that the available choices are more limited than they actually are. In technical terms, this yields two ways for the socialist to reply to *Better Information*, depending on how you interpret Hayek. You might interpret the conclusion as just saying that, *if you are choosing* between markets and democratic control without markets, economic decisions will be better with markets. In that case, the market socialist could simply agree with the conclusion, as far as that goes, because the market socialist is not choosing between those two alternatives. The market socialist says we can have markets and democratic control. On the other hand, you might interpret premise (1) as presupposing that those are the *only* alternatives: that you either have markets or you have democratic control, but not both. In that case, the market socialist should just reject that premise as false.

Friedman: The Better Incentives Argument

Hayek argued that markets utilize more information, but the more common argument for capitalist free markets has to do with *incentives* rather than information. The basic idea behind the argument is popular among conservatives and libertarians, but I will trace it to some things said by

THE CASE FOR MARKETS   183

another capitalist hero, Milton Friedman. In *Free to Choose*, Friedman and his wife, Rose, lay out the following chart of possibilities for spending, where we assume that you are the spender:[7]

	You	**Someone Else**
Yours	I	II
Someone Else's	III	IV

The Friedmans say that if you are spending your own money on yourself (box I) then you will be highly motivated to economize and get good value. You will watch carefully the total amount spent, and you will endeavor to make sure that you get the best value you can for that amount. But the Friedmans say that these incentives break down as soon as your spending fits into one of the other boxes. If you are spending your money on someone else—for example, buying someone a gift—then you will watch carefully how much you spend (it's your money!) but you won't have "the same incentive to get full value for your money."[8] (This does make me wonder about the quality of the gifts that the Friedmans bought for each other, let alone for someone not in their household, but I'll leave that aside.)

The thought, as applied, to government would be something like this: if our democratically elected government were to take over or heavily regulate many economic decisions, then this would mean that those decisions would be in box IV. For the legislators who vote to approve such decisions, it is not really their money at stake and the economic decision will typically benefit the legislators themselves in a relatively minor way. It is definitely not the same as you spending $100 from your own bank account on something you alone plan to use. Moreover, once past the legislative process, regulations or outright public operation of the means of production will not be done by legislators but by administrators of some sort, and they will likewise be making economic decisions with money that is not their own and does not directly benefit themselves. The Friedmans claim that this means their incentives will be poor: they will have neither the incentive to economize nor to get value for the money spent: "The bureaucrats spend someone else's

[7] Milton Freidman and Rose Friedman, *Free to Choose: A Personal Statement* (New York: Harcourt, 1980), 116.

[8] Friedman and Friedman, *Free to Choose*, 116.

184 CAPITALISM AND HUMAN WELL-BEING

money on someone else. Only human kindness, not the much stronger and more dependable spur of self-interest, assures that they will spend the money in the way most beneficial to the recipients. Hence the wastefulness and ineffectiveness of the spending."[9]

As an argument for free markets and against democratic control of economic decisions, the idea seems to be quite similar to *Better Information*: people will tend to make better economic decisions in free markets because they will be motivated by self-interest, and capitalists assume that selfishness and greed are better motivators than caring about other people. We can lay out the argument as follows:

Better Incentives 1.0

(1) To the extent that economic decisions are made under free markets rather than under democratic control, people making economic decisions have a direct financial stake in those decisions. [P]

(2) To the extent that people making economic decisions have a direct financial stake in those decisions, the better the decisions will be. [P]

(3) To the extent that economic decisions are made under free markets rather than under democratic control, the better the decisions will be. [1,2]

Like Hayek's *Better Information*, this argument seems to presuppose a stark dichotomy between free markets and democratic control, whereas the market socialist says that you can have both. However, that presupposition might be somewhat less dubious in the context of *Better Incentives* than it was in the case of *Better Information*. Under most versions of D-socialism that still incorporate markets, it is arguably true that economic actors have *less* of a financial stake in market decisions. This is for two reasons. First, at least under some forms of market socialism (e.g., Schweickart's), those making decisions in the market still do not fully own the enterprises of which they are a part, in the sense that they cannot sell the capital assets and walk away with a huge profit. Though workers running the worker-controlled enterprises will be subject to profits or losses in market decisions, there is less possibility of *extreme* riches. Second, for any form of D-socialism with markets, there

---

[9] Friedman and Friedman, *Free to Choose*, 117–118.

will presumably be much more egalitarian distribution of resources (since that is one of the defining axes of socialism), and thus a much greater social safety net in general. Any particular actor in the market will thus have less fear of devastating and abject poverty. Of course, one might well think of this as a positive advantage of the socialist economic system, but it is true that it means that people have somewhat *less* of an extreme financial risk or stake involved in market transactions under socialism. The Friedmans might well claim that this is enough for premise (1) of the argument: under a more free market, people making the economic decisions have a much more direct financial stake.

Despite the argument's relative immunity to the charge of a false dichotomy, there are other problems. It is first worth noting that premise (2) seems to be a rather dreary assertion about human nature, if meant as a general and universal claim. Consider, for example, someone who is handling the investments for a nonprofit institution, like a private college. According to premise (2), even if that person is doing a good job in making investment decisions for the college, she would do better if it were her own money at stake. The financial officer might beg to differ and claim that she is doing the best she can with the college's money and would not do it any differently if it were her own money, but I guess the Friedmans don't believe her. After all, they are explicit in saying that decisions made on the basis of mere "human kindness" will be less good than those made on the "much stronger and more dependable spur of self-interest." Of course, even the financial officer has an indirect financial stake, in that she might hope that if she makes a lot of money for the college, she will get raises or better job offers elsewhere; she at least wants to do well enough to keep her current job. But those sort of things could be true of government administrators as well, and the Friedmans clearly think such incentives are inadequate, or at least far less good than if it were your own money at stake.

If anything, Friedman doubles down on the point. In a talk show appearance, an interviewer (Phil Donahue) asked Friedman: "Did you ever have a moment of doubt about capitalism and whether greed is a good idea to run on?" Friedman replied: "Tell me, is there some society you know that doesn't run on greed?" He answered his own question by declaring, "The world runs on individuals pursuing their separate interests."[10] If all societies "run on greed" and if the whole world "runs on" people acting simply in their own self-interest, then the picture seems to be this: people are, at root, selfish.

[10] "Milton Friedman and the 'Greed' Question," YouTube.com, https://www.youtube.com/watch?v=TZDXvgUxAgQ.

186 CAPITALISM AND HUMAN WELL-BEING

Perhaps Friedman allows that you do a few things for your immediate loved ones without thinking about how it will benefit you, but he certainly seems to suggest a vision in which people rarely do things because it is the right thing to do or because it will help other people. We might hope instead that some people see us as being in this together; that we care about the welfare of others because they are people like us; that we value doing unto others as we would have them do to us, and without first signing an enforceable contract *obliging* them to reciprocate. All of this is evidently foreign to the thought of Friedman and his followers insofar as they affirm premise (2) of *Better Incentives*.

We might be more optimistic and hope that we could emphasize and learn to harness humanity's better impulses, as philosopher G. A. Cohen suggests in *Why Not Socialism?* It seems to me that there is empirical evidence that Friedman is wrong, and that the quality of people's decisions does not always depend on the decision being about their own financial interest. In particular, I have in mind here healthcare workers, teachers, clergy, and many others. Of course, each of these people gets a salary for their work, but it is rarely as if raises or bonuses are tied incredibly closely to performance levels. In my own field of academia, there may be a very rough correlation between one's salary and the number and influence of one's publications. But how well you teach seems to have almost no correlation at all with the degree of your compensation. And yet nearly every academic I know puts a large amount of effort into teaching. In the end, the view of human nature embodied in premise (2) of *Better Incentives* is an empirical matter, and I will make no assumptions about it. That is to say, I will argue that *Better Incentives* is unsound, even if you grant premise (2).

Better Incentives, like Hayek's argument *Better Information*, glosses over a crucial distinction between whether a decision will be better *for the person* making it or whether it will be better *in general*. Premise (2) perhaps has some plausibility if the claim is that the decisions will be better for the individual whose money is at stake in the decision; but we only have reason to care about the conclusion in (3) if we are talking about decisions being better for everyone. More specifically, the conclusion of *Better Incentives* will only be relevant to refuting the *Democracy Argument for Socialism* to the extent that the conclusion is that the economic decisions made in a free market will be better for overall human well-being. To take care of this point, we will need to revise *Better Incentives 1.0* in a way analogous to the revision of *Better Information*:

THE CASE FOR MARKETS 187

Better Incentives 2.0

(1) To the extent that economic decisions are made under free markets rather than under democratic control, people making economic decisions have a direct financial stake in those decisions. [P]

(2) To the extent that people making economic decisions have a direct financial stake in those decisions, the *better for them* the decisions will be. [P]

(3) To the extent that each person makes economic decisions that are *better for them*, the decisions will cumulatively be *better for all*. [P]

(4) To the extent that economic decisions are made under free markets rather than under democratic control, the *better for all* the decisions will be. [1,2,3]

For some economic circumstances and transactions, all three premises might look plausible. I'll give you an example from my childhood. Like many American kids in the 1970s, I collected baseball cards. Sometimes a few of my friends and I would get together and engage in some economic transactions with these cards—that is to say, we would make trades. Some trades seem like no-brainers: I might have two Rod Carew cards but no Willie Stargell; my friend Steve might have two Willie Stargells but no Rod Carew. Given that both Steve and I want to have as many distinct cards as possible, and we especially want to have one of each of the great players of the day, it makes perfect sense for both of us if I trade him one of my Rod Carews for one of his Willie Stargells. Other trades get more complicated and might involve different motivations. My favorite player was Tom Seaver, whereas Steve was a Royals fan; accordingly, I might be willing to trade him my George Brett card for his Tom Seaver card, even though neither of us has duplicates, and he might be willing to make the trade as well. Nonetheless, after each trade, both of us should end up happier with our set of cards than we were before; otherwise we wouldn't have made the trade. If a bunch of friends, or strangers, get together and trade cards, the situation does not change: each person goes into each trade with the aim of improving their own set of cards, and that should result in a net improvement overall. All of this is in accord with what the Friedmans call "Adam Smith's key insight," namely that "that both parties to an exchange can benefit and that, so long as cooperation is strictly voluntary, no exchange will take place unless both parties do benefit. No external

188 CAPITALISM AND HUMAN WELL-BEING

force, no coercion, no violation of freedom is necessary to produce cooperation among individuals all of whom can benefit."[11]

In this market of trading baseball cards, each of us making transactions had a direct stake in the transaction, and one can well imagine that premise (2) is true for such a situation: if I were making trades on behalf of Steve, then I might not know his preferences as well, and, perhaps, you might doubt that I would be as vigilant about making good trades since it was not my own collection at stake. Each of us would do better handling our own trades because we know better what we want. And with each of us maximizing our own individual interest, everything works out better for all of us as well. That is to say, in that case it does seem that premise (3) of *Better Incentives* is plausible: if each kid makes transactions that are *better for them*, then the cumulative result should be *better for all*. Insofar as the capitalist free market writ large works like baseball card trading, one can certainly see the plausibility of the move from each actor working in their own self-interest to the conclusion that the welfare of everyone is improved.

However, in the broader world beyond adolescent youth and their baseball cards, the situation can become much more complicated. Over the next three chapters, I will discuss a number of areas where markets fail—where we do *not* expect to maximize overall well-being simply by having each economic player act in their own self-interest. If I am right, then at least in these areas the capitalist argument will fail. Then, without a special reason to think that democratic control is a bad idea when it comes to major economic decisions, we will have reason to affirm the *Democracy Argument for Socialism* from the previous chapter, and we will have reason to say that we should move in the socialist direction of increasing collective control over the means of production and the economy.

Key Takeaways

- Contrary to the *Democracy Argument for Socialism* for more democratic control of major economic decisions, capitalists argue for the superiority of markets, markets in which individuals make major economic decisions affecting multitudes of people.

---

[11] Friedman and Friedman, *Free to Choose*, 1–2.

- F. A. Hayek argues that markets utilize more information than could ever be done by democratic (or nondemocratic) planning of economic decisions.
- Milton Friedman argues that markets are superior because people will have better incentives—specifically, they will be acting on the "stronger and more dependable spur of self-interest" rather than mere human kindness.
- Both arguments rely on a crucial assumption: that if each person does what is best for them, we will arrive at a situation that is best for everyone. I will question that assumption in the chapters to come.
- Tom Seaver was the best player the Mets ever had, and I have his (autographed!) baseball card displayed on the wall of my study.

10
Market Failures I: Public Goods

The Argumentative Situation

Here's where we stand. In Chapter 8, I put forward an argument based on the value of democracy for why we should allow citizens to have democratic control over major economic decisions. That argument went as follows:

> *Democracy Argument for Socialism*
>
> (1) Human well-being is maximized by allowing those fully rational beings affected by a decision to have democratic control over the decision, unless there is special reason to think that there is a nondemocratic way of making this type of decision that is better for overall human well-being. [P]
> (2) There is no special reason to think that there is a nondemocratic way of making major economic decisions that is better for overall human well-being. [P]
> (3) Human well-being is maximized by allowing those fully rational beings affected by major economic decisions to have democratic control over them. [1,2]

But then in reply there were two arguments, each of which was aimed at showing that premise (2) of the *Democracy Argument* is false—that when it comes to major economic decisions, there *is* a special reason to think that nondemocratic ways of making those decisions are better. The first argument, from F. A. Hayek, starts from the premise that more information is available in a free market than any governmental planner would be able to have. The second argument, from Milton Friedman, assumes that in a free market people will have better incentives, because they will be motivated by the "stronger and more dependable spur of self interest," rather than merely by kindness or a desire to do one's job well. I noted that one can question both of those premises, but that another possible problem area for each argument lay in a different premise, namely that when each person makes an economic decision that is *better for them*, then economic decisions will be *better for all*. Here was the full version of the Friedman argument:

Better Incentives 2.0

(1) To the extent that economic decisions are made under free markets rather than under democratic control, people making economic decisions have a direct financial stake in those decisions. [P]
(2) To the extent that people making economic decisions have a direct financial stake in those decisions, the *better for them* the decisions will be. [P]
(3) To the extent that each person makes economic decisions that are *better for them*, the decisions will cumulatively be *better for all*. [P]
(4) To the extent that economic decisions are made under free markets rather than under democratic control, the *better for all* the decisions will be. [1,2,3]

If *Better Incentives* or *Better Information* (the Hayek argument) is right, then we will, in general, be better off if we allow economic decisions to be made under a free market, free from democratic control or regulation, and we will also see that premise (2) in the *Democracy Argument for Socialism* is false.

Having put forward *Better Incentives* and *Better Information* on behalf of the capitalists, let me note that almost nobody except a few radical libertarians and anarchists think that a completely unrestrained market is the right way to go for *all* economic decisions. There are some areas where nearly everyone admits that we do not want a free market approach—that this is not what will lead to maximizing human well-being. Capitalists will think of these as exceptions to the general rule of deferring to the invisible hand of the market, but I think it is important to investigate the *reasons* that these seem to be exceptions, for I think that this will lead us to the conclusion that there are more things in this category than the capitalists typically want to admit. This chapter will be devoted to discussing *public goods*—those goods and services that we have come to expect that government will provide. The next two chapters will consider other areas where markets fail.

Hayek and the Diffuse Benefit of Some Services

Hayek himself notes that "there are fields in which the desirability of government action can hardly be questioned," and he includes here

> all those services which are clearly desirable but which will not be provided by competitive enterprise because it would be either impossible or difficult to charge the individual beneficiary for them. Such are most sanitary and health services, often the construction and maintenance of roads, and many of the amenities provided by municipalities for the inhabitants of cities. Included also are the activities which Adam Smith described as "those public works, which, though they may be in the highest degree advantageous to a great society, are, however, of such a nature, that the profit could never repay the expense to any individual or small number of individuals."[1]

Let's consider one of his examples: construction and maintenance of roads. Hayek suggests that, if they were operated privately through the free market, it would be "impossible or difficult to charge the individual beneficiary for them." On the face of things that might seem false: someone could build a road, and then set up a toll collection system, thereby charging each user. That might have rightly seemed infeasible to Hayek writing in 1960: while it is one thing to have toll booths on long stretches of highway, it would be less practical to place a manned toll booth on the little street where I live. These days, it would be more feasible to have tolls even for minor neighborhood streets, for we could put in an automated electronic tolling system.

However, I don't think even the most automated and simple toll collection system would fundamentally change Hayek's point about roads as a public good. The real issue is this: even if we can charge individual drivers for the cost of the construction and maintenance of each road they drive on, that would not *really* amount to charging the beneficiaries. The drivers are indeed a principal beneficiary, but they are far from the only ones. If I have a friend who drives to my house to pay me a visit, then I benefit from the roads being there as well, even if I don't have a car at all. I also benefit from police and firefighters having roads to drive on, even if I rarely or never have to use their services directly. More generally, we all benefit from other people being able

---

[1] F. A. Hayek, *The Constitution of Liberty* (Chicago: University of Chicago Press, 1960), 332–333. For a similar pronouncement, see Hayek, *The Road to Serfdom*, 87.

to get to work, children being able to get to school, goods being transported, and potentially from our military being able to use the roads to get in position to fend off an attack. So, even if there is one set of beneficiaries a private company could charge for its services in road construction, the true set of beneficiaries of a good road system goes far beyond those who are being charged. (I'll also mention one other point specific to roads: if the road in front of my house were privately owned, and the owner charged me a toll every time I used it, then the owner of the road would be in a position to suddenly raise the toll to extremely high levels, either forcing me to pay or effectively locking me in my house, unless I can fly out by helicopter. It would be an extreme case of a monopoly, on which topic, see the next chapter.)

Hayek's basic point is true for many public goods: the only feasible way to charge individuals for the service in a free market setting would mean charging only a proper subset of those who would actually benefit from the service. That by itself is perhaps not an insurmountable challenge; we could privatize those things anyway, hoping that it would all more or less work out in the end. But this feature of paying for public goods gives rise to a problem. I'll attempt to illustrate this with an artificial and abstract example, and then apply the points back to situations from real life.

For purposes of this example, we will operate with the convenient fiction that there is some sort of unit by means of which we can measure human well-being, which we call *utiles*, and we will assume that for people of moderate means having an extra dollar is approximately equivalent to having an extra utile. To keep things simple, let's suppose we are dealing with a town of 100 people. There is some service, S, and we will assume the following about it:

Service S

It costs $1,000 to provide S.
Those using it directly get 18 utiles of benefit.
Those who don't use it directly get 12 utiles of benefit.
50 people would use it directly
50 people would benefit indirectly
Thus, the average benefit of S would be 15 utiles per person

So there is a cumulative increase of 1,500 utiles (15 per person multiplied by the 100 people)—a good deal for the townspeople, since they paid $1,000 cumulatively, and we have stipulated that a dollar of purchasing power is generally worth 1 utile. So we would have this:

Scenario 1: S as a public good.
Payers: each of the 100 townspeople
Price paid per payer: $10
Average utiles gained: 15
Net gain in utiles: 500

Now suppose that the town decides to privatize S. S is one of the services of which Hayek seems to speak: there are the 50 direct users, and they could be conveniently charged a point-of-service fee, but there are also the other 50 who indirectly benefit. The cost of the overall service was $1,000, so to make it profitable, the private company would need to charge each of the 50 direct users $20 just to break even. So the direct users would pay $20 each, and would gain the same 18 utiles as in Scenario 1. The other half of the town that enjoys S only indirectly would not have to pay and would get 12 utiles per person. This would yield the following:

Scenario 2: S is privatized.
Payers: 50 direct users.
Price paid per payer: $20
Utiles gained per direct user: 18
Utiles gained per indirect user: 12
Net gain in utiles: 500

There would still be a net gain of 500 utiles: $1,000 in total would be paid (costing 1,000 utiles), but the 50 direct users would gain 18 utiles each, for a total of 900 utiles, and the 50 indirect users would gain 12 utiles each, for a total of 600 utiles; so we would still have 1,500 utiles, which would be 500 more than the 1,000 lost because of the payments.

Both the public and private scenario thus have the same gain in utiles, and it looks like it should work to privatize S. However, there is a catch: note that the 50 direct users are now forced to pay $20, but they only get 18 utiles in return. It's not worth it to them. So, being economically rational agents under capitalism, they will stop using S and stop paying for it. And S will just disappear. So instead of Scenario 2, we will soon have this:

Scenario 3: After S is privatized.
Payers: nobody
Price paid: $0
Price paid per payer: $0
Utiles gained per direct user: 0
Utiles gained per indirect user: 0
Net gain in utiles: 0

Although it first seemed that privatizing S did no harm, once the direct users realize that they are not receiving enough well-being to compensate for the money they are paying, they will stop using the service. After all, they would, under Scenario 2, lose 2 utiles per person, since they would pay $20 to get a benefit of 18 utiles. But once they stop paying for S, the private company will naturally stop providing it, and thus the indirect users will lose the 12 utiles they would have gotten from S. So, the net effect of privatizing S is that there will be a loss of 500 utiles in comparison with public provision of S.

The fundamental reason that it didn't work to privatize S was that the benefits of S were diffused throughout the community, but only a subset of the community could be billed to pay for S at the point of service. Of course, not all economic transactions are diffuse in this way. To return to my favorite beer, if I go to the beverage store and buy a six-pack of Rothaus Pils, then unless someone else in my household drinks some or I give one to a friend, I am the only one who will appreciate the Tettnang and Hallertau hops in the beer I purchased. Even in this case, there could be minor benefits to others: insofar as being able to find my favorite beer makes me a happier person in general, that benefits others around me, and might even make me more productive for my employer. (On the other hand, if I were to drink the entire six-pack in one evening, I might not be as productive the next day, let alone if I were to drink the six-pack when I am supposed to be at work. Worries about systematic abuse of alcohol would lead to thinking of even individual purchases of alcohol as being economic decisions whose costs and benefits involve everyone, but I'll leave that aside.)

I don't think there is a way to draw a sharp line dividing economic transactions between these two extremes, individual and diffuse:

Individual: Transactions where an identifiable purchaser is the exclusive beneficiary.

Diffuse: Transactions where the benefit is spread equally throughout the people living in a region.

What our abstract example shows is that for some goods or services where the benefit is sufficiently diffuse, then if we make decisions about that good or service under a free market we will actually lower overall utility or well-being. For such goods or services, the conclusion of the *Better Incentives* and *Better Information* arguments will be false: if we treat this good as an economic decision made under free markets, it will not turn out to be *better for all*. The argument fails for goods like these because premise (3) in both arguments is false: under a privatized market approach, we would have a case where each person makes economic decisions that are *better for them*, but this does not add up to a situation where the decisions are cumulatively *better for all*. For such goods or services, we will all be better off if we treat them as public goods—controlled and paid for collectively and democratically.

Applications

To which goods and services does this line of reasoning apply? Another area that Hayek mentions as a public good is sanitation. My town collects trash and recycling each week; in my neighborhood the trucks come by on Wednesdays. Why not let this service be provided by a "competitive enterprise"? It seems that it would not be difficult: if the town stopped collecting garbage, private companies might appear and offer to take my garbage away for a fee. On the face of things, this would seem to be a matter of a private economic transaction in which it is possible "to charge the individual beneficiary," since everyone produces garbage and is thus a direct user of the service by which it is taken away and put in a landfill (and some of it hopefully recycled).

But even with trash collection, I think the benefits are also diffuse in the sense defined above. Suppose we made trash collection entirely private, and that my next-door neighbor decides it isn't worth it to her to have her trash picked up weekly; she instead finds some cut-rate operation that would come by and get her trash once every few months, and in the meantime she lets it pile up in her backyard. Her trash becomes an eyesore for everyone in the neighborhood and, especially in the summer, does not smell so good. For whatever reason, she doesn't mind too much (perhaps she has anosmia—a word I first learned during the coronavirus pandemic), and it is worth it to her to save the money.

What this hypothetical shows: even though my neighbor could be charged at point of service for the removal of her trash every week, she is by no means the only beneficiary of her trash being removed. It would only take a few people in a neighborhood deciding to pile up their trash in their yard before the entire neighborhood would smell and look like a landfill, perhaps complete with rats and other critters that would be attracted to the garbage. And once a few started doing it, and the neighborhood already stank to high heaven, there would be less reason for the rest of us to pay for the more expensive weekly trash collection. Thus, if we made trash collection into a service handled by the free market, then we could easily once again have a situation in which each person acting in their own best interest resulted in a situation that was much worse for everyone. This means that premise (3) of *Better Incentives* and *Better Information* will also be false for this sort of service.

One area that Hayek does not mention is education. As things now stand in Western countries, there are publicly owned and operated schools that educate all children, and the schools are typically funded by tax dollars paid by everyone, not by a fee for those using the schools. Of course, there are also private schools, but in the United States and the United Kingdom, these are typically nonprofit, often associated with churches; indeed, the United Kingdom does not allow for-profit primary and secondary schools. In principle, we could leave education of children to the free market, having enterprising individuals start for-profit schools, charging each child a fee. Why don't we do this? By charging the students for the service, it might seem that this would be an economic transaction in which the exclusive beneficiary of the product receives the bill.

However, it is not so simple. Suppose that Kerry is six years old and eligible to start at the local for-profit primary school. Kerry will indeed be the *primary* beneficiary of the value of receiving an education, but she is rather unlikely to have much money herself; moreover, unless she is a very exceptional six-year-old, she is probably not the most rational consumer, ready to plan the purchase of 12 years of education. So, right away, rather than the transaction being one where the consumer who pays is the one who benefits, with education we would need to rely on the kindness of Kerry's parents to pay the price of an education in a for-profit school. That might not trouble the die-hard capitalist, for they sometimes like to think of nuclear families (by which they mean: dad, mom, and kids) as the *unit* in capitalist economic transactions.[2] (Seeing the traditional nuclear family as the economic unit has another great advantage for the capitalist: they can completely ignore all the labor involved in raising the next generation of kids, labor mostly provided by women. By hiding that inside a family considered as an economic unit, they can pretend that it is not "real" labor where any talk of compensation should arise. "Women's work" just becomes something internal to the workings of the economic unit, no more worthy of compensation than is my stomach for its admirable job of digesting my food while I work and make money. Many people tend to miss how dehumanizing it is to put care work inside the home on that model.)

But even if we grant the capitalist the fiction that families are the independent unit rather than people, it is far from true that Kerry and her parents are the only ones who will benefit from her education. When Larry Page is hiring people to work for Google, he does not need to teach his new employees to read, write, and do basic arithmetic. If he hires Kerry, he benefits from her already having the skills she learned in school, but he won't directly pay the schools for that product. In general, pretty much everyone benefits from the fact that we have an educated electorate and workforce. Education is not just some perk that we give to families with children. Just as I don't want to live in a neighborhood where many people decide to pile up their trash or burn it in their yards, I don't want to live in a community where many voters are simply uneducated and, moreover, incapable of doing the work that society needs to function.

That is to say, the benefits of education are likewise diffuse—many people benefit beyond those who could be expected to pay for it at point of service. This leads to all kinds of dire possibilities if we were to treat education merely as a free market good. First, some significant number of parents might decide not to pay the price that the for-profit educational institutions would decide to charge for their child—perhaps they simply can't afford it, or perhaps they think they have better uses for the money (or they might pay for the educations of their sons over their daughters as happens in some countries where school fees are high and public support for education is low). Thus we could end up in a situation where we have a substantial portion of the electorate and workforce that has no basic education. Second, especially in smaller towns or rural areas, it might not seem profitable to anyone to set

---

[2] See, for example, Milton Friedman, *Capitalism and Freedom* (Chicago: University of Chicago Press, 1962), 193: "There are approximately 57 million consumer units (unattached individuals and families) in the United States."

up a school and charge the residents; it might well be that the profit could only come with the economies of scale provided by having enough willing customers (i.e., students) in each grade. Third, precisely because education might require such economies of scale, then even if a for-profit educational operation showed up in a small town, it might be the only one—giving it an effective monopoly on education in the area. On the problems with monopolies, see the next chapter. Finally, in an era of increasing online learning and automation, you could imagine a world in which poorer children get only virtual schooling while the kids of wealthier parents get actual teachers in actual classrooms.

I have been discussing primary and secondary education, but I think that some of the same points would apply to college education. A college education can, in principle, be paid for at the point of service by the person who will *primarily* benefit from it, namely the student. A prospective college student is likely to be an adult (or nearly so, depending on one's age criterion for adulthood and depending on when one starts college), and thus might be presumed to be rational consumer, unlike the primary or secondary school pupil. Nonetheless, we might still see the benefits of tertiary education as diffuse as well. Prospective employers benefit from having a college-educated workforce, and we might think all of us benefit from being in a society with many people who are educated beyond the secondary level, particularly if these people train in critical fields like medicine, engineering, science, and other fields where advanced levels of education fuel innovation and improvements in overall quality of life for everyone. It is also worth noting that, although the prospective college student can be billed at point of service, they are very unlikely to have the resources necessary to pay for the education; in practice, colleges will again rely on parents to pay the bills. There are, of course, publicly run educational institutions in the United States and Europe already, but, particularly in the United States, publicly run universities still demand large payments from the students. If tertiary education is, as I have suggested, a diffuse good, then the cost should arguably be picked up collectively and tuition for students should be minimal (as it is in most other advanced capitalist countries).

How many other services have the right sort of diffuse benefit that makes them less practical for a free market? This is an empirical question. But I think that once we understand *why* these goods and services should be public, and *why* the *Better Incentives* and *Better Information* arguments fail for these goods and services, then I think we can see that they might well extend beyond what we already do widely acknowledge as public goods. That is to say, once we understand Hayek's own reason for saying that not everything will be better under a capitalist system, I think we will see that the exceptions are broader than he and Friedman think.

Hayek himself mentioned roads, but I think that, by pretty much the same set of considerations, we could include a good system of public transportation. If it is good for all of us to have an adequate system of roads, even for those who drive rarely or not at all, then it is likely to be also good for all of us to have a good system of public transportation, even for those who rarely use it. How does public transportation benefit you if you don't plan to use it? Well, if nothing else, you will have less automobile traffic to deal with if more of your fellow citizens are taking the subway or buses. If you take any pleasure in breathing cleaner air or having the climate less impacted by the greenhouse gas emissions from cars, then you benefit from others of us taking public transportation. If many people are getting to work or shopping or dining by means of public transportation, then that is benefiting the economy and all of us, including you. Finally, you might someday find yourself in a situation in which you do want to use public transportation, and it can't just be conjured up the moment you decide it would be useful to you. Note what this suggests: since the benefits of public transportation are diffuse, we should provide public transportation and *not* aim to make it pay for itself through point-of-service purchases; there should be no reason to expect fees by direct users to cover the cost.

Somewhat surprisingly, since he is a conservative hero, Hayek includes "health services" as among the public goods where "the desirability of government action can hardly be questioned." Hayek is not explicit about what he would include under health services, but I think we can make an argument for the claim that some reasonable degree of healthcare, especially of the preventative version, is not just a nice thing for government to provide to its citizens but is a service where the benefit is diffuse. On the face of things, it might seem otherwise: the person who pays for a doctor's services or for a pharmacist's drugs is surely the primary beneficiary. But, again, it is not so simple. If we treat healthcare as another free market good, then, unless we have a level of redistribution that would already tend strongly in the socialist direction, there will be people who cannot easily afford routine doctor's visits either for preventative care or when they start to feel ill, or they might not be able to easily afford the medicine that they need. How does this affect the rest of us? First, if they do not seek medical help but instead just attempt to power on through work, then they might infect others of us. As we know from having lived through the coronavirus pandemic, that can be quite serious indeed. In countries where there is little preventative care, many people also wait until they are seriously ill before they go to the hospital, usually to the emergency room. Emergency care for seriously ill people is very expensive, and if the patients have no insurance and cannot pay for their care, the cost of that care is passed on to the rest of us, either through higher prices for medical services or through higher insurance premiums. In addition, if a person avoids medical care because of the expense, and then falls seriously ill when this could have been avoided, this means that they will miss work. If they don't have paid sick leave, then this is terrible for them; but it is also bad for us, for we lose the benefits of their economic activity. Finally, if women must stay home to provide unpaid nursing services for their sick children, husbands, or parents, we also lose the benefits of their formal economic activity in the labor force (this is what happened during the coronavirus pandemic when labor shortages at least partially reflected women's disproportioned withdrawal from the workforce). The point is this: just as we all benefit from having an educated electorate and workforce, there are general benefits to all of us from having a healthy population.

Those conservatives in the United States who see government-provided universal healthcare as creeping socialism do have a point. It would be a case of moving something away from the free market model and toward a socialistic model of democratic ownership and control. But it would be justified on precisely the same grounds on which even most arch-conservatives, including F. A. Hayek himself, will accept when it comes to public goods like education or sanitation.

Key Takeaways

- Capitalists argue that free markets give people better incentives to make better economic decisions for themselves, and that this ultimately benefits us all.
- However, the capitalist argument in favor of markets breaks down for goods and services where the benefit is *diffuse*—where the benefit goes well beyond the person who might be able to be made to pay for it at point of service.

- Most capitalists acknowledge these areas where the market fails, but they tend to underestimate the extent of such cases.
- I don't suspect that either of my actual next-door neighbors would ever let trash pile up in their backyards. Concerning a few others in my neighborhood, I'm not so sure.

11
Market Failures II: Monopolies and Monopsonies

Monopolies

A monopoly exists when there is effectively only one seller of a given good or service within a given market. Such situations can easily result in a circumstance in which premise (3) of the capitalist arguments in *Better Information* and *Better Incentives* is false: each person acting in their own best interest will not result in a situation which is better for all. I'll illustrate with a hypothetical example.

Suppose that there is a community of 1,000 people, and within the community there are four suppliers of widgets. Widgets are, we will stipulate, a good thing; they bring a certain amount of happiness and well-being to each consumer who has one. With good capitalist competition, the price of the widgets is reasonable, and all 1,000 people buy a widget from one of the four suppliers. The suppliers sell the widgets at $10 each, and make a reasonable profit of $1 per widget. Thus everyone has a widget, and the four suppliers together take in $1,000.

But then the suppliers decide to merge into one company, which they call Widgorama. Widgorama is now the only source of widgets to the town. Widgorama immediately jacks up the price fourfold to $40. There is a great cry of outrage. The majority of the people decide that either they cannot afford the widgets at this price, or that the price is simply so high that the widgets aren't worth it anymore. But some people, let us say 250 out of the total 1000, decide to buy the widgets anyway. (As I write this, a new iPhone costs about $1,000. Suppose all the smartphone manufacturers merged into one company and began to charge $4,000 for a smartphone. If your current phone dies, do you pay the inflated price?) Widgorama loses 750 sales, but its profit margin has skyrocketed from $1 per widget to $31 per widget. By selling only 250 widgets, its overall profit nonetheless jumps from $1,000 to over

Socialism. Scott R. Sehon, Oxford University Press. © Oxford University Press 2024.
DOI: 10.1093/oso/9780197753330.003.0011

$7,500. What a great business move for them! They have, just as Friedman advocates, acted in their own self-interest and have made a killing.

However, although the owners of Widgorama are now happier (since they have more money), there are a lot of people who are less happy in this scenario than they were under the original scenario: namely *all* of the consumers. Three-quarters of the people now no longer have the widgets that brought them some happiness and well-being, and even the 250 people who do still have widgets have parted with $30 more than they would have otherwise to get them. (Well, a few of those 250 might actually feel somewhat happier, for now widgets have become a symbol of wealth, only possessed by a few; for those who like gloating over the misfortune of others, perhaps they think that paying the extra $30 for a widget was worth it.) We can easily imagine that the overall happiness in the town is now lower than it was before the grand merger: the owners of Widgorama are happier, but this may be more than counterbalanced by the unhappiness of the other people in the town.

Note that even after Widgorama formed and started charging outrageously high prices, we still had a free market, in the baseball-card-trading sense: each transaction whereby a widget was sold was done freely on the part of both the seller and the buyer, and each presumably feels that they are better off after the transaction than they were before. After all, nobody was *forced* to pay $40 for a widget; each consumer who chose to do so must have thought that their life would be better with the widget and without the $40 than it was before, when they had no widget but had the extra $40 in their wallet. We may assume that each person is still making a rational choice, acting intelligently in their self-interest. The point of the example is to show that each person acting in this way need not add up to a situation in which human well-being is maximized. True, after each transaction with Widgorama, human well-being went up a little bit over what it was immediately before (assuming that nobody made a stupid choice and regretted their purchase). But we know that human well-being would be higher overall in a different scenario in which the price of widgets been lower and profits smaller.

If we move from the hypothetical widgets to an essential good or service, then the negative effect of monopolies on overall happiness will be even more obvious. If there is only one provider of electric power where I live, and if they start charging outrageous prices, then my options are pretty bleak. I can either pay the price, try to do without electricity, or try to sell my house and move somewhere else. The power company would have me over a barrel; at some point, if their prices are too high, I will indeed give up electricity or move, but those actions come at such a high cost to me that I would rather pay their high prices until they get absurdly high. The owners of the power company would be acting in an economically rational way by setting the price so as to maximize revenue for the company—probably just at that level where most customers agree to pay the wildly inflated price, while a few others decide either to move or do without commercially provided electricity (by buying solar panels, windmills, or some other technology). The net effect: the owners will become quite rich and will enjoy to some extent the extra dollars. But they will be making many other people much less happy. So this will be a case where each person acting in an economically rational way nonetheless decreases overall well-being. (A situation like this actually happened in some rural parts of Eastern Europe after the fall of communism when the previously state-owned grid was privatized to monopolistic firms. A popular joke went: "Question: What did people use to light their houses before they used candles? Answer: Electricity.")

Even the most ardent capitalists recognize that at least some monopolies are a bad thing; Friedman, for example, supports use of antitrust laws to stop businesses from creating monopolies via collusion.[1] This is an important acknowledgment, for it means that even in the eyes of someone like Milton Friedman, there is nothing *sacred* about the freeness of the market. A completely free market would, after all, presumably mean that each person or business is free to make agreements and contracts with anyone they choose; there would be no law against so-called collusion, for such collusion is just a freely made agreement between two or more companies. Instead, it seems that even on Friedman's view, we let individuals and companies in the market act free of any form of collective control *to the extent* that this is for the benefit of everyone, rather than saying that there are rights in the trump-card sense involved here.

Pure monopolies, where a number of consumers can buy a given good or service through only one provider, are relatively rare; but it is not infrequently the case for utility companies (or cable/broadband providers in the United States). For this reason, utilities, when privately owned, are typically regulated, and price increases often need to go through some regulatory approval process. That might be enough to prevent the worst abuses of their monopolistic power, but if the regulatory board is stocked with people who

[1] Friedman, *Capitalism and Freedom*, 131.

formerly worked in the industry and might hope to work there again, then we might wonder how effective this is. Moreover, to the extent that we regulate the prices such a utility can charge, we thereby lose a big part of the advantage that free markets were supposed to provide to everyone. Hayek claimed that, through the magic of prices in a market, economic actors would have better information than if there is central planning. That alleged advantage is completely gone if there is a monopoly, regulated or otherwise. Similarly with Friedman's *Better Incentives* argument: the central idea was that economic actors make better decisions when they have a direct financial stake; but if the final price the utility company can charge is set through a regulatory process, then crucial actors in that field (the regulators) do not have a direct financial stake. If, within a given realm of business, the motivation for private control has already been undone, then you have to wonder what further advantage there is for having a private utility company whose prices are subject to public control. Why not just have collective control of the process to begin with? (More on utilities in chapter 12.)

Finally, although pure monopolies may be rare, the negative effects of monopolistic considerations can arise far more often. If there are only a small number of providers of a good or service within a market area, then they will realize that it is in each of their economic interest not to undercut the other's prices and to effectively act as one company with a pure monopoly. In a famous line from Adam Smith that Friedman quotes, Smith says, "People of the same trade seldom meet together, even for merriment and diversion, but the conversation ends in a conspiracy against the public, or in some contrivance to raise prices."[2]

If there is collusion between the only two makers of widgets, and if it is quite easy for another company to start making widgets, then price collusion will be unstable. That's what the capitalist counts on: they hope that monopolies will be unstable and thus rare. But there are a number of factors that make this hope seem a bit naive. First, if making widgets requires a huge infrastructure to get started (think of the utilities again, and the cost of laying your own power lines or water pipes), then it may be far less practical for another company to jump in. Second, Widgorama might just buy any start-up company that starts to compete successfully or artificially lower its prices so that the start-up cannot make a profit and will be run out of business—doing

---

[2] The quote is from *The Wealth of Nations*, Book I, Chapter X. Friedman quotes it in *Capitalism and Freedom*, 131.

so will be economically rational for Widgorama, and they may be in a position to make it economically rational for the owner of the start-up to accept the buyout. But once the start-up is gone, Widgorama just increases its prices again. Third, Widgorama might use other strategies to block the start-up. For example, it might threaten the suppliers of materials necessary to make widgets: "If you sell anything to the start-up, we won't buy anything from you!" Or, fourth, the new start-up maker of widgets might—either with an explicit agreement with Widgorama or not—charge the same artificially high price as does Widgorama.

What this means: wherever monopolistic power even begins to threaten, then the positive arguments for the benefits of the free market fall apart. Here was Hayek's argument again:

Better Information 2.0

(1) To the extent that economic decisions are made under free markets rather than under democratic control, more information is available and used in making those decisions. [P]
(2) To the extent that more information is available and used in making decisions, the better the decisions will be for the person making the decision. [P]
(3) To the extent that each person makes economic decisions that are *better for them*, the decisions will cumulatively be *better for all*. [P]
(4) To the extent that economic decisions are made under free markets rather than under democratic control, the *better for all* the decisions will be. [1,2,3]

The mechanism of prices, where there are multiple competitors, arguably does provide a huge amount of information that would be difficult for democratically elected planners to gain, even if we do make the assumption that the alternative to free markets is central planning. But in a monopoly situation, prices are artificial and don't give the same kind of information. So premise (1) of *Better Information* is false under such circumstances. The reasoning behind the *Better Incentives* argument also collapses. The first premise of that argument, that free markets mean that each person making an economic decision has a direct financial stake, would still be true. but, like *Better Information*, the *Better Incentives* argument relied on premise (3), according to which what is best for each individual (under those circumstances) gives us the best result overall. We've seen that this will not be true under circumstances where there is a monopoly or near monopoly.

Where Shopping Is Impractical

When one company has a monopoly on a particular good, shopping—in the sense of comparing multiple offers for price and quality—is simply impossible, for there is only one source of the good or service in question. But there can be many circumstances far short of a pure monopoly where shopping is quite difficult or impractical, and these can have the same net effect as a monopoly: in such circumstances, sellers and buyers can do what is individually rational for them, but the net result can be far less than optimal for human well-being generally. Monopolies are just the degenerate, limit case of difficult shopping circumstances.

To illustrate, let's go back to the example from the last chapter of me trading baseball cards with my friend Steve. I know that Steve really wants my George Brett card, so imagine that I offer him this deal: "I'll give you this George Brett card plus three other cards, and in return you will give me the cards that I have on this list," I say, gesturing at a piece of paper.

Steve, being a rational kid and baseball card collector will ask, "What are the other three cards you are offering? And can I see that list of the cards of mine you are asking for in return?" However, suppose that I simply refused to show him the other three cards or the list, or suppose that time was short. Suppose I knew that he had to get home very soon, lest his parents ground him, and that for some reason Steve could be talked into making trades like this, where I knew all of the information, and he only knew a little bit of it. If that was a regular pattern, and if all I cared about was my baseball card collection rather than any friendship with Steve (if, that is to follow Friedman, I was not so much motivated by human kindness but only by "the much stronger and more dependable spur of self-interest"), then I would be motivated to choose the other three cards and write up the list so that it was substantially to my advantage. And if, for some reason, I am in a position to make trades like that with all sorts of other collectors, then I will be happy with my collection, but they might be substantially unhappy after they learn what was really in the trade.

Of course, that's just a strange and silly hypothetical; nothing could really work like that in the free market, could it?

Let me switch to a different story, a true one this time. Shirley, the mother of a friend of mine, was experiencing significant chest pain. Her husband took her to the local ER. After some tests, the doctor said, "I think you need an emergency angioplasty. We need to take you into surgery right now."

Shirley looked at the doctor. "I want a second opinion." Then she turned to her husband and asked, "What do you think?"

He said, "I think we should do it."

Shirley turned back to the doctor and said, "Okay, let's go!"

For those who knew Shirley, it came as no surprise that she could make a joke, and such a good one, even at a time like that. But my point is merely that it was, of course, a joke. Even calling in another cardiologist from the same hospital to give a second opinion would have cost valuable time and perhaps cost her life. Needless to say, she likewise did not have time to ask how much the procedure would cost and then to compare costs with other hospitals in town, if there were any, which there weren't.

Seeking medical care, especially in an emergency, is not like shopping for shoes. (I have heard tell of people who report clothes-shopping emergencies, but I trust that they are speaking figuratively, or that at least the stakes in the "emergency" were not as high as they were for Shirley in the ER.) I have yet to see a price list at my doctor's office or in a hospital. If you are like me, you pretty much do what your doctor advises, at least in terms of tests and procedures (physician-suggested lifestyle recommendations can be less expensive but not always as easy to follow).

In other words, seeking medical care, when viewed as a commercial transaction, is often quite a bit like me giving my George Brett card to Steve, where I also give him a couple of other cards that he doesn't see in advance, and he gives me 10 of his cards, but he doesn't know which ones until after the trade is complete. Shopping for medical care in the United States is difficult for the consumer: time is often short, there may be limited options in the area, and you usually don't even know how much things will cost. That is to say, the fundamental premise behind Hayek's *Better Information* argument is completely false in these circumstances: a free market for healthcare does *not* lead to greater information, for circumstances often leave consumers no real opportunity to consider information based on prices, even if they are given such information. In the baseball card situation, that meant that for me, given that I had all the information about the cards, it was in my interest to arrange the trade quite unfairly to Steve. Similarly in the medical case: if healthcare is done on the free market, then the incentive is for the healthcare industry to charge much more than it would be able to get away with if it were the case that shopping for medical care were more practical. To the extent that providers follow Friedman and act "on the dependable spur of self-interest," they will enrich themselves, but at the expense of the rest of us. We, like Shirley, will act as rationally as possible, and so will they; but the common good on the whole will not be served. This means that circumstances like this will be places where the capitalist has lost any argument they had for the claim that better incentives will lead to greater happiness overall.

For those of us in the United States lucky enough to have health insurance, immediate price tags on medical services may not be as much of a shopping issue: so long as our insurance covers the procedure, then, for us, it is a matter of deductibles, out-of-pocket limits for the year, and so on. It would still be relevant to see the price list in many cases, but less so than for those without insurance. But this does not change the fundamental situation, for it is often next to impossible to do any serious shopping for health insurance policies. Like many Americans, I get my health insurance through my employer; I have a couple of substantial options and a few minor choices to make each year in that respect, but, basically speaking, I am stuck with the health insurance that my employer offers. I could pay for my own, but that would be enormously more expensive. I could try to switch jobs if I was unhappy with the health insurance, but that is a highly impractical option (see the section below on monopsony and labor). I might hope that my employer at least did careful due diligence when purchasing health insurance plans to cover all its employees. But note that this situation too means that the crucial premise in Friedman's argument is false, for the administrative officials in charge of finding health insurance plans at my institution are acting on the collective behalf of numerous employees, rather than having a direct financial stake in the outcome.

Healthcare and health insurance provide obvious examples of where shopping is difficult, and where the alleged benefits of a free market approach disappear. This is in addition to the reason provided in the last chapter: having a healthy population is a diffuse good, one whose benefits are spread beyond the person who can be made to pay at point of service, and this is also a ground for making healthcare a public good, subject to democratic control. But there are other areas where shopping is, or would be, quite difficult without substantial collective regulation of the economy. In some of these areas, even most typical conservatives accept the need for these limitations on the free market.

As a prime example, consider shopping for a car and imagine that this decision was in a market free from government regulation of any sort. Perhaps the automobile manufacturer would offer you the option, at an extra price, of having seatbelts installed; perhaps it would offer airbags, and perhaps even make sure that the airbags are truly functional in a way that would save your life in an accident. Perhaps the car would have what is known as a "safety cage" and a good crumple zone. But I would hardly be able to inspect the car myself and ascertain whether the manufacturer is telling the truth and has done a good job of installing such things. Even if the car dealer was willing and honest enough to lay out a long list of safety devices that I could decide to purchase or not, and give the prices, I would have a tough time doing those calculations. I already find shopping for a car to be difficult, but it would be much, much more difficult if we did not have collectively decided regulations on automobile safety, and collectively determined standards and tests for things like gas mileage. In theory, we could leave all of that to a purely free market; we might hope that some manufacturers would develop good reputations, and maybe private organizations would arise that would, for a fee, give you what they claimed to be reliable information about the various safety offerings on various makes of automobile. At best, though, automobile shopping would become a hideously complicated affair, and at worst, the manufacturers would take full advantage of the fact that they have much more knowledge and control of the situation than you do. It would not be unlike my strangely concocted baseball card trade with Steve. The owners of car companies would likely make some more money under such a situation, but the rest of us would suffer. If nothing else, we would spend way more time thoroughly investigating any automobile purchase (and that would be time not spent doing things we might like better), but we would also be much more likely to have less-safe automobiles.

We could make similar points about several other industries and products. Shopping is often difficult and impractical, and sellers often have way more information than buyers do—meaning the decentralized information celebrated by Hayek is distributed in a one-sided way that undermines the advantage of the free market. Though it comes in degrees, in a free market we are often like Steve, who really wants the George Brett card but is not in a position to understand the full nature of the trade. In such cases, the capitalist argument about incentives likewise fails: each person doing what is in their economic self-interest is unlikely to result in maximizing overall human well-being.

Monopsony and Labor

As noted above, even most capitalists are uncomfortable with allowing monopolies to develop through the free market. *Monopsony* is a less commonly used concept. Whereas a monopoly exists when there is only one seller of a particular product, monopsony means the existence of only one *buyer*. For a typical good or service, being the only buyer of a thing would not give you any real advantage. If there is suddenly only one person who wants to buy wooden pencils, then that is a bit of a problem for companies that have produced and are sitting on a large stock of wooden pencils; they can either sell the pencils to that person at whatever price she offers, or they can throw them away. If that is the only product that a company has to sell, then their income is dependent on the one person who wants to buy them and how much she is willing to pay. But in the long run there would be little problem here for the market: those companies would stop making pencils and make other things instead.

However, under capitalism, many people have one and only one thing available to sell: their labor. In fact, it is built into the very nature of the situation that, at least at some point in your life, that will be the only thing you have to sell; unless you have inherited money or goods from your parents (or someone has given you some), you couldn't possibly own anything to sell, and you wouldn't have any raw materials with which to make anything on your own. If you can sell your labor effectively, then perhaps you can build up enough capital to be able to produce things on your own and sell something other than your labor. Certainly there are success stories like that, but I think it is fair to say that the majority of us, for the majority of our lives, have basically only our labor to sell. This makes monopsonies much more important in the case of labor than in the case of pencils.

I argued above that under conditions of monopoly, the supposed advantage of decentralized information via prices disappears, and that premise (3) of both *Better Information* and *Better Incentives* is false: everyone acting in their own economic self-interest does *not* generalize into everything being better on the whole. The same points apply in reverse to a monopsony on labor. If, within a given market, there is only one employer, then they are able to offer to buy labor at very low prices, for those selling their labor *must* sell it to someone, and they will have no other option. In the purest case of a monopsony on labor, the one employer would have every reason to offer wages that are just high enough for the workers to manage to survive and come back to work the next day, and this would be largely irrespective of how much money the employer profited by selling widgets that the workers made (a Marxist point). This will clearly be bad for human well-being overall: the employer might add to her wealth, but at the cost of keeping the entire market of available laborers in a miserable state.

Of course, the capitalist will reply that monopsonies don't exist: there are many employers out there. If you don't like the price that your employer is willing to offer for your labor, you can offer it to another employer. The market will take care of everything. But we also know that it is, to say the least, far more complicated than that. Suppose you live in a small town or rural area. As Anne Case and Angus Deaton write: "The most obvious place where employers might be able to pay less than market wages is in rural areas where there may be little work of any kind, perhaps only at a fast-food restaurant, a chicken-processing plant, or a state prison. Schoolteachers or nurses in rural areas or small towns may find themselves in a similar position."[3]

Workers might move away if they don't like the options for selling their labor where they currently live, but that also involves substantial costs, both of the financial and nonfinancial sort. If you have a home, it might be hard to sell, and obtaining housing at a new location might be yet more costly. You might not want to leave your family and friends, not to mention the possibility that your spouse might not be keen on leaving, especially if they have a job in town.

Even apart from those who hope to sell their labor in a rural area, selling one's labor can be difficult for other reasons. It is not as if we each just have a certain supply of this thing called "labor" which is perfectly fungible. Suppose you are in your late 50s and have worked in one field most of your adult life; if you are laid off you might find that very few employers seem to be interested in the skill set you have developed, not to mention that the companies that are hiring might prefer to hire younger workers.

All of this is to say that the effects of monopsony can be felt far from the pure case where there is literally one employer buying local labor at dirt cheap prices. There can be many circumstances in which employers clearly have the upper hand: they can do what is economically rational for them, namely offering very low wages, while the net effect on the overall well-being of humanity is much lower. Once again, the point is that in circumstances

---

[3] Ann Case and Angus Deaton, *Deaths of Despair and the Future of Capitalism* (Princeton, NJ: Princeton University Press, 2020), 236.

like these, the relevant premises in *Better Information* and *Better Incentives* are false, and these arguments for why markets are better than collective control fail.

The power of monopsony threatens to become ever larger as more and more of our jobs are automated. To an ever-increasing extent, those who are buying labor in the marketplace can now get it from robots or other forms of automation, meaning that they make an initial purchase but then need to pay no wages whatsoever. This is not science fiction. Computer scientist Kai-Fu Lee predicts that within the next 15 to 20 years 40% of jobs worldwide will be replaced by automation—artificially intelligent technology in particular."[4] ChatGPT was released in November 2022, with other similar products soon following; such technologies raise even more concerns about lost jobs.[5] We might hope that replaced workers will find other jobs. After all, in 1800, over 30% of the workforce in England was in agriculture; today that figure is 1.2%,[6] but this does not mean that 29% of the workforce is now simply unemployed. For the most part, other jobs arose, jobs that people in 1800 would have scarcely been able to imagine. But note: that was a matter of 29% of the workforce gradually moving to other jobs over the course of 200 years, whereas we now face the prospect of 40% of jobs disappearing within a couple of decades.

If there is massive unemployment caused by automation, then that is another way of saying that there is a huge glut of labor on the market. In the free market of trading baseball cards, if there is a glut of Ed Kranepool cards—if all collectors already seem to have one or more card of this journeyman Mets first baseman—then Ed Kranepool cards become all but worthless. Nobody will give you much of anything for your Ed Kranepool card, for they already have more than they need. And if you only have Ed Kranepool cards to sell or trade, then you are pretty much out of luck; nobody is buying. And, by analogy, if you are living in a world where everything is determined by the market, and if there is a complete glut of the only

---

[4] Scott Pelley, "Facial and Emotional Recognition; How One Man Is Advancing Artificial Intelligence," CBS News, January 13, 2019, https://www.cbsnews.com/news/60-minutes-ai-facial-and-emotional-recognition-how-one-man-is-advancing-artificial-intelligence/.

[5] Megan Cerullo, "These Jobs Are Most Likely to Be Replaced by Chatbots Like ChatGPT," CBS News, February 1, 2023, https://www.cbsnews.com/news/chatgpt-artificial-intelligence-chatbot-jobs-most-likely-to-be-replaced/.

[6] Max Roser, "Employment in Agriculture," Our World in Data, https://ourworldindata.org/employment-in-agriculture.

thing you have to sell—your labor—then you will be pretty much out of luck. (Apologies to Ed Kranepool for the analogy; he was one of my favorite players when I was growing up.)

What sort of government (collective) solutions might help? The answers will vary with the specific circumstances. One might start with reasonable minimum wages and limitations on other ways employers have to exploit the position of those who have little leverage with which to bargain in a free market (such as forcing workers to sign noncompete clauses). We also might work to level the playing field in more ambitious ways. Often enough, a key difference between the position of an employer and a prospective laborer is that the laborer desperately needs the job: their survival, and the survival of their children, depends on them finding someone who will buy the only good they have to sell, their labor. By contrast, when Amazon is seeking to fill a position in one of its fulfillment warehouses, the survival of Jeff Bezos or his kids is most definitely not on the line. When one side of a bargaining situation is far more desperate, then that gives a distinct advantage to the other side, the sort of unfair advantage that means that each person acting in their own self-interest is likely not to result in a situation in which human well-being overall is maximized. We could change that bargaining situation by making sure that we have an extremely good social safety net, such that prospective employees, like the prospective employer, are not worried that they will starve or lack healthcare for their kids if this particular negotiation does not go their way. This might be an argument for universal basic income, or at least universal healthcare and sufficient programs to alleviate poverty. Of course, there is also the possibility of going much further in the direction of collective ownership: if the government operates enough of the means of production themselves, they could, in principle, guarantee full employment by hiring those able and willing to work. That would mean that anyone seeking a job in the private market would not have their very survival at stake in the negotiation.

I'm not suggesting that any of these options is clearly correct, simple to implement, or would obviously be most effective. As I've said, this book is not the place for detailed considerations of specific policies that we might democratically adopt. Rather, the point is simply that we can see that there are broad swaths of the economy where we cannot expect market incentives alone to maximize human well-being, and especially in those areas, consideration of collective action seems warranted.

"Government Is Not the Solution"?

Even if one grants that monopolies and monopsonies pose problems for capitalist free markets, one might still be inclined to echo Ronald Reagan's sentiment that "government is not the solution." We would not want to immediately infer that merely because capitalism has a problem with situation X that socialism will do better with X.

Friedman, for example, grants that "The great danger to the consumer is monopoly" but goes on to add that the consumer's "most effective protection is free competition at home and free trade throughout the world."[7] He suggests that the solution to a monopoly developing in one country is allowing more competition globally. He adds, "A monopoly can seldom be established within a country without overt and covert government assistance in the form of a tariff or some other device. It is close to impossible to do so on a world scale."[8]

You might wonder about this prescription for avoiding the effects of monopoly or monopsony. Monopolies can function *locally* in a quite effective way. As we've seen with the case of utilities, in some cases what makes a local monopoly possible is locally constructed infrastructure. Officially allowing international utility companies to compete will not have an obvious effect on this. Not all goods and services can easily be provided on an international scale. With local monopsonies on labor, the point is even more clear: if there are a very limited number of employers in my area, then it is far from clear how more international free trade will provide any relief to workers stuck in underpaid jobs or laid off when the employer decides to outsource jobs. Perhaps the thought is that workers should always be ready to move to whatever country is now doing this sort of work for which they have been trained; but such uprooting comes at quite a cost to human well-being. Moreover, the circumstances noted above where shopping is impractical are not obviously solved by more free trade; in those cases, even where competition is possible, the consumer may not have the luxury of ascertaining all the information she needs to make a rational economic decision.

But even if Friedman's preferred solution to monopolies and monopsonies seems unlikely to be successful, one might still doubt the inference from "Markets don't work ideally here" to "We should have more collective control."

---

[7] Friedman and Friedman, *Free to Choose*, 226.
[8] Friedman and Friedman, *Free to Choose*, 53.

Jason Brennan echoes a popular thought when he says that "governments are often incompetent." He adds: "even when governments want to fix problems, there is no guarantee they will succeed. Libertarians worry that governments often make things worse, not better."[9]

To evaluate this worry, it is worth reviewing where things stand in the overall argumentative situation. We had the *Democracy Argument for Socialism*:

> *Democracy Argument for Socialism*
>
> (1) Human well-being is maximized by allowing those fully rational beings affected by a decision to have democratic control over the decision, unless there is special reason to think that there is a nondemocratic way of making this type of decision that is better for overall human well-being. [P]
> (2) There is no special reason to think that there is a nondemocratic way of making major economic decisions that is better for overall human well-being. [P]
> (3) Human well-being is maximized by allowing those fully rational beings affected by major economic decisions to have democratic control over them. [1,2]

This seemed plausible enough, but the capitalist claimed that there were strong reasons to doubt premise (2). Through the *Better Information* and *Better Incentives* arguments, the capitalist suggested that there were quite specific reasons that the market is superior to democratic decision-making in this area. But we have now seen that there is ample reason to say that those arguments fail. There are many circumstances in which decentralized information and the incentive of self-interest *might* produce better results for each participant in a given economic transaction, but where the overall result is far from ideal. Premise (3) of those argument is just not true:

(3) To the extent that each person makes economic decisions that are *better for them*, the decisions will cumulatively be *better for all*.

---

[9] Brennan, *Libertarianism*, 56.

So *Better Information* and *Better Incentives* are unsound arguments. But it was precisely those arguments that was supposed to provide the reason for thinking that premise (2) in the *Democracy Argument for Socialism* was false. So we might run the following quick argument:

> *No Special Reason*
>
> (1) If *Better Information* and *Better Incentives* are unsound, then there is no special reason to think that there is a nondemocratic way of making major economic decisions that is better for overall human well-being. [P]
> (2) *Better Information* and *Better Incentives* are unsound. [P]
> (3) There is no special reason to think that there is a nondemocratic way of making major economic decisions that is better for overall human well-being. [1,2]

The conclusion of *No Special Reason* just is premise (2) of the *Democracy Argument for Socialism*. With that premise newly defended, we might conclude that the latter argument is sound: human well-being is maximized by allowing those fully rational beings affected by major economic decisions to have democratic control over them.

Of course, the capitalist can still insist that even in cases where we can see that the market is far from ideal, government will be worse. But they have lost the *reasons* that they gave for making that claim. They might point to *other* reasons for distrusting government. One might suggest the famous dictum from Lord Acton: "Power tends to corrupt and absolute power corrupts absolutely." You could dig into that observation as the basis for a different argument for the superiority of markets over government, but you would at least need to note two things. First, even if Lord Acton's psychological observation is correct, it is not to be taken for granted that the only sort of power out there is that wielded by government. In a capitalist society, those who control large chunks of the means of production have a great deal of power, whether they are government officials or not. So if power corrupts those in government, we might conclude that power likewise corrupts those with large shares of the means of production. Second, we should at least note that this would point to a quite general reason to distrust government—that is, democratically made decisions. There would be no *more* reason to distrust democratically made *economic* decisions than there is reason to distrust democratically made decisions about other matters. What started as specific reasons to favor market mechanisms over democracy has devolved into an inchoate reason to doubt the goodness of any exercise of power, including governmental functions that capitalists usually do not question but also including the power exerted by those who control a disproportionate share of the means of production. We no longer have what we were promised: a specific argument against moving in a socialist direction.

Key Takeaways

- The capitalist arguments in favor of free markets (*Better Information* and *Better Incentives*) break down when monopolies arise and there is only one seller of particular goods or services.
- Even short of monopolies, there can be many situations in which shopping among different providers of the same good or service can be quite difficult or impractical. Healthcare is a prime example, but there are others as well. In such situations, a premise behind the capitalist arguments is false: economic decisions that are in the interest of each participant (as best they can determine under the circumstances) will not yield the situation that is best for overall well-being.
- A monopsony arises when there is only one buyer of a good and is particularly dangerous when there is just one buyer (in a given market setting) of the good of human labor. Here too the capitalist arguments for the superiority of markets fail.
- The capitalist might insist that government is not the solution even where markets fail. But this would then seem to be fueled only by a general skepticism about power, and they have undercut their specific reason for denying the *Democracy Argument for Socialism*.
- Ed Kranepool had a lifetime batting average of .261 over an 18-year career with the Mets; I have one of his baseball cards proudly displayed on a wall, near my Tom Seaver card.

12
Market Failures III: Neighborhood Effects and Climate Change

Negative Externalities and Neighborhood Effects

We have been exploring the *Better Information* and *Better Incentives* arguments for markets and capitalism, especially their share premise (3).

(3) To the extent that each person makes economic decisions that are *better for them*, the decisions will cumulatively be *better for all*. [P]

In many simple economic transactions, it is true that if the parties to the transaction act in their own self-interest, then this will be better for everyone, in accord with the Adam Smith's observation that if a transaction is purely voluntary, then both parties will benefit. For example, if I offer Myles $20 to mow my lawn, then, if this is a voluntary transaction and we are both being rational, I will benefit overall from having my lawn mowed (but having lost $20) and Myles will benefit overall from having the $20 (but having spent the time and effort mowing my lawn). Since Myles and I are the only parties to the transaction, if it benefits each of us, then it can seem reasonable that it will be better for everyone overall. And this is probably right for the lawnmowing case. To the extent that anyone else cares if Myles mows my lawn, they will probably benefit from it: my neighbors will have to put up with the noise of someone mowing the lawn, but they would probably prefer that to me letting my lawn become an overgrown jumble of weeds.

However, some economic transactions have costs that go well beyond the immediate participants. For example, suppose I next contract with Myles to build a shed on my property. I will pay him a sum much larger than $20, and he will provide the materials and the labor to create the shed. Both Myles and I presumably benefit from this transaction. However, this time other people are somewhat more affected. First, the construction process might be somewhat noisy and disruptive, and might constitute a bit of an eyesore for a couple of months for my immediate neighbors. Second, it might be that the large shed, once constructed, has long-lasting effects. For example, it might be that it will block the sun from my neighbor Susan's garden, and her garden will die. In this case, it might well be that the benefit to me (from having the shed) and the benefit to Myles (from having the money he was paid) quite outweighs the temporary harms to my neighbors from the construction process and even the longer-term harm to Susan; so it *might* still be a case where Myles and I making an economic transaction that is better for each of us is still, on balance, better for everyone.

In other cases, the economic transaction between the main parties might have much more significant negative effects on third parties. Recall Sarah and her widget factory from Chapter 5; Sarah uses the factory to make widgets, which she sells for $10 each. There is a large array of economic transactions involved here: Sarah's purchases from suppliers, maintenance work on the factory, payments to the workers, and, of course, each of the sales of a widget. We might suppose, along with Adam Smith, that in each of these transactions the parties immediately involved benefit. But now suppose further that, during the operation of Sarah's factory, the factory dumps effluent directly into the local river, and that this pollution has significant health consequences for those downstream. These people were not parties to any of the economic transactions, but it could very well be that, once the downstream effects are considered, it turns out that the economic transactions created more harm than good overall. This would be a case where premise (3) is false: economic decisions that are better for the immediate parties are not *better for all*.

In economic terms, these sorts of effects are termed *externalities*: costs or benefits to those not directly involved in the transaction. The examples just given have been of *negative externalities*, or negative effects on the other parties. One could also have positive externalities, which would essentially be what I was calling "diffuse goods" in Chapter 10: economic transactions where there are benefits to people who are not directly involved in the economic transaction. I prefer Milton Friedman's term: *neighborhood effects*.[1] "Negative externality" sounds so technical and not very descriptive, whereas "neighborhood effect" is a little more immediately comprehensible.

In some cases, the third party could be brought into the economic transaction. For example, when I arrange for Myles to build that large shed, we

---

[1] Friedman, *Capitalism and Freedom*, 14.

could bring Susan into the negotiations: I could offer her some compensation for the lost sunshine on her garden. It would be possible that all three of us would think that we had benefited from the deal, and we might even stipulate from the outset that I won't have the shed built until we reach a three-way agreement.

In many other cases, however, it would be much more difficult, or impossible, to bring the affected neighbors into the original economic transaction. In the case of Sarah's widget factory, we might think we can identify the people that are harmed by the effluent, for we know where the river goes. But it would not be so simple. The effects of the pollution might be more severe on some rather than others in ways that are not easy to predict, and some people might move to the downstream locations after the factory has been built and many widgets sold. And suppose that, because of the pollution, people start abandoning the downstream town, and that this affects the livelihood of many local businesses. Should each of them be brought into the negotiations concerning each sale of a widget?

Even Friedman acknowledges that neighborhood effects are a case where the market does not function perfectly by itself. He would, in cases like this, advocate having the government impose effluent charges on Sarah.[2] He urges caution, however, when bringing government into issues like this: "It is hard to know when neighborhood effects are sufficiently large to justify particular costs in overcoming them and even harder to distribute the costs in an appropriate fashion. Consequently, when government engages in activities to overcome neighborhood effects, it will in part introduce an additional set of neighborhood effects by failing to charge or to compensate individuals properly."[3] Friedman is basically suggesting the claim that I raised at the end of the previous chapter: that even where markets and capitalism have difficulty, it does not immediately follow that government will do better. And that much is correct: from the failure of market incentives it does not follow that democratically enacted laws and regulations will be superior. But there are a couple of things to note about the situation. First, the sort of scenario we are contemplating is one where we *know* that markets will not reach the best possible result overall—when there are sufficiently negative neighborhood effects, we know that leaving things to the market will result in a situation that is far from optimal for overall human well-being. Second, it requires

---

[2] Friedman and Friedman, *Free to Choose*, 217.
[3] Friedman, *Capitalism and Freedom*, 31–32.

considerable skepticism about government to be convinced that democratically adopted solutions will be *even* worse. In situations like this, we know that premise (3) of both *Better Incentives* and *Better Information* is false—i.e., we no longer have any argument for the claim that markets will promote overall human well-being. If one still insists that government action will be worse, this would seem to stem from a quite general skepticism about democracy. If you harbor that degree of doubt about the value of democracy, then the issue goes far beyond capitalist versus socialist ways of handling major economic decisions—you are skeptical about democratic government in general, not just in the marketplace.

Other Examples

Having granted that there are cases where the market fails because of neighborhood effects, the obvious question is how widespread such cases are. In a literal sense, just about anything we do will have *some* effect on others, so this means that there is always the possibility of a negative neighborhood effect. It clearly comes in degrees. But I think that such cases are much more widespread than the sort of pollution cases that conservatives like Friedman tend to mention.

Many decisions by large companies can have significant effects on many people. Consider, for example, utility companies in Texas in the winter of 2021. In February of that year, some unexpectedly cold weather hit Texas. The temperatures were not super cold by Maine standards (where I live), but much colder than usual for Texans. And much colder than usual for Texas utilities, which had been largely deregulated in prior years. Power plants could not handle the cold, and shut down, leaving customers without electricity and heat for days. Those power companies that managed to stay online charged exorbitant prices, with some customers receiving bills for thousands of dollars for a few days of electricity.[4]

Texas had experienced a similar cold snap in 2011, with power companies likewise being forced to shut down, so the power companies knew that such cold temperatures could occur. And keep in mind that these temperatures

---

[4] Giulia McDonnell Nieto del Rio, Nicholas Bogel-Burroughs, and Ivan Penn, "His Lights Stayed on during Texas' Storm. Now He Owes $16,752," *New York Times*, February 20, 2021, https://www.nytimes.com/2021/02/20/us/texas-storm-electric-bills.html.

were still not so bad compared to places much further north. My power goes out in Maine sometimes during storms when tree branches fall and knock down power lines, but the power plants themselves do not simply shut down because of cold weather. It is not in the nature of power plants to be inoperable in cold weather; the power companies in Texas *could have* winterized their plants. They chose not to do so.

Why not? Why wouldn't the market provide the incentive for them to be better prepared? If their plant is shut down, they have no power to sell, meaning that they lose money. Given the deregulated prices, they would be able to sell at higher prices than normal if they managed to continue to operate while their competitors were shut down. The magic of the market was supposed to be perfect for this situation.

In fact, I think, the market incentives worked just fine—for the power companies. They had a financial decision to make: they could spend money winterizing their plants, or they could not spend that money and risk losing some revenue during an unseasonably cold spell. They decided that winterizing the plants was not worth the extra revenue they might gain later. To some extent, this may have been the normal shortsightedness that often goes with market-based decisions: with investors coming and going and current owners being mostly concerned with their profits in the relatively near term, possible storms 10 years from now might seem less of a significant worry. But the decision might have also been economically rational: perhaps the companies did save more money in the long run by not winterizing and just accepting the loss of revenue whenever weather gets too cold.

The power companies, by making the economic decision *not* to winterize, did what they thought was *best for them*. But this ends up being a case where what was *best for them* was not *best for all*, thus giving another example of the falsity of premise (3) in *Better Incentives* and *Better Information*. One might initially think otherwise: that what is economically rational for the power companies would be economically rational for the consumers as well. The consumers enjoy slightly lower prices most of the time (because the company saved the cost of winterizing) and then simply do without electricity for a few days once every few years. As an analogy, I might be willing to have a few days (or weeks) every decade or so where I simply couldn't buy beer or shampoo if it meant that prices were lower the rest of the time.

But, of course, electricity and heat are not simple consumer goods like beer or shampoo. I can easily do without a beer in the evening, and my hair can just be dirty for a few days. But if you have no heat, especially during a period of intensely cold weather, then things are not so simple. For one thing, you might suffer other enormous costs: if your pipes freeze and burst, then that will be a homeowner's disaster. (I had it happen once; it's not pretty.) But there are also noneconomic costs. It is, to put it mildly, no fun to spend several days and nights in frigid temperatures, especially if you have small children or are yourself elderly, or if your health requires oxygen tanks that run on electricity. People died in Texas for lack of power during the cold spell of 2021.[5] The massive costs to some consumers, the inconvenience and discomfort of many others, and the deaths of a few were neighborhood effects of the economic decisions that were in the economic self-interest of the power companies making those decisions.

Cases like the Texas utilities are unlike the typical example of a neighborhood effect in this way: it is not exactly a case of a two-party transaction that nonetheless has significant effects on a third party. Instead, it was an essentially *unilateral* decision made by each utility, a decision *not* to engage in the series of economic transactions that winterizing the plants would have required. But it is nonetheless a case of an economic decision that was best for the actors involved (just one, in this case) but having substantial effects on people who were not party to the decision. Thus it is still a neighborhood effect, and is another circumstance in which premise (3) of *Better Incentives* and *Better Information* is false.

Many other unilateral decisions by major companies will have neighborhood effects. Suppose that a business owner, call her Sheryl, is deciding whether to lay off hundreds of workers in a small town. Sheryl might stand to add tens of thousands of dollars to her already considerable wealth if she takes this action. In a sense, there are other parties to the transaction, in that there were the employees who were no longer selling their labor to Sheryl. But, of course, these employees had no say in the transaction, meaning that any effect on them was a neighborhood effect, rather than an initial part of the transaction. And, of course, the effects on the laid-off employees are likely to be quite negative. As noted in Chapter 11, labor is often not a completely fungible good; the laid-off workers may not be in a position to simply sell their labor to someone else in town now that Sheryl no longer wishes to buy it. Moreover, even if they move away to seek a new job, they may find the

---

[5] Giulia McDonnell Nieto del Rio, Richard Fausset, and Johnny Diaz, "Extreme Cold Killed Texans in Their Bedrooms, Vehicles and Backyards," *New York Times*, February 19, 2021, https://www.nytimes.com/2021/02/19/us/texas-deaths-winter-storm.html.

process of uprooting from their friends and family gut-wrenching. The stress of being unemployed can be devastating as well, both for the person laid off and their loved ones. There could also be ripple effects throughout the local economy: if the former employees have little money to spend or move away, this could affect other business owners in town.

I am not saying that Sheryl was morally at fault for laying off workers without considering the nonfinancial misery she caused. We might blame her for that, depending on the circumstances, but that's not my claim. Rather, I'm just making the more obvious point that decisions that are economically rational for the self-interest of the individual making them might have significant nonfinancial impacts on others, and this makes the capitalist's arguments even more dubious. And if the capitalist incentive system does not work for improving overall human well-being, then we lack the special reason that the capitalist claimed to have for thinking that there is a nondemocratic way of making major economic decisions that is better for overall human well-being. This indicates that the *Democracy Argument for Socialism* will be sound, and we have reason for more democratic control over major economic decisions.

What form should this democratic control take in cases where significant nonfinancial values are at stake? These could vary with the circumstances, and, as I've said, this book is not the place for detailed policy proposals. But a few things come to mind. First, with respect to utilities, I think there would be a case to be made for simply running them publicly (as they do with electricity in France). We should not let market forces dictate that people will occasionally be without electricity or heat during the winter simply because that was the risk that seemed financially best to a private corporation. With something so dependent on a huge infrastructure, there is also always the danger that utility companies will tend toward monopolies, and for that reason they are often more heavily regulated than other industries, including regulation of prices. But once you have that kind of regulation, most of the claimed advantages of the free market system are already gone.

The No-Brainer? Future Generations and Climate Change

I'm now in the seventh chapter since beginning the discussion of whether socialism or capitalism is best for overall well-being, and I haven't yet discussed climate change. Perhaps it should have been the lede, since in some ways it is the most obvious reason for moving in the direction of more socialistic control of the economy. This is hardly a new thought. Danny Katch writes: "The future of all life on this planet is losing to the short-term opportunity for a few people to make even more money. This fact alone should make the case against capitalism a no-brainer."[6] As early as 2007, the one-time World Bank chief economist Nicholas Stern said, "Climate change presents a unique challenge for economics: it is the greatest example of market failure we have ever seen."[7]

In this chapter and the previous two I have been exploring various circumstances under which the capitalist's assumption fails—the assumption that each person making economic decisions that are *better for them* will result in decisions that are cumulatively *better for all*. Neighborhood effects of the sort I have discussed provide examples where this assumption will fail: cases where people beyond the immediate economic transaction (and who have no say in that transaction) are nonetheless harmed by it. In fact, even if each of us successfully acted to maximize our own self-interest, and *even if* that was guaranteed to add up to greater happiness for all of *us*, there is one set of people noticeably left out of this equation: future generations. You and I might engage in an economic transaction that does fine for each of us. But that business matter might have consequences for people decades or centuries from now, and none of those people played a role in the transaction.

Even apart from neighborhood effects on existing people, the capitalist is, in effect, presupposing that what is economically best for humans right now will likely be best for the overall well-being of people that exist in the future. Obviously, there is no guarantee that this is true. It might, for example, be economically best for people *right now* to buy and burn fossil fuels with abandon: they are cheap, and they provide energy that makes life much easier. For us. But if a side effect of burning those fuels is that we drastically change the climate for our descendants, and if we make life much, much worse for them, then what is best for people now could easily be worse for human well-being in general. Since the incentives of the market so lauded by capitalists (in Friedman's words, the "stronger and more dependable spur of self-interest") so clearly leave out the interests of future generations, we cannot count on the market to maximize human well-being once future generations are also

---

[6] Katch, *Socialism . . . Seriously*, 6.
[7] Nicholas Stern, *The Economics of Climate Change: The Stern Review* (New York: Cambridge University Press, 2007), vii–viii.

228   CAPITALISM AND HUMAN WELL-BEING

counted. Besides incentives, the other argument for markets stemmed from the decentralized information provided by prices; but I don't think anyone would claim that markets and prices provide information about the effects on future generations.

The Claim That Climate Change Is a Ruse

In fact, some capitalists today seem to acknowledge that the scientific consensus on climate change means that there is a very good case for socialism rather than capitalism. You can see this when they insist that claims about climate change are just a ploy to advance the socialist agenda. For example, Dinesh D'Souza claims that "climate change is the ruse to get the public to go for full socialism."[8] Senator Rand Paul makes similar claims. He titles a chapter of his book on socialism "If Socialists Can't Find a Crisis, They Will Create One," and within the chapter he uses scare quotes around the word "crisis" to indicate his opinion that claims of such a crisis are false: "In their own words, climate alarmists are using the 'crisis' of climate change to scare people into relinquishing the freedom and prosperity of capitalism in exchange for a global socialist welfare state."[9]

D'Souza and Paul thus suggest that socialists are making something like the following argument:

> *Climate Change and Socialism*
>
> (1) If climate change is real, then there is a good case for socialism. [P]
> (2) Climate change is real. [P]
> (3) There is a good case for socialism. [1,2]

What seems to be happening is this: capitalists like D'Souza and Paul, implicitly or otherwise, accept the truth of the first premise—they implicitly accept that we cannot count on free markets to help save us from the great suffering that will ensue if climate change is as the scientists say it is. If they thought (1) was false, then they would not need to be so concerned to claim that premise (2) is a ruse; in the context of writing about socialism (and both

---

[8] Dinesh D'Souza, *United States of Socialism: Who's behind It. Why It's Evil. How to Stop It* (New York: All Points Books, 2020), 20.
[9] Paul, *The Case against Socialism*, 256.

D'Souza and Paul were in exactly that context), they could simply point out (if they thought it true): if climate change is a real challenge for humanity, then capitalism is the solution. Because they see the truth of (1), but they despise socialism, they are absolutely intent on denying (2). Not only do they deny climate change so as to save the case for capitalism, but they suggest that it has all been made up (a "ruse") or at least deliberately exaggerated precisely to argue for socialism.

Paul explicitly suggests that the motive behind what he calls the "climate change industry" is suspect: "Considering the desire of so many in the climate change industry to silence debate, as well as their antipathy toward capitalism, one has to wonder if there is another motive behind their efforts.... Perhaps global redistribution of wealth or a worldwide socialist welfare state?"[10]

In an argumentative context, accusations about the other side's motivations are interesting. At first glance, it might just look like an example of what is referred to as an argument *ad hominem* (see chapter 1), in which, rather than directly dealing with the premises or inferences of an opponent's argument one instead simply attacks, for example, the moral character of the opponent. But in some cases, there might be some reason for looking at the motives behind someone making a claim. You cannot do your own independent research for every claim; at some point you must rely on the testimony and expertise of others. (Doing your own climate change research would *not* be a matter of checking out the latest YouTube videos by climate change deniers, since that would likewise be relying on testimony. Instead, doing your own research would mean taking your own temperature measurements, collecting your own data relevant to past temperatures, doing experiments concerning greenhouse gases, constructing your own mathematical models, etc.) Given that we must ultimately rely on assertions of others (even if we do our own logical analysis of what follows), it does make sense to look with some scrutiny at whether your sources are trustworthy, and one indication of that might be whether the source has some ulterior motive. So, for example, if your source of information about climate change is solely from people who are antecedently committed to socialism, and if you are convinced that the reality of climate change would provide a strong case for socialism, then that is at least a reason to check some other sources as well. Perhaps those who say

---

[10] Paul, *The Case against Socialism*, 265.

that climate change is real are honest but hopelessly biased, or perhaps it is, as D'Souza claims all a ruse—it is a conspiracy to put socialism into place.

It is one thing to grant that as a possibility, but it is another thing to take it seriously after doing even a modicum of reading about climate change. Any conspiracy would have to be vast indeed. There was a tweet that passed around a few years ago:

> Plot idea: 97% of the world's scientists contrive an environmental crisis but are exposed by a plucky band of billionaires & oil companies.[11]

The tweet's 97% figure appears to stem from some widely cited studies saying that, among published scientific papers on the topic, 97% of them concur that the climate is warming and that humans are causing it. The 97% figure is perhaps mistaken. A more recent study analyzed thousands of peer-reviewed scientific papers in the first part of 2019 and found that fully 100% agreed with the consensus view.[12] So not only have socialists concocted a crazy theory to allow them to propound *Climate Change and Socialism*, they somehow have 100% of climate scientists on board.

Senator Paul's "Refutation" of Climate Change Claims

Senator Paul alleges that he can raise legitimate doubts about climate change simply by asking difficult questions:

> My question to the alarmists is, how much of climate change is related to nature and how much to man? The alarmists gaze back confused at the question. I egg them on—"no, really, what percentage? Is climate change 90 percent nature or 90 percent man or perhaps we don't know?"[13]

The suggestion seems to be that if we can't put a reasonably precise number on the percentage of the climate effects that are due to human beings, then

---

[11] Scott Westerfield, Twitter post, March 20, 2014, 8:27 PM, https://twitter.com/scottwesterfeld/status/446805144781348865?lang=en.

[12] James Powell, "Scientists Reach 100% Consensus on Anthropogenic Global Warning," *Bulletin of Science, Technology & Society*, November 20, 2019.

[13] Paul, *The Case against Socialism*, 263.

we would be justified in seriously doubting that the percentage coming from human beings is significant.

In its extreme form, this is a version of a standard sort of argumentative move:

No Proof 1.0

(1) There is no proof that p. [P]
(2) If there is no proof that p, then it is rationally justified to believe not-p. [P]
(3) It is rationally justified to believe that not-p. [1,2]

Whether or not we accept such arguments depends on the meaning of the word "proof" in each of the premises. There is a strong sense of the word "proof" according to which one has proof of a proposition only if one can demonstrate conclusively that the opposite of p is contradictory or otherwise completely indubitable. Call that "$proof_s$" for "proof in the strong sense." This is basically the sense of proof that one gets in mathematics or formal logic. One might mean "proof" in a much weaker sense, according to which proof of a proposition only requires a reasonable and rational justification for believing the proposition (even if one cannot demonstrate that the negation of the proposition is contradictory). Call this "$proof_w$" for "proof in the weak sense."

The argumentative trick that sometimes occurs is to conflate the two senses. For almost *any* proposition outside of mathematics or pure logic, including propositions about climate change, there is no $proof_s$; so for any such proposition, premise (1) of *No Proof* will be true: there is no $proof_s$ that p. But as a general statement, premise (2), read with proof in the strong sense, is surely false. There is no $proof_s$ that Ronald Reagan existed. Sure, there are lots of people who say they saw him and interacted with him, and books are filled with straightforward references to him. But it is not *logically contradictory* to suppose that all such reports are mistaken or that what we thought was Ronald Reagan was a cleverly designed hologram or a body double or his secret twin brother Edward. These may be absurd suggestions, but they are not logically impossible (and provide many pivotal plot points for fans of the soap opera genre). But, of course, it is far from rationally justified to believe that Ronald Reagan never existed. The basic point here is simple: $proof_s$ is far too high a bar to require for rationally justified belief; if we do require $proof_s$, then we will believe very little.

However, in the weak sense, "proof$_w$" just means that you have a rational justification for believing p. In that sense, premise (2) would look plausible: if there is no proof$_w$ that p, then it is rationally justified to believe not-p. Surely it is right that if there is no rational justification for believing p, then it is rationally justified to believe not-p. But if we mean proof$_w$, then of course the scientists (and the rest of us) who think that climate change is real, largely due to humans, and very serious will disagree with premise (1): we believe that there is adequate, rational justification for these beliefs about the climate.

The sneaky thing one can do is to switch between the two senses of proof:

No Proof 2.0

(1) There is no proof$_s$ that p. [P]
(2) If there is no proof$_w$ that p, then it is rationally justified to believe not-p. [P]
(3) It is rationally justified to believe that not-p. [1,2]

Now, for most propositions, both premises are true. But it is, of course, a trick, because now the argument is not valid; it is an example of equivocation, using a word with one meaning in one premise, but a different meaning in a different premise. People are not usually so obliging as to lay out their premises in such explicit fashion so that the equivocation becomes clear, but I think that something like this line of thought lies behind a great deal of seemingly rational sounding skepticism. For example, one might say, "You can't prove that God exists, so it is rational to believe that there is no God." Or one might say the converse: "You can't prove that God does *not* exist, so it is rational to believe in God."

My suggestion is that something like this pattern of thought seems to underlie the pronouncements of those who profess what they claim to be reasonable skepticism about climate change. They note, quite correctly, that it has not been proven (in the strong sense) that climate change is serious, and they infer that it is rational to believe that there is no problem with climate change.

In any event, back to the question with which Senator Paul says he eggs on climate change "alarmists" (as he calls them): What percentage of the warming is nature and what percent is from the activity of humans? Paul seemingly suggests that there is no way to know this. In fact, climate change scientists can, with appropriate caveats about degrees of certainty, answer that question. In the 2021 Intergovernmental Panel on Climate Change, a United Nations report from 234 scientists building on 14,000 scientific papers, the authors write the following:

> It is unequivocal that human influence has warmed the atmosphere, ocean and land. Widespread and rapid changes in the atmosphere, ocean, cryosphere and biosphere have occurred.
> The *likely* range of total human-caused global surface temperature increase from 1850–1900 to 2010–2019 is 0.8°C to 1.3°C, with a best estimate of 1.07°C. It is *likely* that well-mixed GHGs contributed a warming of 1.0°C to 2.0°C, other human drivers (principally aerosols) contributed a cooling of 0.0°C to 0.8°C, natural drivers changed global surface temperature by −0.1°C to +0.1°C, and internal variability changed it by −0.2°C to +0.2°C.[14]

So, while we of course do not know for sure, the likely answer is that −0.1°C to + 0.1°C of the warming is from natural causes and the rest is human caused. That is to say, the most likely hypothesis is that 100% of the increase in surface temp since the 19th century is human caused.

It is clear from reading this report or any of the other scientific literature that the dangers of climate change are quite real. If we continue on our current path of greenhouse gas emissions and global warming, there will be hugely adverse effects on the lives of millions or billions of people. When people like Hayek and Friedman were writing, they *might* have had reason to assume that, subject to the earlier exceptions already discussed, whatever maximizes the economic interests of those currently making the major economic decisions will maximize the interests of everyone, including future generations. But if that was ever plausible, the looming climate catastrophe shows that it is clearly wrong.

---

[14] "Summary for Policymakers," in *Climate Change 2021: The Physical Science Basis. Contribution of Working Group I to the Sixth Assessment Report of the Intergovernmental Panel on Climate Change*, ed. V. Masson-Delmotte, P. Zhai, A. Pirani, S. L. Connors, C. Péan, S. Berger, N. Caud, Y. Chen, L. Goldfarb, M. I. Gomis, M. Huang, K. Leitzell, E. Lonnoy, J. B. R. Matthews, T. K. Maycock, T. Waterfield, O. Yelekçi, R. Yu, and B. Zhou (New York: Cambridge University Press, 2021), 4, 5.

Capitalism as the Answer to Climate Change?

In the face of ever-growing evidence about the seriousness of climate change, some defenders of capitalism are now taking a different tack: rather than insisting that it is all overblown or even a ruse, some now implicitly acknowledge the threat, but claim that capitalism is the solution. The Australian prime minister Scott Morrison recently claimed the following: "Climate change will ultimately be solved by 'can do' capitalism, not 'don't do' governments seeking to control people's lives and tell them what to do, with interventionist regulation and taxes that just force up your cost of living and force businesses to close."[15] Morrison was not explicit on how capitalism would manage this, and there is obvious reason to think the opposite: after all, the long-term damage to the environment and climate is being caused by practices that are, in the short-term, genuinely beneficial and cost-effective.

Nicolas Loris, writing for the Heritage Foundation, likewise suggests that "Capitalism Helps Protect the Environment," and it does so as follows: "Markets incentivize efficiency by rewarding people for coming up with ways to do more or do better with less. People choose—and businesses make—more efficient products because it saves them money while delivering what customers want."[16] Loris goes on to note that coal production, as a share of energy production in the United States, has dropped significantly, and that this has resulted from "companies providing consumers with the goods and services they want while using fewer resources and emitting fewer unwanted emissions."[17]

We might note that, since Loris wrote his article in 2019, coal production has been on the rise again,[18] but that would not be the main point. Loris's suggestion, and presumably the implicit suggestion of Prime Minister Morrison, is that capitalist markets will provide what people want, and will provide it with maximum efficiency. This means two things: (i) if people want energy, markets will provide the most efficient sources of energy—i.e., the ways of

---

[15] Rob Verdonck, "Capitalism—Not Government—Will Fix Climate Change, Australia Says," Bloomberg, November 9, 2021, https://www.bloomberg.com/news/articles/2021-11-10/let-capitalism-fix-climate-australia-says-as-cop26-nears-finish.

[16] Nicolas Loris, "Breathe Free: Capitalism Helps Protect the Environment," Heritage Foundation, October 23, 2019, https://www.heritage.org/environment/commentary/breathe-free-capitalism-helps-protect-the-environment.

[17] Loris, "Breathe Free."

[18] Kayla Desroches, "U.S. Coal Production Is Up Sharply after Hitting a 50-Year Low Last Year," NPR, October 22, 2021, https://www.npr.org/2021/10/22/1048108267/u-s-coal-production-is-up-sharply-after-hitting-a-50-year-low-last-year.

providing the most energy for the least money; (ii) if people want energy with fewer emissions, then markets will provide that.

There is a glaring problem with the first point: it is far from guaranteed that the most efficient (i.e., cheapest) ways of producing energy are the ones that do the least damage to the climate. In fact, it is precisely because the contrary is true that the climate is changing so drastically, for, at least up until now, the cheapest source of massive amounts of energy is to burn fossil fuels. When capitalists say that markets "incentivize efficiency," that sounds good, for one can be soothed into thinking that *efficient* energy will have the least effect on the climate. Not only does that not go without saying, it seems obviously false. (It might be true in the future, *if* we can get to the point where we can produce energy without creating greenhouse gases and more cheaply than burning fossil fuels.)

Loris's second point is somewhat more complicated. It is true, for example, that if everyone in my part of Maine refuses to buy electricity produced by the burning of fossil fuels, then that provides a market opportunity for a business enterprise to provide electricity in a renewable way that does not involve burning fossil fuels. It's also true that if consumers simply cut down drastically on the sorts of behavior that cause climate change, then this would help; this is another sort of market solution, namely the market responding to lower consumer demand, perhaps motivated by consumers' desires to help fend off a looming climate disaster.

One might even try to parlay these points into a general argument that capitalism is better, or at least no worse, than socialism when it comes to climate change, even granting that climate change is a serious problem. The key points behind the capitalist argument would be these: if people *want* solutions to climate change, then the market will provide those solutions. If there are solutions and it is not too late. But even if it is too late to completely avert a climate disaster, the capitalist claim would be that markets will provide the best means of mitigating climate change *if people want that*. And if people do not seriously want solutions to climate change, then it is hard to see why socialism will do any better than capitalism on this problem. Socialism provides democratic control of the economy, and thus a *potential* means to taking the sort of broad-scale action that will be necessary; but if consumers don't want solutions to climate change, then there is little reason to think that they, as citizens, will use their democratic control of the economy in a way that will ultimately help. Or so the capitalist might argue. We could lay out the argument as follows:

Capitalism and Climate Change

(1) If people want solutions to climate change, markets will provide solutions to climate change. [P]
(2) If markets will provide solutions to climate change, then, with respect to climate change, capitalism is at least as good as socialism. [P]
(3) If people want solutions to climate change, then, with respect to climate change, capitalism is at least as good as socialism. [1,2]
(4) If people do not want solutions to climate change, then socialism will fail to provide solutions to climate change. [P]
(5) If socialism will fail to provide solutions to climate change, then, with respect to climate change, capitalism is at least as good as socialism. [P]
(6) If people do not want solutions to climate change, then, with respect to climate change, capitalism is at least as good as socialism. [4,5]
(7) With respect to climate change, capitalism is at least as good as socialism. [3,6]

The capitalist argument is in the form of a dilemma for the socialist: if the people don't really want solutions to climate change, then giving them more democratic control over the economy won't especially help; but if people (consumers) really do want solutions to climate change, then the market would be a good mechanism for producing those solutions, either through drastically reduced consumption or technological advances toward energy that is less damaging to the environment. The capitalist does have a point with premise (4): giving the people more democratic control over the economy does not guarantee that we will democratically make the best decisions we can with respect to climate change. Anyone who is paying attention to climate change has to hope that we can convince people of the seriousness of the problem and get them to take action, but there are no guarantees that we will be successful.

The socialist's best bet is to choose the first horn of the dilemma—that people do want solutions to climate change—and then to deny premise (1) of *Capitalism and Climate Change*, the claim that markets will provide solutions to climate change if consumers want that. There are two problems with the premise. The first has to do with infrastructure and monopolies, as discussed in Chapter 11. As I suggested above, if everyone in my state of Maine refused to buy electricity produced by burning fossil fuels, then this would create a business opportunity for anyone who could bring online more renewable and less damaging ways of producing electricity. But if the current utility company has, in effect, a monopoly, has the infrastructure in place, and has various means by which to make life difficult for potential competitors, then it is much more difficult than it sounds for a company producing greener energy to get established, even if that is what consumers want. This has already happened in some markets where electricity producers try to prevent the mass installation of solar panels.

Monopoly and infrastructure issues do not, of course, stop consumers from drastically reducing energy consumption and changing other behaviors that contribute to climate change, and one might assume, with premise (1), that if people really wanted to help with climate change, then they would do this; the market would work fine for that as well, for if people are using far less energy, far less will be produced, with far fewer greenhouse gas emission as a result.

The real issue with premise (1) has to do with collective versus individual sacrifice. Yes, we can take public transportation (when it is available) rather than drive, limit the meat in our diet, and dutifully recycle our cans, etc. We could also attempt to drastically lower energy consumption by downsizing and better weatherizing our abodes, never taking planes, etc. These actions obviously involve sacrifices, some more significant than others. Even with the best of intentions, it can be difficult to follow through or not start backsliding, especially if one sees that some of one's neighbors are not engaged in similar sacrifices.

Consider an analogy. Suppose that the best weather forecasting and scientific evidence indicates that the town where you live is likely to be devastated by a flood within the next few weeks. However, the scientists tell us that we can likely avert the worst damage by placing hundreds of thousands of sandbags along the bank of the river. For whatever reason (perhaps the town is quite isolated), there is no realistic prospect of hiring outside workers. But if all able-bodied adults in the town will devote an hour a day to stacking sandbags over the next two weeks, then this will likely get the job done. There is uncertainty in all of this: we don't know exactly how bad the flood will be, and we don't know exactly how much good stacking sandbags will do; but it is, according to the best research and scientific consensus, our best bet.

Once all of this information is known, some good citizens will undoubtedly start stacking sandbags voluntarily. Others think that the whole thing is a ruse and that there is no flood coming; they refuse to take an hour out of their day to stack sandbags. Still others might start stacking some sandbags occasionally, but they look around and see that not nearly enough people are similarly engaged in the project. They *might* take this as reason to redouble their efforts, stacking for two or three hours a day to make up for the people they see as slackers. But, after a while, they might grow to resent the fact that they are making this sacrifice while others are not, and they might really come to doubt that the efforts of those who are stacking sandbags will be enough. Since so many people are not stacking sandbags, it feels to them that their efforts are in vain. There will be a natural tendency to cut back on their efforts, with the likely net result: the flood comes, there are not nearly enough sandbags, and the damage is severe.

By contrast, instead of just asking for volunteer labor on an individual basis, suppose that the town considered the evidence from the scientists and weather forecasters and then put the issue to a vote: they held a referendum on a law that would *require* all able-bodied adults to spend an hour a day stacking sandbags. Then the results might be quite different. Voters would know that if the law passes, they will not be unilaterally deciding to make sacrifices that their neighbors are not, and they might well pass the law. It's one thing to vote for policies that require a certain amount of sacrifice from all of us in one way or another and then to abide by the laws that have been passed; it's another to make, and continue to make, your own sacrifices when so many around you seem not to be taking the situation seriously, and when this threatens to mean that your own sacrifices were in vain.

The same applies to climate change and expectations of individual versus collective action. All of this is reason to doubt premise (1) of *Capitalism and Climate Change*: it could very well be that most people either want, or can be convinced that they should want, some sort of way out of the impending climate disaster—or at least some way of mitigating its effects on people. But this does *not* mean that the market, based as it is on individual decisions in the absence of collective action, will provide those solutions.

Of course, there is no guarantee that increased democratic control of the economy will move us adequately in the right direction; just as future generations, being not yet existent, do not engage in market transactions, they also do not yet vote. If current voters think only of themselves and not future generations, then they will only become adequately concerned about climate change when it becomes so urgent that it affects their own immediate future; that's likely to be too late. But more democratic control at least gives us hope.

Key Takeaways

- We say that an economic transaction has a *neighborhood effect* when it affects people who were not parties to the transaction.
- In circumstances where the neighborhood effects are significant and there is no effective way to bring harmed parties into the negotiations over the economic transaction, the market fails: transactions that are better for the immediate participants are not better for human well-being in general.
- Many economic transactions involve neighborhood effects, including obvious cases like industrial pollution, but also including unilateral corporate decisions, like a utility company not winterizing its power plants and routine decisions to lay off large numbers of workers.
- Climate change is the biggest and most dangerous example to date of a neighborhood effect.
- It is quite dubious that capitalism and free markets can address the looming disaster imposed by climate change.
- Socialism, via more democratic control of the economy, at least gives us some hope.

13
Conclusion

When I started high school in Lawrence, Kansas, back in 1979, I joined the debate team. This was great fun. Across the country, high school students participated in tournaments with carefully structured debates, all with the same topic. My first year the topic was this: resolved that the federal government should significantly change its foreign trade policies. We would debate in pairs, switching from the affirmative side to the negative side each round of a tournament. The affirmative team would try to convince the judge (often a parent of one of the debaters from the school hosting the tournament) that the resolution in the topic was true, and the negative team would try to show that the affirmative team had failed to do this. The debates were carefully structured: the affirmative team would start with an eight-minute speech, the negative team would follow with an eight-minute speech in opposition, and so on, for a total of 48 minutes of speechifying and interspersed periods of question and answer or cross-examination. Then onto the next round, taking the opposite side. We brought with us for each round hundreds or thousands of carefully organized index cards with quotations and statistics ready to pull out and be read as evidence for our claims.

It's hard to go through a year of debating the same topic in that format without realizing that there are always two sides to most complicated issues. A structured debate was a reasonable way of bringing out considerations on each side, but there were, of course, certain limitations. After the initial affirmative speech, which was written in advance, all other speeches were hastily prepared or improvised under extreme time pressure. The ability to speak smoothly and confidently was paramount, even if you knew next to nothing about the particular point you were discussing. *Gotchas* were highly prized: instances where you could undermine your opponent's sources or make a clever or elegant retort to a particular point. One simple strategy in these debates was to talk very fast, covering more points than your opponent could respond to in their next speech, and then claim that their lack of response means that you "won" that point.

After my debate career and high school were over, I left Kansas for Harvard. I was too intimidated to try competitive debate there, but I discovered something much better: philosophy. During my first year I took formal logic and a class on the history of modern philosophy. In these classes, I was introduced to the idea of reconstructing arguments into numbered steps and the ability to rigorously formalize and check logical inferences. After three years of throwing around claims and arguments in high school debate, this was like having the scales fall from my eyes: with the tools of argument reconstruction and logic, I could see the underlying structure of the reasoning philosophers and others put forward. This allowed me to better understand their claims and also to see more clearly any weaknesses in the argument.

The beginnings of my philosophical education put into my head a sort of fantasy about arguments: that with careful construction of arguments and strict attention to logic, we had a recipe to follow for resolving any philosophical or political dispute. In abstract terms, it would go like this. Suppose I believe some proposition, p, and that you are inclined to disagree about p. If I believe p, then I must have reasons for doing so. If I don't have reasons for p, then I should not affirm it; if I have reasons I should be able to put them into the form of a numbered step argument for p. You must then either agree with my argument (and thereby change your mind about p) or tell me which premise is false (or show that my argument has a logical fallacy and is invalid). Suppose you dispute one of the premises of my argument. Then I should be able to produce a *further* argument for that premise. If you can't dispute the premises of that argument, then you should now agree with p. If you do dispute one or more of those premises, then we continue the process further. With enough patience and clarity of thought, we should be able to settle our dispute this way; surely we can get down to premises that are obvious enough that both sides will agree about them. After that, it's just logic.

Fast-forward a number decades into the present, and we see that political debate is almost the opposite of my undergraduate fantasy about rational discourse. We live in a polarized political world where there is little or no genuine engagement with people in the opposite political camp. In the United States, a 2019 Pew survey found that solid majorities of both parties view the people in the other party as "closed-minded"; 55% of Republicans think of Democrats as generally "immoral" (or at least more so than other people), and 47% of Democrats think the same about Republicans.[1] If you think of the other political side as immoral and closed-minded, you aren't very likely to engage with them in a possibly protracted analysis of the arguments each of you will put forward for your position. Moreover, it may also seem increasingly unlikely that we can use the process of logical analysis to get down to premises on which we can both agree, for the political polarization is such that politically opposed people may not be able to agree on sources of basic information. A 2018 Gallup poll reported that over half of American said they could not even think of one objective news source.[2] When people are content to just stay within their own information silo, dispute that there are *any* neutral sources of information, and regard the other side as immoral and closed-minded, the prospects for meaningful reasoning with each other seem slim. Though perhaps not to the same degree as in the United States, polarization also affects politics in many European countries.[3] There too observers have noted "the brutalization of political debate" and "the spread of disinformation."[4]

We have all grown to accept the sorry state of public discourse, but I think this is a huge mistake. By way of analogy, when citizens are gathered together as jurors, attempting to decide the fate of an accused criminal, the lawyers for the state and the lawyers for the defense will, we hope, make arguments and substantiate their claims with evidence and testimony of experts. Imagine a courtroom where nobody agrees on what counts as evidence, and the lawyers spend the whole trial insulting one another's character, and where the side with best zingers and the most disinformation wins. It would be obviously ridiculous and fundamentally unjust to have such a process decide the guilt or innocence of people accused of crimes. Why have we allowed our political culture to operate in this manner?

---

[1] "Partisan Antipathy: More Intense, More Personal," Pew Research Center, October 10, 2019, https://www.pewresearch.org/politics/2019/10/10/partisan-antipathy-more-intense-more-personal/

[2] "American Views: Trust, Media and Democracy," Gallup/Knight Foundation, 2018, https://kf-site-production.s3.amazonaws.com/publications/pdfs/000/000/242/original/KnightFoundation_AmericansViews_Client_Report_010917_Final_Updated.pdf

[3] Ezra Klein, "What Polarization Data from Nine Countries Reveals about the US," *Vox*, January 24, 2020, https://www.vox.com/2020/1/24/21076232/polarization-america-international-party-political

[4] Heidi Schulze, Marlene Mauk, and Jonas Linde, "How Populism Affects Europe's Liberal Democracies," *Politics and Governance*, vol. 8, no. 3 (2020): 5.

In any event, my undergraduate fantasy—that with reason and analysis we could trace back any disagreement to its root and eliminate it—was always unrealistic, to say the least. Sometimes our reasons for believing something do not fall into neat logical steps, and this does not necessarily mean that we are being irrational. Sometimes it might be quite reasonable to trust basic feelings or intuitions more than the results of a narrowly focused argument. To take an extreme but trivial example, there are mathematical "proofs" for the claim that $1 = 0$; even if each of the steps in the proof seem reasonable to you, you would not be well advised to conclude that $1 = 0$. Sometimes we might be justifiably confident that a conclusion is false even when we cannot pinpoint a mistaken premise or faulty logic. (In the seeming proofs that $1 = 0$, the trick is usually to have a step that amounts to dividing by zero.)

Moreover, when an argument comes down to empirical premises, the empirical claims over which we differ are not likely to be something like "There are five chairs in my dining room"—i.e., the sort of claims where we can just go to my dining room and count the chairs and we will both agree on how many are there. As seen in Parts III and IV above, that a claim is empirical does not mean that it is easy to answer. Finally, when an argument comes down to normative rather than empirical premises, this does not necessarily make things any easier. When I explored the question of whether capitalism violates rights in Chapter 5, I myself was ultimately left uncertain about a key normative premise.

All this said, I remain convinced that we can make great progress by using the philosophical tools of analysis and logic, and that more of this in our political discourse would help us greatly in the challenging times ahead. This is not just a matter of being civil in our debates, though sticking to the arguments does tend to lessen the tendency to replace reason with name-calling and abuse. Being civil is generally good, but one can be civil by simply "agreeing to disagree," walking away, and then muttering to yourself how stupid the other person is. One can pepper one's conversation with things like, "I can see your point of view," or "That's an understandable claim." All well and good to do. We could use more of it. But I'm talking about something further: defending your own positions through rational argument and trying to understand and grapple with the other side's argument, even if you have to piece it together for them.

Why bother? For at least four reasons. First, by carefully working through the arguments, you might actually convince someone. It's been known to happen. It is admittedly rare that someone hears an argument and immediately changes their mind. But reasons are like seeds; once planted, and given the proper environment, some of them grow. Second, even if argumentative opponents don't completely change their view, they might at least now better understand your view and the motivations for it; they might be less likely to think of people holding your view as immoral and closed-minded, and even that much is progress. Third, you might change your own mind. That's been known to happen too. Some people regard changing their mind as almost akin to a character flaw, as something only weak and vacillating types do. Of course, changing your mind does mean admitting that you were wrong about something and that you are not infallible, but it doesn't seem that those should be *such* big concessions. Fourth, if you don't change your basic position, you will hopefully at least better understand your own reasons for your position, and that seems valuable. When you better understand the reasons for a view, then you are also presumably less likely to change your mind for bad reasons.

Our question in this book was a very big one: How ought we to structure our political and economic system? After all that has been said about this question over the centuries, it would be surprising indeed if one relatively short book could effectively lay out all the issues and arguments, let alone do so in a way that would, in accord with my undergraduate fantasy, simply settle things. But I do hope we've made progress. I'll close by recapping some of the major pieces.

One of my principal aims was to defend this basic argument for socialism:

Master Argument for Socialism

(1) Socialism better promotes human well-being than extant alternative styles of governance. [P]
(2) Socialism does not violate moral rights of individuals. [P]
(3) Given two styles of governance, if the first better promotes human well-being than the second and does not violate moral rights of individuals, then it should be chosen over the second. [P]
(4) Socialism should be chosen over extant alternative styles of governance. [1,2,3]

This aim required that I also rebut the parallel argument for capitalism:

> *Master Argument for Capitalism*
>
> (1) Capitalism better promotes human well-being than extant alternative styles of governance. [P]
> (2) Capitalism does not violate moral rights of individuals. [P]
> (3) Given two styles of governance, if the first better promotes human well-being than the second and does not violate moral rights of individuals, then it should be chosen over the second. [P]
> (4) Capitalism should be chosen over extant alternative styles of governance. [1,2,3]

Both arguments share the third premise, and I tried to make a case for that premise in Chapter 3.

Premise (2), in both cases, is a negative claim. There is the old slogan that you can't prove a negative. That's true, first and foremost because you can't *prove* much of anything, if one means prove in a strong sense (see the discussion of the word "prove" as it comes up in the discussion of climate change in Chapter 12). But even apart from questions of *proof*, it is admittedly difficult to provide a positive argument for a negative claim like, "Socialism does not violate the rights of individuals." So, in Chapter 4, I did what I could by seeking out arguments *for* the claim that socialism *does* violate rights, and then I tried to show that those arguments were implausible. The arguments considered included *Socialism Violates Political Rights, Socialism Will Restrict Speech, Socialism Violates Property Rights,* and a couple of arguments based on the libertarian Nonaggression Principle. All of these arguments had serious problems; that is to say, the popularly given reasons for thinking socialism violates rights are dubious. Does that mean that socialism does *not* violate rights? No. Even if I am correct to reject the arguments I considered, perhaps I missed an argument that does show that socialism violates rights. I welcome such attempts, even if I suspect that they will likewise be unsuccessful.

In Chapter 5, I considered premise (2) of the *Master Argument for Capitalism* in analogous fashion, by seeking out the arguments that socialists have given for the claim that capitalism violates rights. My final version of what I took to be the most promising argument in this regard was *Capitalism Exploits 4.0*. For my own part, I was not entirely convinced by this argument, though I was also not convinced that the argument was mistaken. I hope to have at least indicated the reasons why one might *think* that capitalism violates rights, but also the reasons that one might be dubious about that claim. But in terms of premise (2) of the *Master Argument for Capitalism*, my own position is to be agnostic.

Since I was agnostic about whether capitalism violates rights and I denied that socialism violates rights, this meant that both *Master Arguments* were still standing, insofar as premise (2) of each was concerned. There is, of course, no inconsistency is saying that premise (2) of both of those arguments is correct: it could be that neither system violates rights. (If the utilitarian is right about morality, then *no* system violates rights, because there are no rights in the sense of something that trumps utility considerations.)

Premise (1) of the respective arguments is a different story. Premise (1) of the *Master Argument for Socialism* states that socialism promotes human well-being better than other systems, whereas premise (1) of the *Master Argument for Capitalism* claims that it is capitalism that does this; since they make competing claims in this way, both premises cannot be right. Parts III and IV were concerned with the question of which system would lead to greater human well-being. This is an empirical question, and I noted in Chapter 6 that there were two broad sorts of reasons one might seek in answering it. First, one might look to evidence that starts with correlations: Where it has been tried, is capitalism correlated with greater human well-being? What about socialism? Where there appear to be such correlations, can we determine that there is, beyond the mere fact of correlation, a genuinely explanatory relationship involved? I.e., can we *attribute* observed increases in well-being to either capitalism or socialism? Second, particularly if empirical correlations do not seem to settle the question, we can look at other sorts of arguments, other sorts of general reasons for *expecting* that one system of the other should typically lead to greater well-being.

Capitalists often propose that there is overwhelming evidence of the first sort, for they note that there is a correlation between the rise of capitalism and a general increase in human well-being over the last couple of centuries. However, when examined more closely as *Capitalism and Progress*, this argument seemed weak: data from the state socialist countries of the 20th century cast considerable doubt on the claim that capitalism *explains* the increases in human well-being that we have seen; it seemed more likely overall that the major explanatory factor was science and technology. In fact, drawing mostly on data presented by Wilkinson and Pickett, I argued in Chapter 7 that the correlational evidence goes the other direction: across a wide variety of indicators of human well-being, more egalitarian distribution of resources is closely tied to greater well-being. I also noted in Chapter 8 that Nordic countries have greater collective ownership of the means of production and greater human well-being, thus giving us a correlation there as well.

Both capitalists and socialists claim reasons of the second sort for the superiority of their system, i.e., general reasons for expecting that their system would lead to greater well-being. On the side of socialism, there is the obvious fact that money has diminishing marginal utility, which speaks in favor of redistribution via taxation—so long as we do not tax at such high rates that we destroy incentives and thereby shrink the amount of wealth available across the board. But evidence about optimal taxation rates indicates that we can go substantially further than most countries do now towards progressive rates of taxation (especially the United States, which has comparatively low taxation rates). These discussions were in Chapter 7 as well.

In Chapter 8, I presented two different general reasons for expecting that socialism would lead to greater well-being: *Community Makes People Happier* and *The Democracy Argument for Socialism*. The first was derived from ideas presented by G.A. Cohen, Albert Einstein, Sam Arnold, and others: socialism might lead to a greater sense of community, and this is better for happiness and well-being than the more predatory and competitive mindset of capitalism. The democracy argument started with the thought that if we think that democracy is a good form of government for traditional governmental functions, then this is presumably because we think that we make *better decisions* when we bring in all of the people who are affected. Perhaps we can say that there are some sorts of decisions that are best made (i.e., will have the best effect on human well-being) if they are made in some non-democratic way, but, insofar as we like democracy, it seems that our default assumption is that democratically made decisions are better. But that would then imply that we would also do well to make major economic decisions—those affecting significant numbers of people—democratically, rather than leaving those decisions up to individual owners of the means of production. This need not mean that we institute a Soviet-style planned economy; *market socialists* propose that we still utilize markets while still having far more collective ownership and control over the economy.

The Democracy Argument for Socialism had a caveat: we trust democracy as the best way of making decisions that affect large numbers of people *unless* we have special reason to think that there is some non-democratic mechanism that would work better in some cases. Capitalists argue that we have just such a special reason, for we have reason to think that a free market will be better for everyone. They claim that it will increase overall welfare if we have individuals own the means of production and make economic decisions largely free of government involvement. In Chapter 9, I considered F.A. Hayek's *Better Information* argument and Milton Friedman's *Better Incentives* argument. If these arguments hold up, then we *do* have a special reason to think that we will do better to let the market do its work.

The *Community Makes People Happier* argument, in effect, had a similar caveat: *if* we can make socialism work to create similar levels of productivity as capitalism, then the greater sense of community might indeed lead to more well-being. The Friedman and Hayek inspired arguments would, if correct, lead us to the conclusion that the caveat is not met and that capitalism and free markets will do better than socialism to maximize well-being.

However, the *Better Information* and *Better Incentives* arguments each relied on a key assumption: that when individuals in a free market make decisions that are *better for them* individually, this results in a situation that is *better for everyone* generally. I admitted that there might be something to that in certain cases, but I went on in Chapters 11-13 to detail a wide variety of circumstances in which the market can be expected to fail in this regard. The most notable of these was the impending crisis posed by climate change.

Where does this leave us? I have certainly not lived my undergraduate fantasy in this context: I have not constructed a series of arguments from largely indubitable premises that logically demonstrates that socialism is better than capitalism. But, after all of the arguments, counter-arguments, empirical considerations, and normative theories, I hope to have made it plausible that the *Master Argument for Socialism* is sound: moving in a significantly socialist direction does not violate rights, and it would better promote human well-being than capitalism. Since we ought to structure our political system in a way that promotes human well-being and doesn't violate rights, we should move towards socialism.

A Brief Annotated Selection of Suggested Readings

Philosophers on Socialism

Arnold, Sam. "Socialism." *The Internet Encyclopedia of Philosophy*. https://iep.utm.edu/socialis/
 An excellent philosophical overview of socialism.
Burgis, Ben. *Give Them an Argument: Logic for the Left*. Winchester, UK: Zero Books, 2018.
 Brief but very valuable introduction to the nature of arguments and how the Left can recapture the language of logic and rationality, with examples of fallacies and bad arguments from the political Right.
Cohen, G. A. *Why Not Socialism?* Princeton, NJ: Princeton University Press, 2009.
 Very short introduction to socialism by a leading philosopher, focusing on the question of whether it would be desirable if we can make it work. Cohen also wrote many other more academic works on socialism; particularly worth checking out is his 1995 collection of essays, *Self-Ownership, Freedom, and Equality*.
Davis, Angela. *Freedom Is a Constant Struggle: Ferguson, Palestine, and the Foundations of a Movement*. Edited by Frank Barat. Chicago: Haymarket Books, 2016.
 Philosopher Angela Davis has many works related to socialism; this is the most recent. Other key texts include *Women, Race & Class* and *The Meaning of Freedom*.
Gilabert, Pablo and Martin O'Neill. "Socialism." *The Stanford Encyclopedia of Philosophy*. Fall 2019. https://plato.stanford.edu/archives/fall2019/entries/socialism/.
 An excellent philosophical overview of socialism by two contemporary philosophers.
Honneth, Axel, *The Idea of Socialism*. Translated by Joseph Ganahl. Cambridge: Polity Press, 2017.
 Honneth is a German philosopher (the book was originally in German) who asks why there seems to be no utopian vision around these days, and he tries to reconstruct the original idea of socialism, with some "conceptual renovations."
Schweickart, David. *After Capitalism*. Lanham, MD: Rowman & Littlefield, 2002.
 Also a mathematician. Proposes a form of market socialism that he calls "Economic Democracy."
Sypnowich, Christine. *Equality Renewed: Justice, Flourishing and the Egalitarian Ideal*. New York: Routledge, 2017.
 Proposes a theory of equality focused on human flourishing, hoping to raise the ideal of equality as fundamental principle.
Van Parijs, Philippe. *Real Freedom for All: What (If Anything) Can Justify Capitalism?* Cambridge, MA: Harvard University Press, 1995.
 A strong advocate of a form of universal basic income. See also his more recent coauthored book, *Basic Income: A Radical Proposal for a Free Society and a Sane Economy*.

Vrousalis, Nicholas. *Exploitation as Domination: What Makes Capitalism Unjust.* New York: Oxford University Press, 2023.
>Argues that capitalism is inherently exploitative and thus unjust.

Economists on Socialism

Corneo, Giacomo. *Is Capitalism Obsolete? A Journey through Alternative Economic Systems.* Cambridge, MA: Harvard University Press, 2017.
>Proposes a version of market socialism in which large firms would be publicly owned, but small firms would remain in private hands.

Piketty, Thomas. *Capital in the Twenty-First Century.* Cambridge, MA: Harvard University Press, 2013.
>Concerned with wealth inequality and how that will continue absent government intervention. His recent collection of essays, *Time for Socialism*, makes his political commitments more explicit. His most recent book, *A Brief History of Inequality*, explicitly argues for a form of democratic socialism.

Roemer, John. *A Future for Socialism.* New York: Verso, 1994.
>An advocate of market socialism; also the author of many other related works, including *Egalitarian Perspectives: Essays in Philosophical Economics*.

Wolff, Richard. *Democracy at Work: A Cure for Capitalism.* Chicago: Haymarket Books, 2012.
>One of a number of books on socialism by leading economist Richard Wolff. Referred to as "required reading" by Cornel West.

Recent More Popular Treatments of Socialism

Ghodsee, Kristen. *Why Women Have Better Sex under Socialism: And Other Arguments for Economic Independence.* New York: Hachette, 2018.
>How's that for a title? But it's not all about sex. Ghodsee is an ethnographer who points to many ways in which capitalism is particularly bad for women.

Katch, Danny. *Socialism . . . Seriously: A Brief Guide to Human Liberation.* Chicago: Haymarket Books, 2015.
>A humorous and brief introduction to socialism.

Maass, Alan. *The Case for Socialism.* Chicago: Haymarket Books, 2010.
>A journalist and author making the case against capitalism and for "a revolution because capitalist society can't be fundamentally and permanently changed in any other way."

Newman, Michael. *Socialism: A Very Short Introduction.* 2nd ed. New York: Oxford University Press, 2020.
>A mostly historical and, as promised by the title, short introduction to socialism. Part of an excellent series by Oxford University Press; you might also look at *Capitalism: A Very Short Introduction*, by James Fulcher.

Paul, Rand. *The Case against Socialism.* New York: Broadside Books, 2019.
>An easy to read, bombastic, and not very rigorously argued attack on socialism. But it is written by a US senator and gives insight into the conservative mindset. For an even more bombastic and even less rigorously argued attack on socialism, one could

read Dinesh D'Souza's *United States of Socialism: Who's behind It. Why It's Evil. How to Stop It.*
Robinson, Nathan. *Why You Should Be a Socialist.* New York: St. Martin's Press, 2019.
Lively and accessible treatment by the founder and editor-in-chief of *Current Affairs* magazine.
Sunkara, Bhaskar. *The Socialist Manifesto: The Case for Radical Politics in an Era of Extreme Inequality.* New York: Basic Books, 2019.
A mostly historical introduction to socialism by the founder of *Jacobin*.
Uetricht, Micah and Meagan Day. *Bigger Than Bernie: How We Can Win Democratic Socialism in Our Time.* New York: Verso, 2021.
The deputy editor and associate editor of *Jacobin* focusing on long-term prospects for socialism.
Wright, Erik Olin. *How to Be an Anti-capitalist in the 21st Century.* New York: Verso, 2019.
A sociologist who, like me, was raised in Lawrence, Kansas. Argues that we need an "emancipatory alternative" to capitalism. Also the author of *Envisioning Real Utopias*.

Books from the Libertarian Tradition

Brennan, Jason. *Libertarianism: What Everyone Needs to Know.* New York: Oxford University Press, 2012.
An excellent and very readable overview. Also worth reading by Brennan: *Against Democracy*.
Hayek, F. A. *The Constitution of Liberty.* Chicago: University of Chicago Press, 1960.
Classic text by the Austrian economist. Sometime in the late 1970s during a meeting of the UK Conservative Party, Margaret Thatcher is said to have interrupted a more moderate member of her party by fetching a copy of this book from her briefcase, slamming it down on the table, and shouting, "*This* is what we believe." See also *The Road to Serfdom* and *The Fatal Conceit: The Errors of Socialism*.
Friedman, Milton. *Capitalism and Freedom.* Chicago: University of Chicago Press, 1962.
Classic text by the American economist and adviser to President Reagan, in which it is argued that economic freedom is necessary for political freedom. See also his coauthored *Free to Choose: A Personal Statement* for a more popular approach to many of the same issues.
Mises, Ludwig von. *Socialism: An Economic and Sociological Analysis.* New Haven: Yale University Press, 1922.
Critique of socialism by the teacher of Hayek. Mises has become something of a hero to libertarians.
Nozick, Robert. *Anarchy, State, and Utopia.* New York: Basic Books, 1974.
Argues that an extremely minimal state could arise out of anarchy, and that anything beyond this minimal state is unjust.
Scott, James C. *Two Cheers for Anarchism.* Princeton, NJ: Princeton University Press, 2012.
One of several excellent books by the political scientist and anthropologist. See also *Against the Grain: A Deep History of the Earliest States* and *Seeing Like a State: How Certain Schemes to Improve the Human Condition Have Failed*.
Tomasi, John. *Free Market Fairness.* Princeton, NJ: Princeton University Press, 2013.
Argues for a view he calls "free market fairness" that combines libertarian ideas about the market while still affirming left-leaning values of social justice.

Index

For the benefit of digital users, indexed terms that span two pages (e.g., 52–53) may, on occasion, appear on only one of those pages.

Tables and figures are indicated by *t* and *f* following the page number

Acton, Lord John, 12
Aesop, 92–95, 96–97
Alaska, sovereign wealth fund, 21–22
All Affected Principle, 161–63, 165–66, 247
Alvaredo, Facundo, 101n.16, 140n.12
argument
   ad hominem, 4–6
   definition, 6–10
   denying the antecedent, 10
   equivocation, and, 91, 180–81, 232
   fallacy, 4–5
   implication, logical, 7–8
   proof, and, 231–32, 245
   sound argument, definition, 9
   valid argument, definition, 9
Ariely, Dan, 155
Arnold, Sam, 20–21, 72, 74, 88, 156–57, 161n.21, 167, 247

baseball cards, 187–88, 189
begging the question, 18–19, 26–27, 38, 69
Bentham, Jeremy, 43, 47–48
Bezos, Jeff, 168–69, 172, 215
Bible, The, 18, 71
Botswana, 12–13, 15
Branco, A.F. 10–15
Brave New World, 45–47
Brennan, Jason, 76–77, 117–18, 155–57, 160–61, 216–17
Brett, George, 187–88, 208, 211
Burgis, Ben, 77–79, 99
Bush, George H. W. 178
Bush, George W. 137–38

Carens, Joseph, 171n.37
Carew, Rod, 187–88

Case, Anne, 213
Causation vs. correlation, 119, 120–22, 147
ChatGPT, 214
Chauvin, Derek, 89
China, 123–29, 130
Churchill, Winston, 160–61
Classic socialism, 25–26, 30–31, 31*f*, 38
Cleese, John, 6–7
Climate change, 120, 226–38
Clinton, Bill, 137–38
Cohen, G. A., 92–93, 95, 97, 154–59, 186, 247
community, 153–60
Constitution, US, 52
copyright protection, 23, 34
Corneo, Giacomo, 171n.37
coronavirus pandemic, 34, 44–45, 51–52, 114, 121, 200–1
corporations, 23–24
Cuba, 14

Dahl, Robert, 161n.21
Darwin, Charles, 178–79
Day, Meghan, 25–26, 32–33, 41, 88
Deaton, Angus, 213
Democracy, 160–69
D-socialism, 26–27, 32–33, 38, 47, 60, 66, 67, 76, 77, 79, 80, 113, 181–82, 184–85
Diamond, Peter, 138
diminishing marginal utility, 133–37, 151, 247
Donahue, Phil, 185–86
D'Souza, Dinesh, 228–30
DuBois, W. E. B. 161
Dworkin, Ronald, 56–61

Einstein, Albert, 5, 153, 247
Eisenhower, Dwight, 29–30
Envy. *See* inequality: envy and
Exploitation and capitalism, 87–109

fallacy of composition, 99
feudalism, 99–101, 102
Fieldhouse, Andrew, 138
Floyd, George, 89
Freidman, Milton, 24, 85, 122–23, 125, 130, 141–42, 156–57, 178, 181, 182–88, 189, 190–91, 203–4, 205, 206, 208, 216–17, 221, 222–23, 233, 247–48
Friedman, Rose, 182–88
Fukuyama, Francis, 124

Gagarin, Yuri, 129
Garbinti, Bertrand, 101n.16, 140n.12
Gates, Bill, 131, 132, 134
Ghodsee, Kristen, 126, 127–28
Gilabert, Pablo, 25–26, 89–90
Gini coefficient, 30–31
Goodin, Robert, 161n.21, 166n.24
grasshopper and the ants, 92–95, 96–97

Harwood, Matthew, 67–70
Hayek, F. A. 85, 131, 141–42, 147, 178–82, 186, 189, 190–91, 192–93, 194, 196, 199–201, 205–6, 207, 211, 233, 247–48
healthcare, 209, 210, 215
health insurance, 210
Heritage Foundation, 152, 234
Hitler, Adolf, 160
Holmes, Oliver Wendell, 131
Huxley, Aldous, 45–47

inequality, 141–49
 child well-being, and, 144, 144*f*
 definition of "socialism", and, 20, 24–25, 30–32
 envy, and, 131–33, 135, 137, 139–41, 147, 149
 health and social problems, and, 146, 146*f*
 mental illness, and, 141–42, 144*f*
 Nordic countries, and, 36*t*, 36–38, 38*t*
 obesity, and, 142, 142*f*, 143
 social mobility, and, 144–45, 145*f*

inheritance, 36–37, 40, 84–85, 100–1, 103–4, 135–36, 140, 212
Institute on Taxation and Economic Policy, 24–25
Intergovernmental Panel on Climate Change, 232–33

Kansas, 5–6, 17, 56
Katch, Danny, 51, 88, 226–27
Kenton, Will, 70–71
Kerry, John, 51–52
Kershaw, Clayton, 101–3
Kollontai, Alexandra, 9
Kranepool, Ed, 214–15, 219

Ladan, Luka, 117–18
Laffer, Arthur, 137–38
Lagerspetz, Erik, 161n.21
Led Zeppelin, 140
Lee, Kai-Fu, 214
libertarianism, 72–79
life expectancy, 115–16, 116*f*, 123–24, 124*t*, 126–27, 129, 130, 143, 146
logical implication, 8
Long, Roderick, 74–75
Loris, Nicolas, 234–35
luck, 100–2
Luxemburg, Rosa, 9

Maass, Alan, 25–26
Maddison, Angus, 124–25
Market socialism, 169–71, 247
Marx, Karl, 3–4, 9–10, 25, 27–28, 39–40, 87, 88, 105–6, 212–13
Mets, New York, 8
Mill, John Stuart, 43, 47–48
Mnuchin, Steven, 137–38
monopolies, 34, 203–8, 216, 236–37
monopsony, 212–15, 216
Monty Python, 6–7
Morrison, Scott, 234–35
Murphy, Robert, 117–18, 122
Musk, Elon, 37, 151

negative externalities. *See* neighborhood effects
neighborhood effects, 220–39
 climate change, and, 226–38
 layoffs, and, 225–26

pollution, 221, 222–23
   utility companies, and, 223–25, 226
Nonaggression principle, 73–79, 86
Nozick, Robert, 76–77, 139–40, 155, 164

Ocasio-Cortez, Alexandria, 7–8, 32–33, 67
O'Neill, Martin, 25–26, 89–90
Orenstein, Mitchell, 126
Oxford English Dictionary, 19–20, 23, 25–26

Page, Larry, 198
Palin, Michael, 6–7
Parfit, Derek, 47–48
Paul, Rand, 32–33, 51, 55, 117–18, 131, 132–33, 228–33
Pickett, Kate, 141–49, 246–47
Piketty, Thomas, 27–28, 138n.10
Pinker, Steven, 115–18, 122, 125, 129–30, 132
polarization, 4, 16, 241–42
public goods, 190–202
   education, 197–99
   healthcare, 200–1
   trash collection, 196–97
Putin, Vladimir, 118–19, 120–21

Rawls, John, 49–50, 102, 103, 106, 107, 155
Reagan, Ronald, 137–38, 177–78, 216, 231
Reeve, Andrew, 161n.21
rights, 41–42, 50–61
   economic rights and socialism, 70–73
   exploitation, and, 91–92, 97–98, 104–8
   healthcare, and, 54–56, 60–61
   legal vs. moral, 52–54
   political rights and socialism, 65–70
   positive vs. negative, 54–56
   trumps, as, 56–58
Robinson, Nathan, 23–24, 40, 133
Roemer, John, 92, 171n.37
rooster, Maurice the, 51–52, 59–60
Rothaus Pils, 167, 173, 195

S-socialism, 19, 38, 66–67
Saez, Emmanuel, 138
Sandel, Michael, 96, 103
Sanders, Bernie, 10–11, 26–28, 32–33, 54
Scholz, Olaf, 8
Schweickart, David, 167, 169–71, 184–85

Scientific revolution, 129–30
Seaver, Tom, 187–88, 189
Smith, Adam, 187–88, 192, 206, 221
Social Democracy, 26, 32–33
Sopo, Giancarlo, 33–34n.22
Soviet bloc, 22–23, 66, 123–29
Soviet Union, 22–23, 31–32, 66, 123–30
Spock, Mr. 7–8
Sputnik, 129
Stantcheva, Stefanie, 138n.10
Stargell, Willie, 187–88
Star Trek, 7–8, 43
Stern, Nicholas, 226–27
Sunkara, Bhaskar, 28–29
Supreme Court of the US, 59–60
Surplus value extraction, 87–89, 104

Taxation
   optimal rate, 137–40, 148, 247
   progressive, 24–25, 27, 29–30, 32–33, 135–37
   redistribution, and, 75–76, 79–85
   theft, and, 73–74
Tereshkova, Valentina, 129
Thatcher, Margaret, 177–78
Tomasi, John, 79–85, 86
Trump, Donald, 51, 62, 137–38, 160

Uetricht, Micah, 25–26, 32–33, 41, 88
UNICEF, 144
universal basic income, 215
US-style capitalism, 29–30, 31f
utilitarianism, 41, 42, 43–50, 73, 106–7
Utilities, 204–7, 223–25, 226

Venezuela, 10–15

Walton, Sam, 84–85, 140
Westerfield, Scott, 230n.11
Wilkinson, Richard, 141–49, 171n.37, 246–47
Wolff, Jonathan, 92–94, 95, 97
Wolff, Richard, 171n.37
World Happiness Report, 148–49
World Inequality Database, 33t, 36t
World Values Survey, 159
Wright, Erik Olin, 171

Zuckerberg, Mark, 37, 101–3, 140–41

Arguments:
Better Incentives, 184, 187
Better Information, 180, 181
Capitalism and Climate Change, 236
Capitalism and Progress, 118, 119
Capitalism and Starvation, 12
Capitalism Exploits, 90, 91–92, 98
Capitalism Violates Rights, 107
Capitalists Will Restrict Speech, 68
Climate Change and Socialism, 228
Community Makes People Happier, 153
Democracy Argument for Socialism, 167–68
Democracy Argument for Traditional Governmental Functions, 164, 165
Economic Liberties and Autonomy, 81
Economic Liberties and Self-Authorship, 82, 83
Free Speech and Autonomy, 59
Master Argument for Capitalism, 42
Master Argument for Socialism, 42
NAP and Redistribution, 75
NAP and Taxation, 76
Putin and MLB Salaries, 118
Socialism and Starvation, 11, 13, 14
Socialism Violate Political Rights, 67
Socialism Violates Rights, 65, 66
Socialists Will Restrict Speech, 68–70
Taxation is Theft, 74